UNFOLDING ISLAM

P. J. Stewart

Unfolding Islam

Published by
Garnet Publishing Limited
8 Southern Court
South Street
Reading
Berkshire
RG1 4QS
UK
www.garnetpublishing.co.uk

Second Edition

Hardback ISBN: 978-1-85964-213-9
Paperback ISBN: 978-1-85964-205-4

British Library Cataloguing-in-Publication Data
A catalogue record for this book is available from the British Library

Typeset by Samantha Barden
Jacket design by David Rose
Cover photo used courtesy of iStockphoto.com/Damir Cudic

Printed by Biddles, UK

INTRODUCTION

A Dangerous World

Whoever planned the events of 11th September 2001, the aim was clear: to provoke the United States into attacking Islamic targets and persuading Muslims that there was a worldwide war on Islam. The plan succeeded brilliantly, and on Sunday 16th September, President Bush warned Americans that 'this crusade, this war on terrorism, is going to take a while'. His minders prevented him from talking about a 'crusade' again, but his army was soon engaged in war on two Muslim-majority countries.

The war in Afghanistan was widely condoned, although the Taliban government had said that it would hand over Osama Bin Laden if they were shown the evidence against him. However, the invasion of Iraq, without either UN authorization or clear and realizable objectives, is almost universally seen as a disastrous mistake. The dismissal of the Iraqi Army and of most of the Civil Service, and the dissolution of the Baath Party left the country without the structures of a state. The resulting chaos has caused the deaths of hundreds of thousands of Iraqi civilians and has left the once-great former capital of Sunni Islam and the most sacred sites of Shia Islam under American occupation. Meanwhile, the United States gives unconditional diplomatic, financial and military support to Israel, which controls the third holiest city of Islam, ignores the claims of Palestinian refugees and continues to colonize the territories occupied in 1967.

Alongside the war of bombs there has come a war of words. The day after the attack on the World Trade Center, an American columnist, Ann Coulter, published an opinion piece which concluded that 'we should invade their countries, kill their leaders and convert them to Christianity'. Franklin Graham, son of Billy Graham and confidant of the President, called Islam 'a very evil and wicked religion'. A number of well-known televangelists have made deeply insulting remarks about Muhammad. Books and websites have appeared, some of them produced by ex-Muslims converted to Christianity, claiming to tell 'the truth about Islam', 'the world's most intolerant religion', 'the greatest threat to world peace', and so on. Repressive legislation in some countries has affected Muslims disproportionately, and Guantanamo Bay has become a permanent grievance.

Some non-Christians have become as vehement as Christians in their criticism of Islam. Atheists claim that Muslims are driven by 'blind faith'. Liberals are convinced that they are particularly illiberal. Feminists imagine that all Muslim women are victims. Supporters of Israel talk of 'ancient hatreds' towards Jews. Hindu nationalists lament their 'wounded civilization' – wounded by Islam. Any story that shows Muslims in a negative light is seized upon by the media. Hollywood uses Muslims as villains in a way that would be denounced as hateful if applied to any other group.

At the opposite extreme, some Muslims call for jihad against the West, and there are preachers who condone suicide bombing (a technique pioneered not by Muslims but by the Tamil Tigers) and who maintain that Islam requires its followers to fight for world domination. Any suspicion of insults to the religion or its Prophet provokes death threats and angry demonstrations. There are enough terrorist incidents to give the impression of a worldwide campaign of violence.

The mood of panic on both sides leads to fears that further attacks are imminent and that world war could result. Terrified people will do terrible things, and there is a grave danger that this could be a self-fulfilling prophecy. Dialogue is urgently needed but seems more difficult than ever. However, there is common ground, in that all parties agree that the fountain-head of Islam is in the example of the Prophet Muhammad. There is also apparent unanimity between crusaders and jihadists that Islam is at war with the rest of the world; if two groups at opposite extremes can agree, must they not be right? The first half of this book examines the Prophet Muhammad's life and teachings in search of an answer.

Sources

Superficially, it seems that we know an enormous amount about Muhammad – far more than about Jesus or Moses, Buddha or Lao Tse or the shadowy authors of the Hindu Vedas. There are enough books recording his words and deeds to fill many shelves. They include *Sira* (biography), law books, Hadith (collections of accounts of particular sayings and doings of the Prophet and his companions, also referred to as Traditions) and commentaries on the Koran, interpreting the text in the light of events in the course of his life. However, none of them was written less than about a century after his death, so they are records of an oral literature, as open to question as any other.

Muslims have always been aware of the problems of oral literature, and they developed a science to deal with them. The collectors of Hadith studied the chain of authorities who had handed down each story. They required each link in the chain to be a person of sound character and reputation, and to have been at some time in the same place as the people above and below them in the chain. They classified chains on a scale from 'sound' to 'weak'. This was an admirable procedure, but three problems remained: some of the oldest and most-respected books, notably the *Sira* and the oldest law books, had been written before the study of chains of authority was established. Secondly, once the essentials of chains of authority had been established, it became possible to attach a sound chain to an untrue story. Finally, once the authority for a story had been accepted, there was little or no critique of its content.

For a modern historian, the study of an oral literature is based on the content of stories. It is assumed that each one was told in a particular community and reflected the interests of its members. True stories were liable to be consciously or unconsciously edited by people leaving out inconvenient details, adding embellishments or changing the context. Untrue ones quickly gained acceptance because they fitted in with the group's outlook. Application of such assumptions to the Bible has cast doubt on many cherished beliefs of traditional Jews and Christians.

One of the roots of Islamic reaction against the West is the fear that critical study of their founding texts would have the same caustic effect as it has had on Christianity and Judaism. They have responded by claiming that their oral transmission was immune to the general problems of such literature. Some rest their case on their unique analysis of chains of authority. Some point to the extraordinary powers of verbal memory cultivated by the Arabs when they lived in the desert with no means of making written records. Some take refuge in the supernatural, saying that Allah did not allow error to be sanctioned by the community. None of these arguments was considered decisive in the third century of Islam, when there was still fierce debate on such matters.

Muslims should not fear the application of modern historical methods to Islam, for they possess something that is missing from every other classical religion: a contemporary record of the teaching of their founder. In the course of this book, I present detailed evidence, mainly from the Koran itself, for the contention that the consonantal text is more or less exactly as it was written down in the lifetime of the Prophet. There are small differences, mainly in pronunciation, but these hardly ever make any difference to the meaning, and they were recognized and catalogued by Muslim scholars eleven or twelve centuries ago.

Western scholars have been examining manuscripts of the Koran for two centuries without finding any significant deviation from the received consonantal text – and it would need only one authentic page from one deviant version to demolish faith in the whole concept of an authentic text. Some scholars still claim that the Koran was written long after the death of Muhammad, but this is simply preposterous. The latest possible date for getting agreement from all Muslims was twenty-four years after he died, since that is when relations broke down permanently between

Sunni and Shia. Both factions, soon joined by a third, the Kharijites, would have dearly loved to possess a Koran that backed their claims against those of their opponents, yet all accept the same text.

The same events that guarantee the authenticity of the Koran require us to be very cautious in using the later literature, all of which was transmitted orally during generations of warfare and repression. The descendants of the Prophet's Companions were all keen to show that their ancestors had been virtuous and that the descent into civil war was the fault of others. Soon there also came to be an urgent need for precedents to establish particular interpretations of Islam, and these could only be accepted if they could be attributed to the Prophet and those who had known him.

The Koran provides us with enough material to give a picture of the Prophet's teaching and to confirm the main outline of his life. I have therefore been very sparing with my use of later sources, but this is not meant to imply a total rejection of them. But it is not for a non-Muslim to tell Muslims which parts of their tradition to question. Currently, there is a tendency to accept all the traditional literatures, but this is partly an understandable reaction to the unremitting hostility with which many outsiders view every aspect of the religion.

An exception is my use of traditional accounts of the Prophet's family life – his relations with aunts and uncles, cousins and daughters as well as wives – which is valuable in filling out a picture of his personality. Ibn Saad's description of the wives' domestic quarters in Medina seems particularly reliable as they were not demolished until about eighty years after his death, so eye witnesses must have been alive when the first accounts were written down.

Author's Bias

The second half of the book describes what Muslims made of their religion in successive eras. Some claim that only a believer can write about any religion, and that is undoubtedly true when it is a question of expressing devotional aspects. However, where there are mutually hostile factions, which seems to be the case in every religion, only a sympathetic outsider can hope to be fair to all of them. Each of the streams of Islam has its special share of the riches of the religion, and it is a pity they cannot all be brought together; but in practice, most Muslims follow the tradition in which they grew up, although there is no priesthood to tell them what to believe or how to act.

Some also hold that only a Muslim can translate the Koran, but really no one can translate it. For this – more, perhaps, than for any other book – it is indeed true that *traduttore traditore*, to translate is to traduce. Muslims have always rightly said that no translation can replace the Arabic original. With its compressed style, its elisions, its echoes and its double meanings, which need to be heard with the ear and not just read with the eye, it poses problems that can never all be solved at the same time. For the purposes of this book, I have tried to bring out the aspect of meaning that is uppermost in relation to the point that is being made.

After much thought, I have decided not to translate the word 'Allah' (nor 'YHWH'). The Christian concept of God is strongly anthropomorphic, partly because of the Biblical statement that 'God made man in his own image' (Genesis 1:27) and partly because of the teaching that God 'was made man' in the person of Jesus (Nicene Creed). The Koranic view is that 'nothing and no one is like Allah' (112:4). Also, Westerners often think of God as being outside the universe. Many Muslims have the same conception, but according to the Koran, 'We created man, and we know what he whispers to himself. We are closer to him than his jugular vein' (50:16).

God, in English, is always a 'he', though some feminists prefer 'her'. The alternative would be 'it'. Any of these is misleading because in Arabic, as in Hebrew, there is no equivalent of 'it'; even inanimate objects have to be either *'huwa'* ('he/it') or '*hiya*' ('she/it'). *Allah* is a masculine noun without any implication of maleness. Instead of a pronoun, I have therefore either repeated the noun or done without. Pronouns are of course only part of the problem. The Koran applies to Allah many verbs and adjectives which imply an animate being. These have long been discussed by Muslim theologians. At one extreme, some have understood them all metaphorically. At the other, literalists have claimed that Allah must have hands and eyes and sit on a throne, since the Koran says so. Our little human minds are at a loss when it comes to talking about the Transcendent.

I have no problem in writing about 'the Prophet', an expression whose primary meaning, according to the Concise Oxford Dictionary, is 'Muhammad'. He was the very epitome of prophethood. I also use the word 'revelation', which readers are free to understand in whatever sense they wish. Muslims mark their respect for him by using after mentions of his name the formula '*salla'llah alayhi wa sallam* – may Allah bless him and give him peace' (Koran 33:56), usually abbreviated in Arabic and similarly in English. In this book, which is written primarily for non-Muslim readers, this formula and the similar ones used after the names of certain other revered people are not used, and neither are the phrases that customarily follow a mention of Allah. Muslim readers are invited to add them mentally.

Some readers may feel that a person who has problems with the word 'God' should not be writing about religion. I might say the same about authors who have no problems with an anthropomorphic god. My book comes of more than fifty years knowing ordinary followers of Islam and appreciating its dedication to the unity of existence, its openness to all people, its passion for justice, its concern for the poor and needy, its devotion to the family, its affirmation of the equality of all believers, its tradition of hospitality, its inculcation of contentment, etc.

Muslims are not always good Muslims, but their failings are those to which all humans are prone, for example complacency, mistrust of the unfamiliar, readiness to find fault, hasty judgement, hypocrisy, short-sightedness, generalization... in fact the very things that Westerners are guilty of when they make demeaning statements about Islam. Anyone who accuses Muslims of violence and aggression should remember the long history of Western incursions into Muslim-ruled territories: Britain in Mughal India, the Netherlands in Indonesia, France in Egypt then in North Africa, Russia in Central Asia, Britain in Egypt, Britain and France in Palestine, Iraq, Syria and Lebanon, Britain and Russia in Iran, Britain, France and Israel in Suez. Complaints of 'Muslim backwardness' should not be made by those whose grandmothers never went out without a hat and waited half their lives to get the vote! And at least, the Koran does not tell people to turn the other cheek.

What is most distressing in the present situation is to see Muslims turning against each other and ready to accuse each other of not being true Muslims. In so doing they forget the often repeated phrase in the Koran: 'Allah knows what is in your hearts'. None of us can be certain of what goes on in the minds of others, and much conflict would be avoided if we all gave our fellow humans the benefit of the doubt.

Other Points

Many readers of my first edition complained that they had difficulty with Arabic words and names. I have therefore removed all but the most necessary technical terms, and I have reduced names to the bare minimum needed to avoid confusion. I have removed the dots on consonants, the over-lining of vowels and the inverted commas of scholarly transliteration, which are meaningful only to those who know Arabic and therefore hardly need them. Where a spelling is familiar in English, for example Mecca, emir, Saladin, I have used it. I have written Koran rather than Quran, as 'qu' stands for 'kw' in English. Otherwise I have kept the 'q' which represents a throaty sound that occurs in no European language. Arabists will notice that I have written aa for a + *'ayn*.

centuries their language had practically replaced the non–Semitic Sumerian. Akkadian differs markedly from the other Semitic languages, but this may partly be the result of its having been taken up by non–Semitic speakers.

The linguistic situation is more confused further west. Tribal names are not a reliable guide, as unwritten languages change over time, and some of the evidence on tribal movements dates from long after their occurrence. The Amorites, for example, were reckoned as Mesopotamians at one stage and Canaanites at another. Similarly 'the Hebrews' seems to have been the name of a tribe before it was that of a language. Linguists disagree about the date of separation of the ancestral forms of Arabic, Aramaic and Canaanitic (including Hebrew). It seems likely that the Semites who settled down to farm in Canaan were the first to separate socially and linguistically from those who still formed the shifting nomad scene. I shall call the early speech of the latter Arabo-Aramaic – a cluster of dialects, one group of which evolved into Arabic, while another under Mesopotamian and Canaanite influence became Aramaic.

These speakers of Semitic languages soon came into contact with speakers of Indo–European languages, of west-Eurasian origin. Three of the latter peoples eventually came to dominate the area politically and culturally: the Persians, founders of the first truly multi–national empire, centred on Mesopotamia; the Greeks, who colonized the shores of the Mediterranean but never achieved political union, except briefly under Macedonian leadership; and the Romans, whose empire eventually came to include the Greeks, Syrians and Egyptians as well as Western Europe and North Africa.

Islam was the last born of the Semitic religions, and it includes many beliefs found in the earlier religions of Semitic peoples and their neighbours. Non–Muslims tend to conclude that Islam is a composite of beliefs taken from various sources. The Muslim version is that the one true religion was announced by successive prophets to various peoples, but that their teachings were diluted and distorted and partially lost. It was only with Muhammad that the truth was repeated and safely preserved for all time in the Koran.

The story of the earliest prophets is told in the Hebrew Scriptures, produced by one of the Semitic-speaking peoples, the Jews. They trace their origin to Abraham, whom the Arabs too claim as their ancestor. According to the Biblical chronology, he was born in around 1800 BCE in southern Mesopotamia and migrated to what is now north-eastern Syria, both occupied mainly by speakers of Arabo-Aramaic dialects. The Bible describes Abram, as he was at first called, as a Bedouin, possessing 'sheep and goats, cattle, asses, male and female slaves, she-asses and camels' (Genesis 12:16). Camels were not fully domesticated for another thousand years, but it is possible that they were already being used for special occasions, as when Abraham is described as sending camels to bring back an Aramaean bride for his son Isaac (Genesis 24:10). His people lived in tents and ranged over an area that stretched from the borders of Mesopotamia to the Eastern Desert of Egypt. They favoured cousin marriage, as many Arabs – and Muslims generally – still do, although Abraham's nephews and nieces remained pagans (for example Jacob's wife Rachel, who stole her family's idols).

Abraham, Moses and the Jews

Apart from the legendary figures of Adam and Noah, Abraham was the first person recorded as believing in only one deity, El or YHWH. Whether the Biblical account of Abraham and his descendants is taken as myth or history, it is significant in reflecting Jewish ideas about tribal relationships at the time the Bible was written. YHWH rewarded him with the promise of a multitude of descendants. The Hebrew Scriptures give two versions of this promise. The first, written by the Yahwist (Genesis 15:18), was given before the birth of the elder son by his Egyptian concubine Hagar, Ishmael – Arabic Isma'il – the ancestor of the Arabs from time to time they came together in a loose confederation to fight a common enemy. The Torah commanded them to enslave the citizens of towns that opened their gates to them, but to kill all the men and enslave the women and children of those that fell after a siege. The whole population of towns that YHWH was 'giving them as an inheritance' was to be annihilated – the Hittites, Amorites, Canaanites, Perizzites, Hivites and Jebusites (Deuteronomy 20:10–18).

The Biblical Book of Joshua claims that the Israelite tribes carried out a large number of exterminations of Canaanite towns and villages, but this is likely to be boastful exaggeration, if not pure myth. The northern tribes intermarried so extensively with Canaanites that they eventually disappeared from history, becoming the 'lost tribes of Israel'. Even the southern tribes, Judah and Benjamin, intermarried with the indigenous people. The Israelites abandoned the nomadic way of life and became settled farmers, though there continued to be Jewish nomads such as Job, who ended up with 'fourteen thousand sheep and goats, six thousand camels, a thousand yoke of oxen and as many she-asses' (Job 42:12). They adopted the local language, out of which developed Hebrew.

Eventually the tribes came together under a succession of three kings: Saul, David and Solomon, who built the Temple in Jerusalem. This united kingdom lasted only a century before it was torn in two by tension between the northern tribes and the tribe of Judah, from which came David and Solomon, and its small ally Benjamin, from which came Saul and which owned the land on which Jerusalem was built. The Northern Kingdom continued to call itself Israel, but its religion was increasingly mixed with idolatry. It lasted only two more centuries before it became an Assyrian colony, to re-emerge as something quite different. The history of the Jews became that of the southern Kingdom of Judah or Judaea (Hebrew *Yehudah*) after which they are named.

Even before Saul was chosen to be the first king, the very institution of kingship was criticized by the prophet Samuel, and throughout the history of the kingdoms a succession of prophets rose up to denounce the wickedness of the kings and many of their subjects. Only David and Solomon achieved something like prophetic status themselves, though most if not all of the writings attributed to them came from later hands. The Northern Kingdom was particularly affected by pagan practices, until it was finally destroyed by the Assyrians in 722 BCE.

The Kingdom of Judah lasted more than a century longer before it was conquered by the Babylonians in 587 BCE. They sacked Jerusalem, destroyed the Temple and deported thousands of the leading Judaeans to Babylon. During their five decades of exile they absorbed much Babylonian culture, including the calendar, and it was no doubt at this time that the replacement of Hebrew by Aramaic began. Most of the Hebrew Scriptures took their final form during or soon after the exile, and Judaism became a fixed system that was to undergo little further change.

The Emperor Cyrus defeated the Babylonians and absorbed their Empire into his larger Persian Empire, which he ran on a decentralized basis, allowing his subject peoples their own culture and institutions. Those Jewish exiles who wished to were permitted to return to Judaea, where they built the Second Temple, but many remained in Mesopotamia to form the community that was to last for the next two and a half millennia. The Northern Kingdom of Israel, however, had disappeared, leaving only the name of its last capital, Samaria. The Samaritans were a mixed population, some of whom continued to revere the Torah. Only in the northern–most district, Galilee, did there persist a form of Judaism recognized by the Judaeans.

The change from Israel to Judaea was of immense religious as well as political importance. The Israelites had battled ceaselessly for worldly power. The Judaeans ceased to desire the revival of their own kingdom, unless YHWH himself sent them an 'Anointed one' (Hebrew *mashiah*, 'Messiah', Greek *khristos*, 'Christ'), and concerned themselves instead with the unworldly values of their religion. When the Persians were replaced by the Greeks, and the

Greeks by the Romans, the Judaeans continued to be content as long as their religious freedom was respected. Interference with it caused periodic revolts, which all ended in defeat but helped to restore some autonomy. The longest of these produced the Hasmonaean kingdom, but its rulers soon ran into trouble with the religious establishment. The Israelite search for worldly power lasted at most five or six centuries, but Judaean unworldliness had survived eleven centuries by the time of Muhammad and was to continue a further fourteen until the creation of the State of Israel.

The essence of Judaism is contained in the Torah. Besides the story of the creation of the world, Noah's flood, the wanderings of the Patriarchs and the exodus from Egypt, the Torah contains a code of behaviour, summed up in the Ten Commandments (Exodus 20:3–17): (1) no worship of other gods, (2) no making of carved images nor any worship of them as idols, (3) no abuse of the name of YHWH, (4) the Sabbath – Saturday – to be kept holy, (5) parents to be honoured, (6) no murder, (7) no adultery, (8) no theft, (9) no false evidence and (10) no lusting after the next person's spouse or property. At the basis of these were the two Great Commandments: (I) 'love YHWH your God with all your heart and soul and strength' (Deuteronomy 6:5), and (II) 'love your neighbour as yourself' (Leviticus 19:18). That this love was to extend to non-Jews is clear from Leviticus 19:33–34: 'When a foreigner settles with you in your land, do not oppress him. Treat him as a fellow countryman and love him as you love yourself.'

There was a mass of other laws covering every aspect of the life of an agrarian society. Two areas are of particular interest here, because they reappear in Islam. Among the many food laws, there was a prohibition on the eating of the meat of pigs or carnivores, and on the eating of meat containing surplus blood, which meant that animals must be bled to death. As regards economic life, there was a prohibition on lending at interest to fellow Jews, which did not apply to loans to non-Jews (Deuteronomy 23:19–20).

A third feature shared with Islam is the circumcision of males, regarded by the Jews as a distinctive practice, part of Abraham's covenant with YHWH (Genesis 17:10–14), though in fact it is a very ancient custom, found in many parts of Africa and south-west Asia and even among the Australian aborigines. This was performed on the eighth day from birth, but the operation was simply the symbolic removal of the tip of the foreskin (Hebrew *milah*). A more drastic and dangerous version (*periah*), involving forcible separation of infant foreskin and glans (which normally remain fused in early years), was introduced two thousand years later to prevent Jews from passing as gentiles.

The system of criminal justice was based on retaliation: 'an eye for an eye and a tooth for a tooth' (Exodus 21:24). Stoning to death was prescribed for those guilty of acts considered particularly wicked: fornicating girls (Deuteronomy 22:21), adulterous couples (22:22) and rapists (22:25). Other capital crimes included idolatry (Deuteronomy 17:2–7) and Sabbath-breaking (Numbers 15:35), which were seen as amounting to apostasy or abandonment of the religion.

To the scrolls of the Torah, which alone reside in the Ark of the Law in synagogues, were added the scrolls of the Prophets (including Joshua, Judges, Samuel and Kings) and of the Writings (Psalms, Proverbs, Job, Song of Songs, etc.). Together these formed the Hebrew Scriptures. Eventually they were written as a *codex* (pages bound in a cover) to form 'the Bible', but the earliest known Hebrew codex dates to about 900 CE. They span perhaps a thousand years, starting with oral literature at least three thousand years old, and ending with books written less than two centuries before the Common Era. They were written and repeatedly revised by many different authors, most of them of uncertain identity. Probably no book in the Bible is preserved just as its original author left it.

There were differences of opinion on which books were canonical. At one extreme, the Samaritans accepted only the five books of the Torah; at the other, some books not accepted in Hebrew were added to the Greek version, the *Septuagint*. Through the copying and recopying of texts, many variant readings were introduced. Modern bibles are based on the Masoretic text, fixed in the eighth century CE, but fragments of older texts survive, and the Septuagint was based on such a text, differing in many details from the Masoretic text. The Samaritans have preserved a third version of the first five books.

In the period following the compilation of the Hebrew Scriptures, many new beliefs were added to popular Judaism, most of them traceable to outside sources. The belief in the resurrection of the dead came in, perhaps from Egypt, together with expectation of the end of the world and the Day of Judgement, or Last Day. From Persia came the belief in eternal reward in Paradise (from Old Persian *pairidaiza*, 'a park or walled garden') and eternal punishment in Hell (*Gehinnom*, the name of a smouldering rubbish dump outside Jerusalem, as opposed to the *Sheol* of the Hebrew Bible, which was just a limbo for the souls of the dead). God's adversary Satan, who made a few late appearances in the Hebrew Scriptures, became – perhaps under Persian influence – the universal Lord of Evil. The Messiah, expected in the Hebrew Scriptures just as a divinely guided king, was transformed into a miraculous being appointed to bring in the Last Day.

The focus of Judaism was Jerusalem, the capital of David and Solomon, where a hereditary priesthood performed animal sacrifice in the Temple. In theory, apart from the priests, no one came between the believer and YHWH. In practice the great complexity of the Law required a scholarly class of rabbis who devoted their lives to study. After the destruction of the Temple, the priestly function came to an end, leaving only the rabbis. Their debates on the finer points of Jewish law form the Hebrew *Mishna* and the *Talmud*, which is the *Mishna* plus voluminous Aramaic elaborations. The two versions of the Talmud – the Palestinian and the Babylonian, were composed in the early centuries of the Common Era.

Jews migrated all over the great empires of which they were part, building synagogues, converting gentiles and becoming one of the most successful of the competing religions in the ancient world. It has been estimated that 10% of the population of the Mediterranean region were Jewish at the beginning of the Common Era. Their expansion would certainly have continued if it had not been halted by Christianity.

Jesus and Christianity

Jesus of Nazareth was a young charismatic teacher and healer who emerged in the outlying Jewish territory of Galilee about forty years before the final destruction of the Second Temple. As with Moses, it is impossible to know his exact teachings or even, for certain, in what language he taught. He certainly spoke Aramaic, of which a few words are quoted in the Gospels, but he may also have been fluent in Greek, the language of the New Testament, for Galilee was virtually a bilingual province. The gospels of Matthew and Luke claim for him two different lines of descent from King David, and it is possible that he came from a Davidic family that had taken refuge in Galilee.

The first generations of his disciples believed that the world was about to end, so for a long time wrote little or nothing about him. The earliest Christian writings are the letters of St Paul, who never met Jesus and who was mainly concerned with theology. There seems also to have been an early collection of sayings of Jesus, possibly in Aramaic, preserved in the Gospels of Matthew and Luke, who also made free use of the Gospel of Mark, the first biography, which was written probably forty or fifty years after Jesus' death. The Fourth Gospel, that of John, is a later work, of mystical rather than historical value, though it may include authentic details. Other gospels failed to be accepted, notably the Gospel of Thomas, preserved in Coptic translation. The Christian New Testament was completed by a few more letters, including one from James the brother of Jesus, the Acts of the Apostles (a history of the first thirty-odd years of the churches, claimed to be written by the author of Luke's Gospel), and the Apocalypse (an end-of-the-world allegory).

There was from the beginning a potential for anti-Jewish feeling, directed not against any supposed 'race' but against those who remained 'stubborn' enough to continue to practise Judaism. For justification, Judeophobes looked to passages like John 8:31–47, in which Jesus is alleged to tell Jews who do not believe in him that they are the children of the Devil, and Matthew 27:25, where Pilate offers to release Jesus and 'the people as a whole answered "His blood be on us and on our children!".' Incidentally, embarrassment over this legacy has led some modern Christians even to alter the Bible; in the *Good News Bible* (New Testament, New York, 1966), St John's references to *hoi Ioudaioi*, 'the Jews', have mostly been translated as 'the Jewish authorities', and the expression has been deleted altogether in John 8:31.

A little less than three hundred years after the death of Jesus, Christianity was adopted as the religion of the Roman Empire by Constantine I, who had won a series of bloody civil wars to make himself its sole master, founding a new capital in Constantinople (formerly Byzantium, today Istanbul). He put pressure on the bishops at the Council of Nicaea to resolve their conflicts over the Trinity, and he used the resources of the state to finance the building of many churches. For the next thirteen centuries, Christian rulers considered it their right and their duty to dictate the beliefs of their people.

The last Roman emperor to embrace religious pluralism was Julian the Apostate. Among his other projects was that of rebuilding the Temple in Jerusalem, probably in order to force Christians to share the city rather than to please the Jews. He reigned only twenty months, dying in battle against the Persians in 363, aged 32. With his death the supremacy of Christianity was restored, and it was soon intensified by Theodosius I, the last man to rule over the whole Roman Empire and the one who abolished the thousand-year-old Olympic Games. By a series of decrees between 380 and 392, he made Nicene Christianity the only approved religion, opening the way to the persecution not only of non-Christians but equally of heretical Christians. This was a long way from the position of the early Christians, who had been persecuted pacifists looking forward to a supernatural kingdom.

For the centuries leading up to the time of Muhammad, Christianity was the religion of the Byzantine territories bordering on Arabia, including Egypt and Greater Syria, which included Palestine and Lebanon. There was a much smaller Christian Empire in Abyssinia and southern Arabia. The Jews were allowed to practise their religion but not to repair their synagogues nor build new ones, and their patriarchate had been abolished. Unable to proselytize or intermarry, they became a closed ethnic group, though as late as 740 CE Jews converted the ruling class of the Khazars – a Turkic kingdom in Central Asia.

Persian Religions

Older than the Roman Empire was that of the Persians. Its founder, Cyrus the Great declared on his accession in 539 BCE: 'I shall respect the traditions, customs and religions of the nations of my empire. While I am King of Iran, Babylon and the four points of the compass, I shall never let anyone oppress any others, and if it occurs I shall penalize the oppressor. I shall never let anyone take possession of the movable and landed property of others by force.' The expansion of this Empire brought it into conflict with Greece, and the lands of the Fertile Crescent were contested between the two sides for centuries. During the lifetime of Muhammad, the Sasanian successors of Persia invaded Syria and Egypt and were then driven back by the Byzantines to the Iranian plateau.

The Sasanians broadly continued the religious tolerance of Cyrus. Both Christians and Jews flourished, especially in Mesopotamia. However, the dominant religion was Zoroastrianism or Mazdaism, which together with the closely related Zurvanism, was the root from which the others derived. It was founded by a prophet called Zoroaster (Zarathustra). More recent Iranian religions, with confusingly similar names, were Manichaeism,

Mazdakism, and Mandaism. They had at first been tolerated but were later condemned as subversive. All these religions shared a philosophy of ethical dualism, dividing all existence into Good and Evil. Some Persian ideas had come into Christianity through post-Biblical Judaism, and there seems to have been some continuing influence. Mandaism was a hybrid between Iranian religion and Gnostic Christianity.

Almost nothing is known of Zoroaster, and his dates are given variously as between 1200 and 600 BCE. He was virtually a monotheist, believing that everything had been created by Ahura Mazda, the Wise Lord, who nevertheless had an antagonist, Ahriman, the embodiment of Evil, and there were lesser deities on both sides. Life was conceived as a war between the People of Ahura Mazda, represented by settled farmers and citizens, and his enemies, represented especially by nomads – the raiders and destroyers of order. It was the destiny of the world that Good would triumph, Ahriman would be destroyed, and the good would be rewarded with eternal joy in Paradise, while the wicked were punished in Hell. Zoroastrians had a holy book, the *Avesta*, including hymns, the *Gatha*s, the original version of which may have been written by Zoroaster himself. Most of the book is later, however, including the lengthy compendium of divinely sanctioned law. There was a male priesthood that presided over the rituals of the religion and defended its orthodoxy.

Zoroastrianism was the principal religion of the Sasanian Empire, but other religions were tolerated. However Manichaeism was proscribed. It had been founded by a Persian, Mani, who was born in Mesopotamia in 216 CE and who died a prisoner under interrogation in or about 276. He was brought up in a Judaeo-Christian sect, but obeyed the order of an angelic messenger to leave it and found a new religion. He regarded himself as the final member of a succession of prophets, including Zoroaster, Buddha and Jesus. Like Zoroaster he saw a universal conflict between Good and Evil, but like the Christian Gnostics he saw soul or spirit as good, and matter as the source of evil, so that the struggle was internal, between the light and darkness in each person. The religion was pacifist and vegetarian. Worship, fasting and giving to charity were the Three Pillars of Salvation – identical with three of the Five Pillars of Islam. Mani was concerned that his words should be preserved, unlike those of previous prophets, and he therefore insisted that all copies of his prophetic books be made from texts that he had prepared with his own hand. Poor Mani! In spite of his efforts, hardly anything of his scripture has survived.

A Manichaean church was organized, and it spread very rapidly, reaching into the Roman Empire and into China. However, its unity was broken by the appearance of Mazdakism, which started out as a reform movement within Manichaeism, and was similarly pacifist and vegetarian. This religion is known mainly from accounts given by its enemies, but it seems to have been founded on the idea that the root of evil is private ownership; property should therefore be held in common. It is said also to have called for women to be held in common, but perhaps it in fact taught the equality of the sexes – a scandal to its contemporaries. Its origins are obscure, but at the end of the fifth century CE its leader, Mazdak, briefly succeeded in persuading the Sasanian Emperor to regulate ownership and liberalize marriage. The reaction from the rich and from the Zoroastrian clergy led to persecution and drove the movement underground. Its ideas lived on in certain Christian and Muslim sects and may have contributed to the origins of socialism.

Sasanian society, like that of the Byzantine Empire, was strongly male-dominated, partly as a result of having possessed abundant female slaves for many centuries. The Emperor and the noblemen had enormous harems guarded by eunuchs – an institution that had spread to Byzantium. Women of the upper classes lived largely in seclusion, and if they went about in public they had to be veiled. Virgin women were much sought after for their sexual value, and the lot of widows and divorcees was not a happy one.

The religions of the Sasanian Empire clearly belonged to the same world of ideas as those of the West, with which they held in common the belief in God, Satan, scriptures, divine law, resurrection, Heaven and Hell, orthodoxy and heresy, the People of God and the Enemies of God. A shared concept of the role of prophet had grown up, defined by the lives and works of those who had been called by this name, yet no prophet had succeeded in leaving an incontestable record of his teachings. Partly because of this there were endless disputes over doctrine and practice. With India and China out of view, there seemed to be nowhere from which to expect a new vision of the unity of religion. However, there was one place that had not yet been brought into the troubled world of monotheism: Arabia, 'the Island of the Arabs'. It was soon to be an island no longer.

by alliances between related groups maintaining an approximate balance of forces. Rough justice was obtained by retaliation against any member of the offender's group, an eye for an eye, a life for a life, but alternatively honour could be satisfied by accepting blood payment, normally in the form of livestock. However, many feuds went on for generations, exploding periodically into warfare. One particularly Arab institution was the raid or *razzia*, whose object was to seize livestock and other property from an enemy group, with killing as a regrettable side-effect rather than the object.

Arab society was collectivist in that the honour of the group was paramount, and its members must be ready even to sacrifice their lives in the common interest. However, society was also individualist in that each person's contribution depended absolutely on his or her personal qualities and capacities. For a man the supreme virtue was manliness, aptly described by R. A. Nicholson as 'bravery in battle, patience in misfortune, persistence in revenge, protection of the weak, defiance of the strong'. An individual could amass wealth, mainly in the form of livestock, but the advantage of doing so was the ability to offer lavish hospitality and to help poorer members of the group. Enemies could be unscrupulously deceived, but keeping faith with friends was a great virtue. One of the Arabs' folk heroes was the Jew Samawal Ibn Adiya, who allowed his son to be killed as a hostage rather than surrender weapons entrusted to him for safe-keeping by the poet Imrul-Qays.

The religion of the desert was animist, involving cultivation of good relations with the spirits, jinns and afrits believed to inhabit rocks, springs, trees and other living things. The desert Arabs showed little interest in more abstract deities. There were various shrines and places of pilgrimage, but the religious significance of these for the Bedouin seems to have been limited, and they may have visited them more for the associated markets and fairs. The most important shrine was the Kaaba of Mecca – an ancient cubic temple around which were ranged idols, said to have numbered three hundred and sixty. The Kaaba was at the centre of a sanctuary where fighting was prohibited and people might seek refuge.

Dotted about the peninsula were hundreds of oases, whose inhabitants had a very different way of life, working their date-palms, fruit trees and fields, storing up surpluses, trading and amassing wealth. To the fierce Bedouin they were a constant source of temptation, and the oasis people had to maintain sound defences and to cultivate alliances with the desert tribes, whether as relatives, clients or confederates. Through trade, some of the oases had contact with the settled peoples of Mesopotamia, Syria or Abyssinia, and foreign cultural influences were felt. In particular there were oases – most notably Yathrib, later to be called Medina – with a nucleus of Jewish inhabitants, including rabbis who knew the Hebrew Scriptures and perhaps some later writings. They may have belonged to a sect that had a special regard for Ezra, probable final editor of the Torah, to whom various apocryphal books are attributed (Koran 9:30). There were also Christians in Najran on the northern borders of Yemen.

Mecca

The most important settled community was that of Mecca, just south of the tropic of Cancer in the western foothills of the mountains of the Hijaz. It was not an oasis, having hardly any cultivable land, nor was it at all a congenial site for settlement, for the air trapped in its steep-sided valley was still and very hot, with daytime temperatures above blood-heat for half the year. It owed its importance both to its possession of the shrine of the Kaaba and to its place at the junction of trade-routes between Yemen and Syria and between Abyssinia and Persia. After a long period of abandonment, it had been repopulated by the tribe of Quraysh. Although their ancestors had quit nomadism and settled down only a century or so before the birth of Muhammad, they considered themselves greatly superior to the Bedouin. Indeed, the Quraysh did not include themselves under the name of 'Arabs', which they reserved for the nomads (see for example Koran 9:96).

Contact with foreign merchants and the possession of the Kaaba had opened the minds of the Quraysh to ideas from outside Arabia. They seem to have seen religion in terms of gods and goddesses rather than local spirits, and they recognized Allah (from al-ilah, literally 'the God') as the principal god. They believed him to be the father of three goddesses – of Allat, whose shrine was at Taif, of Uzza who was worshipped in the form of a sacred tree at Nakhla, on the way to Taif, and of Manat, enshrined in a white rock between Mecca and Yathrib. The Quraysh had an economic interest in the cult of these and other deities.

Literacy was rare or non-existent among the desert Arabs, for there was nothing except rocks and skins for them to write on, and they had developed their powers of memory to a point where writing was hardly needed. In the oases things were different. The Quraysh in particular, with their business interests, needed to draw up contracts and keep accounts. A North Semitic alphabet had been adapted for use in Arabic, and it seems that quite a number of Meccans could write. However, there is no evidence of their having had any schools, still less libraries.

The social system of Mecca was essentially that of the desert Arabs. The family tree of Figure 2 shows the principal subdivisions. Muhammad's great-great-great-grandfather, Qusayy, was credited with having led the process of settling Mecca, which had previously been a camp-site for the periodic fairs centred on the Kaaba. The clans that descended from him had the leading role in the community, though they had been weakened by a split between the sons of Abd-al-Dar, who held the keys of the Kaaba and those of Abd-Manaf (including Hashim, Muhammad's clan) who had the privilege of providing food and water to pilgrims. Outside the clans descended from Qusayy, the most prestigious was Makhzum, whose leader, Walid, was the most powerful man in Mecca during the earlier part of Muhammad's life. There had been shifting alliances of clans, but the one that was most important in his time

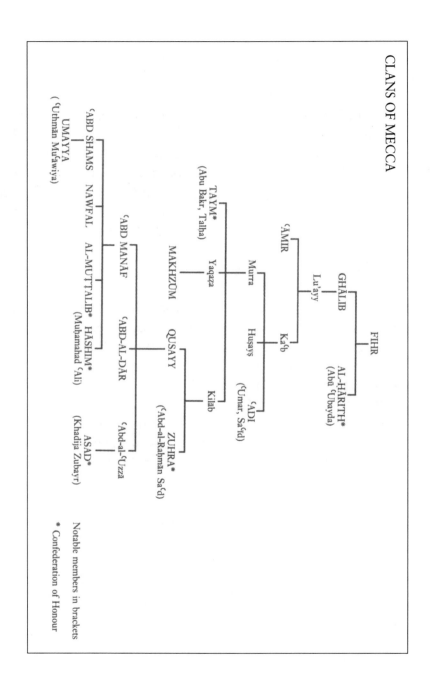

FIGURE TWO

CLANS OF MECCA

Notable members in brackets

* Confederation of Honour

was the 'Confederacy of Honour', in which Muhammad's clan was joined with Asad, Zuhra, Taym and Adi. Its object was to enforce honest dealing by Meccan financiers and traders.

The leading men of the most powerful families formed a council that functioned as a rudimentary government for the city. Many Western writers have referred to the Meccan 'aristocracy', but that is a concept foreign to the Arabs. Each of the main families considered itself the best, and the standing of each in the eyes of the others fluctuated from generation to generation with changes in the number of men, in the force of character of their leaders and in the size of their fortunes. Muhammad's clan, Hashim, was on its way down before his prestige caused it to be permanently raised above the others.

In the course of their short history of settlement, the Quraysh had prospered enormously through commerce and finance. The richest had become wealthy in ways and to an extent unknown to the desert Arabs. They lived in large houses divided into rooms or apartments grouped round a courtyard. They called the rooms 'tents' and the whole house a 'circle' [of tents]. Some families also owned land and secondary residences in the nearby oasis of Taif. We do not have descriptions of the contents of houses in the time of Muhammad, but it is safe to assume that they were richly furnished with things made from the produce of the desert: woollen carpets, cushions and curtains, and all manner of leather goods. There would also be a wide variety of utensils, ornaments and jewellery in metal, glass or pottery, made locally or imported from Syria, Mesopotamia or Yemen. The rich could even possess furniture made from fine woods and clothes of imported fabrics, and they could consume exotic foods, spices and drinks, within the limits of conservation during transport, perfumes, oils and balms and other products for toiletry and beautification.

There was a shocking contrast between this wealth and the poverty of the poor. With their nomadic background, the Quraysh had no inherited system for the redistribution of wealth. In the desert even the rich enjoyed little luxury, and fortunes ebbed and flowed with the slow changes brought by the breeding and consumption of livestock and with the sudden advent of raids, disease or depredation by wild animals. Moreover, the harshness of desert life maintained consciousness of the obligation to help the poor, since failure to do so would condemn them to death. In Mecca the rich were offensively rich and they tended to neglect their duty to the less fortunate. Widows, orphans and the disabled could be driven to begging, prostitution or theft.

Lower even than the poor were the slaves, who had no legal protection against bad owners. The desert Arabs had slaves, but nothing like the numbers to be found working for the wealthier families in Mecca, who hardly needed to do any physical work. Many of the women slaves and practically all the men had been born into slavery or captured as young children. A high proportion of them were of African origin. A slave had little prospect of being freed, and a female slave was likely to be forced to be her master's concubine and to see her children grow up as slaves.

The problems of the poor and the slaves may have been worsened by an economic decline. Arabia was surrounded by three great powers: the Byzantine Empire, the Sasanian Empire in Iraq and Iran, and the much smaller Christian Empire of Axum, in Abyssinia. The Axumites had controlled Yemen and southern Arabia, but they were driven out by the Sasanians soon after the birth of Muhammad. This led to a reduction in trade through Mecca between Yemen and the Byzantines. The position grew still worse some forty years later with the Sasanian capture of southern Syria and Egypt.

CHAPTER THREE

THE PREPARING OF THE PROPHET

The Orphan

We know little for certain about Muhammad's early life. The Koran tells us the essentials (93:6): 'Did [Allah] not find you an orphan and protect you, find you wandering and guide you, find you in need and enrich you?' Accounts written down long after the event offer plenty of detail, much of it credible. As a great-great-grandson of Abd-Manaf, Muhammad came from one of the most important groups in Mecca. His great-grandfather, Hashim, had been destined to share leadership in the family caravan business with his three brothers, taking Syria as his specialist domain, but he died young, leaving Muhammad's grandfather, Abd-al-Muttalib, to be brought up by his mother's people in Yathrib (later Medina), an oasis several days journey to the north, where he had been born.

Abd-al-Muttalib was brought to Mecca as a boy, to serve his uncle Muttalib – hence his name, 'Muttalib's Servant'. From this humble beginning he rose to establish himself as one of the leading figures of the town. He re-discovered the long-lost sacred well of Zamzam in the precinct of the Kaaba. He also inherited his uncle's privilege of providing food and water to the poorer pilgrims, which was paid for by a sort of tax levied on the wealthy families of Mecca. He is said to have acted as a spokesman negotiating on behalf of the town with Abraha, who brought an Abyssinian expeditionary force, complete with elephants, into the area in the year of Muhammad's birth – 'the Year of the Elephant', usually taken to be 570 CE.

Abd-al-Muttalib had ten sons and six daughters by five wives. Muhammad's grandmother, Fatima, came from the powerful clan of Makhzum. Besides Muhammad's father, Abd-Allah, she bore two of the other boys and five of the girls. Abd-Allah came somewhere in the middle of the family, but we know little about him, except that he is said to have died staying with his grandmother in Yathrib on his way back from a trading visit to Syria.

When Abd-Allah died his wife was expecting their first child, Muhammad. She was Aminah bint Wahb of clan Zuhra, of whose short and sad life little is known. She had lost her parents and been brought up in the home of her uncle Wuhayb, whose daughter Hala must have become very close to her. Soon after the baby was born he was sent out for two or three years to a Bedouin foster mother, Halima. It was the custom among the wealthier families of the Quraysh to have their sons fostered in this way, as the desert was reckoned healthier than the town – morally as well as physically. Because of this Aminah only enjoyed her little boy for a short time. She died when he was six, on her way back with him from a visit to his great-grandmother's people in Yathrib.

During Muhammad's brief years with his mother, it seems that they lived with her people. When she died he came to the home of his grandfather Abd-al-Muttalib. Besides five camels and a few sheep, the little orphan's sole inheritance was his father's African slave, Baraka, who was only a little older than him. She mothered him through the rest of his childhood, and provided his deepest link with the past.

Muhammad's aunts and female cousins played an important part in his childhood, something that probably taught him to enjoy the company of women throughout his life. Foremost among these figures was his mother's cousin Hala bint Wuhayb, who had married Abd-al-Muttalib. Hala's son Hamza, an unusually big, strong boy, was only a little older than Muhammad and was probably his protector and champion in childhood, as he was in later life. Her daughter Safiya was a little younger than Muhammad, and he felt a special affection for her. She was to become one of the first and most ardent Muslims. Two other aunts of Muhammad, Arwa and Atika, may also have taken a special interest in him and were to be among his early converts. His aunt Umayma was clearly fond of him too, and all of her children became Muslims, though she herself appears not to have accepted the religion. Muhammad eventually married her daughter Zaynab.

Besides Hamza, three other uncles played an important part in his boyhood and later life. The eldest of these was Abu Talib, a full brother of Muhammad's father. The other two, Abu Lahab and Abbas, were born of two different Bedouin mothers. Abu Lahab was the elder, and does not seem to have been close to Muhammad in childhood, being perhaps specially jealous of his father's attention to the orphan. Abbas was closer to Muhammad in age, and seems always to have had cordial relations with him. His great-great-grandsons founded the Abbasid caliphate, which ruled at the time when most of the Hadith literature was written down, so it is hard to know how much to credit in the reports about him.

Abd-al-Muttalib had himself grown up without a father and must therefore have understood better than anyone his grandson's feelings. The old man used to spend his day reclining on a couch in the shade of the Kaaba, watching over the Well of Zamzam and the feeding and watering of pilgrims. The only person who was allowed to share his couch, having his back rubbed, was little Muhammad – provoking the jealousy of the old man's sons. Unfortunately Abd-al-Muttalib's protection was not to last; he died only two years after Muhammad's mother, when Muhammad was eight. His property was divided between his sons, with nothing going to Muhammad, for there was no provision in Arab custom for an orphan to inherit a deceased parent's share. Actually the deprivation seems to have been more symbolic than material, for none of the sons ended up wealthy. The one who did best was Abbas, who inherited his father's position as guardian of Zamzam.

Muhammad now joined the household of Abu Talib and his wife Fatima. It is not clear whether this meant moving to different premises or simply to a different part of Abd-al-Muttalib's establishment. At any rate, his faithful nurse, Baraka, was still with him. Abu Talib's son Talib may have been jealous of the newcomer, and never seems to have been close to him. Much the same is true of the next son, Aqil, born a couple of years after the arrival of Muhammad, though he did eventually become a Muslim. The two youngest sons, Jaafar and Ali, born respectively a little before and a little after Muhammad left the household, were to become his very close friends. There were also three daughters. We know little about Muhammad's life in his uncle's household, but there is a story of Abu Talib taking him on a business trip to Syria when he was twelve.

Abu Talib's commercial ventures were apparently a failure; indeed it is said that he was reduced at one time to driving camels out to pasture – a humiliation for a man from a good family. Certainly, he was not in any position to help his nephew to start a career. Muhammad too worked as a herdsman, whether with the animals he had inherited or to earn his living, and this may have been the beginning of his later custom of musing alone in the hills around Mecca – a first hint of his future vocation.

The Busy Family Man
In the course of time, Muhammad overcame the disadvantages of his orphan childhood and acquired a reputation for honesty and competence. He was nicknamed 'al-Amin, the Trustworthy'. By his mid-twenties his good character had attracted the attention of a wealthy widow, Khadija of clan Asad, who was several years older than him. She had heard a great deal about him from her sister-in-law, his young aunt Safiya. Khadija was a prosperous business-woman on her own account. She put Muhammad in charge of a caravan to Syria and, following his successful return, a marriage was arranged.

Khadija, who already had children by previous marriages, bore Muhammad four daughters, Zaynab, Ruqayya, Umm Kulthum and Fatima. There were also two (possibly three) sons, none of whom survived infancy. The household was soon increased by the addition of Ali, son of Abu Talib. The latter had fallen on such hard times that his half-brother Abbas agreed with Muhammad that the two of them should go along and offer to take over the upbringing of his two younger sons, respectively Jaafar, born about 590, and Ali, born about 600. So it came about that Ali grew up like a son to Muhammad and like a brother to his future wife Fatima. The great significance of this will be seen when the origin of Shia Islam is considered.

There was another virtual son in the household, Zayd Ibn Haritha. He had been a Bedouin child, captured and sold as a slave in Syria, brought back to Mecca, acquired by Khadija and given as a present to Muhammad. Zayd's father eventually traced him and asked for him back, but the boy said he was so happy with Muhammad's family that he preferred to stay. Muhammad was so touched that he gave him his freedom and adopted him as a son. Zayd, who was at most fifteen years younger than Muhammad, was in effect the oldest of the children. For most of his life he was known as Zayd Ibn Muhammad.

The household was completed by its slaves, in particular Salma, who assisted Khadija in the birth of all her children, and Rafi, who eventually married Salma when both had been given their freedom by Muhammad. As for his dear Baraka, whom he had freed when he married Khadija, and for whom he had arranged a marriage, she had come back to his household after losing her husband and was now called Umm Ayman after her son. Zayd then married her, though she may by then have been in her early forties, and she bore him a son, Usama, whom Muhammad loved like a grandson.

Only one incident is reported from this time. The Kaaba was in a dangerous state and needed to be completely rebuilt. The clans agreed a division of labour that left none of them feeling disadvantaged, but their agreement broke down when the time came to replace the Black Stone – the most sacred part of the structure. Fighting was about to break out when the leaders agreed to seek arbitration from the next person to enter the precinct. At that moment, in came Muhammad. They appealed to him, and he proposed that the Stone be placed on a cloak, that a representative of each clan should hold a corner of the cloak to lift it to the right level and that he himself should then set the Stone in place. His solution was adopted and battle averted.

It is frustrating to know so little about this period, but we have a picture of a devoted family man with a growing reputation in the community for wisdom and straight dealing. He was no doubt still occupied to some extent with running his wife's business, but her wealth afforded him considerable leisure. He could happily have continued on this course, enjoying a well-deserved prosperity, working quietly to improve society in small ways and influencing people by his personal example. However, he was dissatisfied by the worldly pleasures of Meccan society and the injustice towards orphans, widows, slaves and the poor. He took to retreating alone into the bare, rocky hills around Mecca to listen in silence for some deeper truth.

It is probable that he was influenced in this by the small circle of Meccans who were dissatisfied with the conventional religion of the town. Two of these, Waraqa and Uthman Ibn al-Huwayrith, were first cousins of Khadija, and another, Ubayd-Allah Ibn Jahsh, was the son of Muhammad's aunt Umaymah. All three men eventually became Christians, Ubayd-Allah after emigrating as a Muslim to Abyssinia, Uthman in Byzantium, but Waraqa without having left Mecca. A fourth man, Zayd Ibn Amr, was alone in continuing to seek for the true religion of Abraham. He went on a vain search for fellow believers in Mesopotamia and Syria and died on his way back to Mecca, before he could hear of Muhammad's call to Islam. His son Said was to become one of the first Muslims and one of those closest to Muhammad. Together, the four seem to have formed a sort of secret society, and Muhammad may have been its fifth member, at least for a time.

The case of Waraqa is particularly interesting, as he became a Christian at quite an early date – early enough to have influenced Muhammad. As there was no Christian presence in Mecca, Waraqa must have been converted by someone passing through the town. According to the *Sira* (p. 99), he read Christian writings, probably just two or three scrolls, perhaps in Syriac (a Christian form of Aramaic). It may have been from Waraqa that Muhammad first heard the Biblical version of some stories.

Whatever the influence of these other seekers after truth, Muhammad followed his own solitary course. Mecca was a small town, and a few minutes walking were enough to bring him out into the stillness of the surrounding hills. These were steep and bare, and few plants had escaped the attention of goats long enough to grow to any size. By day the sun beat down with tropical strength. By night the temperature fell steeply as the stars came out with desert brilliance. It was a wonderful place to realize the majesty of the world, the miracle of life and the fragility of humanity. Muhammad took to spending whole days in the hills, and he sometimes slept there, wrapped in his cloak. According to one account he used to stay there for the whole month of Ramadan, with his family bringing him food and water. One is reminded of Moses meditating in the Egyptian Desert, and of Jesus going alone into the hills of Galilee to pray.

CHAPTER FOUR

THE MESSENGER

The Call

Islam is founded on the belief that Muhammad received the message of Allah for humanity, a message that had been brought before by other prophets including Abraham, Moses and Jesus. For many centuries, non–Muslim accounts of this were based on Christian or Jewish assumptions that, since Muhammad's mission was by their definition false, he must therefore have been either fraudulent or deluded. Such a view does not bear examination, for his task was to put an end forever to comfort and security for himself, his family and his associates.

What happened to Muhammad was outside normal human experience, and we cannot hope to obtain more than a very approximate idea of it. One must distinguish between his original experience, his later attempts to describe and explain it, and the standard picture that was eventually adopted. The first of these three levels of description can only be arrived at through the second and third. The oldest evidence by far is that of the Koran itself, which is the divine message that Muhammad understood himself to have received. Next comes the account by the historian Zuhri, preserved by Tabari, based on personal acquaintance with those who had known Muhammad's companions. Finally there is the narrative of Ibn Ishaq, written a generation later, which is the basis for all later descriptions.

The crucial event was the coming of the first Koranic passage, which took place, according to all accounts, in the month of Ramadan, probably in the year 610 CE, when Muhammad was about forty. However, this followed a long period of preparation. According to his widow, Aisha, as reported by Zuhri, Muhammad's experience began with true vision, which used to come like the dawning of day. It was after this that he became attached to solitude and took to staying in a cave on Mount Hira to practise mortification for several nights, before going back to his family to get provisions for another stay.

On one of these occasions, Muhammad was overwhelmed by a tremendous presence. The earliest account of such an encounter is given by Koran 53:1–18 (though it has also somewhat improbably been claimed as a reflection of his vision of a visit to Jerusalem):

> By the star when it goes down,
> Your companion has not erred nor gone astray,
> Nor does he speak out of desire.
> It is nothing but revelation revealed,
> Taught by the Mighty of Power,
> Possessor of Strength. He stood
> On the highest horizon,
> Then drew near and came down
> So that he was two bow-lengths off or nearer,
> Then revealed to his servant the revelation.
> The heart has not lied about what he saw,
> So will you dispute with him about what he sees?
> Also he saw him on a second descent
> By the furthest zizyphus bush
> By which is the Garden of the Abode,
> When That which pervades covered the zizyphus;
> The eye did not flinch nor did it strain.
> He saw one of his Lord's greatest signs.

There is a remarkable parallel here with Moses' vision of a radiant bush: 'He led his flock beyond the wilderness and came to Horeb, the mountain of God. There an angel of YHWH appeared to him in a flame of fire out of a bush; he looked, and the bush was blazing, yet it was not consumed' (Exodus 3:1–3).

A similar account is given by Koran 81:15–25, where the Presence is referred to as a messenger (*rasul*), a term soon to be applied to Muhammad himself:

> I swear by the stars
> That move and are hidden,
> And by the night when it fades,
> And by the day as it dawns,

It is the speech of a noble messenger,
Powerful, established with the Enthroned,
With authority there, faithful.
Your companion is not possessed,
And he indeed saw that on the clear horizon.

In Koran 26:193 this messenger is described as the Faithful Spirit:

It is indeed a revelation from the Lord of the Worlds;
The Faithful Spirit brought it down
On your heart, that you might be one of the warners
In a clear Arabic tongue.

These passages are taken by Muslims as referring to the Angel Gabriel (*Jibril*). However, Gabriel is mentioned by name in the Koran in only two places, both of them dating from after the Prophet left Mecca twelve years later (2:97–8 and 66:4). It may well be that he made no public claim to have received his message from an angel while he lived in Mecca, for the Meccans are represented as asking why no angel has been sent down to him (25:7–6:8):

They say: 'What is wrong with this messenger who eats food and goes in the market-places? Why has not an angel been sent down to him to be a warner with him?'

Whatever form Muhammad's experience of the Presence may have taken, the fact that it eventually came to be described in terms of a visitation from the Angel Gabriel does not require us to suppose that he saw a winged, man-like creature of the kind familiar from Western paintings and Persian miniatures, which is a simple way of representing something far outside normal experience. It is true that the Koran describes angels as 'winged messengers' (35:1), and says that eight of them will carry the Throne on the Last Day (69:17) but there is no need to take such statements literally.

Taking the common elements from the historians' accounts, one can say that one night on Mount Hira, probably just as day began to dawn, Muhammad was overwhelmed by a Presence. Either on this or a subsequent occasion, he had the experience of receiving words from the Presence. In the most commonly quoted account, he was told: '*Iqra!*' This can mean either 'read' or 'recite'. Muhammad is said to have replied: '*Ma aqra?*' which could mean either 'What am I to recite/read?' or 'I cannot recite/read'.

Three times, seeming to crush him, the order was repeated, and three times, with increasing agitation, Muhammad replied in the same way. The Presence then supplied what was to be Koran 96:1–5. It is possible that this was not chronologically the first revelation, and that it was later designated because of the appropriateness of 'recite' as the first word of the Recitation, which is the literal meaning of *qur'an* – Koran:

> Recite/read in the name of your Lord who created,
> Created humankind from a clot of blood.
> Recite/read! Your Lord is most generous,
> Who taught by the pen,
> Taught humankind what they did not know.

An important element in all the accounts of the first revelation is the pain and anxiety that it induced. Muhammad hurried home to Khadija feeling strangely cold and utterly drained. She covered him with a blanket until the terror had passed, and she gave him the most valuable support he could have hoped for – her belief in his mission. She contacted her cousin Waraqa, and he is said to have reassured Muhammad that he was indeed the prophet for his people.

Whatever the exact course of events on that momentous day, the starting point of the Prophet's mission was the conviction that he had been given Allah's message to his people. This implied a whole view of the world, familiar throughout the empires by which Arabia was surrounded: that there was a Supreme Being, the source of all existence, with implications for human behaviour that were transmitted by revelation through prophets. It is an open question whether, at this early stage, Muhammad foresaw that the recitations he was to receive would add up to form a scripture (*al-quran*, 'The Recitation'), but the reference to 'the pen' (96:4) in this early revelation does already suggest something to be written down.

A somewhat later passage, Koran 68:1–5, mentions the pen. This is also the first of 29 Koranic chapters to begin with letters of the alphabet, known as 'Quranic initials'. The letter N is pronounced 'noon', which is the Arabic word for 'ink'. The tone of reassurance confirms the account given by Zuhri and Ibn Ishaq of the distressed and self-doubting state of mind induced by the first experience of prophethood:

> N! By the pen and what they write,
> You are not, by the grace of your Lord, possessed,
> And for you there is indeed a reward not counted on.
> You are engaged in a mighty enterprise;
> Soon you will see and they will see
> Which of you is deluded.

The Embryonic Community

From the outset the Prophet always distinguished between the revelations, which came to him involuntarily, and his own thoughts. Western critics have gone through a succession of abusive interpretations. In the Middle Ages they claimed that Muhammad was possessed by a devil, which put words in his mouth. A later claim was that he hallucinated under the effect of epilepsy. Nineteenth-century writers suggested that he made up the Koran to suit his own purposes. A modern version is that his hearing voices of angels was a symptom of schizophrenia. None of this stands up to examination. On a number of occasions he is reported to have been surprised or even dismayed by the words that came to him, and the message certainly spelt the end of an easy life for him. As for his sanity, it is evident in his excellent practical judgement and his immense gift for friendship.

The fact that Muhammad so clearly distinguished between two kinds of utterances should convince rationalists that he experienced the revelations as not being his own conscious thoughts, whether or not he always felt an angelic presence. A way of understanding this that might satisfy both sides is to suppose that a deeper reality underlies the surface patterns of existence, and that Muhammad was one of those rare people capable of entering a state in which this reality uses their faculties to express itself.

The revelations took the form of verses of variable length and rhythm, each ending in a rhyme. They do not use the metres of Arabic verse, but they are anything but prosaic. Their language is highly compressed and forceful, with strong but constantly varying rhythms. An early passage (73:4) instructs Muhammad to intone the Koran in a regular, measured way. Chanted in Arabic, it has an almost mesmeric quality. The effect can never have been greater than on this first occasion, when these extraordinary words suddenly burst forth from a quiet and sober citizen who had never shown any inclination or gift for poetry or rhetoric. The notion that the Koranic verses were miraculous soon took root. Given the immense importance of language and eloquence in Arab culture, no more persuasive miracle could have been offered.

After one or two first revelations there was a painful silence, which may have lasted as long as two years. Muhammad almost despaired at this apparent withdrawal of divine favour. According to Zuhri he was several times tempted to throw himself over a precipice, but each time his Angelic Presence saved him. The Koranic verses that broke this silence may have been the following (93:1–11), with their assurance that Allah is not displeased.

> By the morning light,
> By the night when it is still,
> Your Lord has not left you nor is displeased.
> The last will be better for you than the first,
> And Allah will soon give you to be pleased.
> Did He not find you an orphan and shelter you?
> He found you straying and guided you.
> He found you needy and enriched you.
> So do not deprive the orphan,
> Nor scold the beggar;
> And proclaim the goodness of your Lord.

At first, Muhammad kept his mission a secret, and the community of the faithful consisted of the members of his household: Khadija and her four daughters, Ali, aged about ten, Zayd Ibn Haritha, aged perhaps twenty-five, Baraka Umm Ayman and one or two slaves. There were probably a few cousins and close friends who were in on the secret, a matter to be discussed below. By acknowledging Allah alone and Muhammad his Prophet, these first believers were in effect bearing Witness, which is one of the Five Pillars of Islam – the five elements that were to define the essence of the religion. The formula that came to be customary for this is attested by the Koran: 'I witness that there is no god but Allah (37:35) and that Muhammad is the Messenger of Allah (48:29)'. It is best not to refer to it as a 'creed' as it is not intended, like the Christian creeds, to distinguish between orthodoxy and heresy.

The Prophet's Angelic Presence soon inspired him with the knowledge of how to wash ritually and to perform Worship, which is another of the Five Pillars. The Arabic, *salat*, is often translated as 'prayer' in European languages, but it is rather different from Christian prayer. It consists of an ordered series of physical movements – standing, bowing, kneeling, prostrating oneself, sitting back on the heels – accompanied by simple formulae, spoken aloud or silently, according to context. Praise and submission are expressed by the whole person, body and mind together, and there is no listing of requests to Allah. The other three Pillars of Islam – Charity, Fasting and Pilgrimage – were not formally imposed on the faithful until later, but they were already present in potential. Generosity to the poor and weak is called for in some of the earliest revelations, fasting seems to have been a private practice of the Prophet long before the fast of Ramadan was instituted, and pilgrimage did not need to be formalized as long as the faithful lived in the neighbourhood of the Kaaba that is its focus. The essence of the religion was thus present even before the public mission began.

The first person outside the family to accept the new religion was Muhammad's great friend and probable business associate,

Abu Bakr, of clan Taym; already the Prophet was reaching out beyond his own clan. The date of Abu Bakr's acceptance of the religion is not clear. Ibn Ishaq brackets it with that of Ali and Zayd, and goes straight on to give a list of men converted by Abu Bakr at an early date. First there were five men who, together with Ali and Abu Bakr, would belong to the group of Ten who were to become the Prophet's closest companions. Then came thirty-six more men, two of them further members of the Ten, and nine women. All these were, according to Ibn Ishaq, converted before Muhammad made his mission public, and they used to worship secretly in wadis outside the town.

It is conceivable that Ibn Ishaq's account is correct, but it seems unlikely that the secret could have been kept with some sixty people knowing it. It is more probable that he telescoped events, and that most of these conversions happened after Muhammad had come forward publicly as Prophet. A hint of this is given in Ibn Ishaq's statement: 'When [Abu Bakr] became a Muslim he showed his Islam openly and called people to Allah and his Messenger.' Abu Bakr may not have entered the faith until shortly before the start of the public mission. The date of his conversion may have been brought forward in order to put him on a par with Ali. The two men were eventually to be seen as having been rivals for the leadership of Islam after the death of Muhammad, and it was to become politically important for the partisans of Abu Bakr to justify his priority. Anyway it seems that both were among the first three male believers. Ali had the advantage of growing up in Muhammad's household and living in the faith from the age of about ten. Abu Bakr had the advantage of being his closest friend among men of his own age and of accepting the religion from the first with the mind of a mature man.

These first Muslims did not just assent to a set of propositions; they were overwhelmed by the power and intensity of the Prophet's conviction, when nothing in their social context favoured his radical message. Soon they would be taking risks and making sacrifices in its name. For more than a decade they were to hold firm as an increasingly embattled minority.

CHAPTER FIVE

THE MESSAGE

Preaching to a Sceptical Public

After having kept his secret for two years, the Prophet was finally instructed by his Angelic Presence to proclaim the religion publicly. It may have been Koran 74:1-10 that gave him the signal, though some accounts made it the very first revelation:

> You who are wrapped up,
> Rise up and warn.
> Magnify your Lord;
> Be pure in your dress;
> Shun the abominable;
> Do not give for profit;
> Endure patiently for your Lord.
> When the Trumpet is sounded,
> That day will be distressful,
> For the ungrateful nothing easy.

According to Ibn Ishaq, the Prophet saw it as his first duty to bring his message to the members of his clan (throwing further doubts on the claim that many conversions outside it were made before the public mission began). He is said to have invited some forty men of the Bani Abd-al-Muttalib to hear him speak. However, apart from Ali, only one of them is to be found in the lists of early converts: Jaafar, the older brother of Ali. There was also a member of the Muttalib clan, Ubayda. They were joined some time later by Muhammad's childhood companion, Hamza, the son of Hala – the only one of his uncles to accept the faith while the Prophet lived in Mecca.

Of the Prophet's other surviving uncles, Abu Talib was unconvinced but protective, and Abu Lahab sooner or later downright hostile, although at one stage his son had been engaged to one of Muhammad's daughters. The position of Abbas is hard to judge, because of the claims made by partisans of his descendants, the Abbasid caliphs. He was probably benevolently neutral, but his Bedouin wife Umm al-Fadl is said to have been an early believer like her sister Maymuna, who eventually married the Prophet, and their half-sisters Salma, who married Hamza, and Asma, who married Jaafar.

Because the clan system traced descent through the male line, the children of Muhammad's paternal aunts and maternal uncles and aunts were not members of his clan, but it is worth noting among the earliest believers his paternal cousins Zubayr, son of Safiya, two sons of Barra, and the three sons and three daughters of Umayma. There were also three sons of Hala's brother Abu Waqqas.

However, the Prophet never valued people by their place in the clan system. From the beginning he saw his message as being addressed to everyone, and for him all believers were equal in the sight of Allah. As soon as he began his public mission, converts started coming in from all the clans of the Quraysh, and from among Bedouin confederates and clients, and from the ranks of the slaves. This is not to say that Muhammad ignored ties of kinship; on the contrary, he always showed a keen sense of their social importance, and in his private life he was conscientious in attending to the needs of his relatives, whether or not they were believers, continuing to send them gifts even after he had become the most powerful man in Arabia. But this was a matter of personal morality; it did not mean that any one was higher in the sight of Allah by virtue of kinship with him.

What was the message that these first believers accepted? It is not possible to know for certain, since we rarely know the dates of particular revelations. The Koran in its final form consists of 114 suras. 'Sura' is often translated as 'chapter', but the division of the Koran is quite different from that of an ordinary book into chapters. The suras are of very unequal length, ranging from three short verses to nearly three hundred long ones. It would be perfectly possible to divide the longer suras into chapters, for their subject matter is very varied, and they were put together out of verses received at different times. Each sura is self-contained, and there is not usually any special reason to read them in a particular order.

The passages accepted as early all have very short verses consisting often of only two or three words, and the rhyme-word is an integral part of the sense. The verses in the late suras may have dozens of words, even occasionally a hundred or more, and the rhyme is usually supplied by adding a rhyming phrase at the end of the verse. On this basis attempts have been made to date suras or even parts of suras by their length of verse and type of rhyme. From this, other features of style, vocabulary or teaching have come to be used as indicators of date. There is a danger of circular reasoning: a feature is deemed early because it is contained in early passages, but a passage is early because it contains early features.

Montgomery Watt in his *Muhammad at Mecca* (1953) adopted the argument that the earliest passages must be those that did not mention opposition, since 'before opposition could arise some message which tended to arouse opposition must have been proclaimed'. On this basis he concluded that the following passages indicate the original message: 51:1–6; 52 (parts); 55; 74:1–10; 80:1–32; 84:1–12; 86:1–10; 87:1–9, 14–15; 88:17–20; 90:1–11; 93; 96:1–8; 106. At the heart of the initial teaching, according to this analysis, is the message that Allah, the source of all being, is benevolent and bountiful (80:24–32):

> Now let humankind look at their food,
> How We pour water down,
> Then We break the soil up,
> And We cause to grow in it grain,
> And grapes and vegetables,
> And the olive tree and the date palm,
> And walled gardens well stocked,
> And fruit and grass,
> Provision for you and your livestock.

Note that this is continuous creation; the Allah of the Koran is not a celestial watchmaker who, having started the Universe off, left it to run by itself; every event – the falling of rain, the germination of seed, the ripening of fruit – is a divine act.

The human response should be one of gratitude, generosity and purification, which find expression straight away in worship. For Islam, this does not just mean indulging in good feelings towards Allah, nor even just giving voice to them in words; it means expressing them with the whole body in *salat*. The difference between believers and unbelievers is thus not that they do or do not assent to this or that abstract statement, but that believers perform worship and unbelievers do not. The faithful were not yet confronted by the problem of hypocrites, who are outwardly but not inwardly believers.

Belief also has ethical consequences. Watt's selection of the earliest Koranic passages give little indication of these, but if the continuation of sura 90 (verses 13–16) is accepted as evidence, the 'steep path' of virtue is:

> The freeing of a slave,
> Or feeding on a day of hunger
> An orphaned relative,
> Or a beggar in the dust.

Another early passage generalizes the distinction between open-handedness and tight-fistedness (92:5–11):

> As for him who gives and who relies on piety
> And affirms the good,
> We shall smooth the way to ease;
> But as for him who stints and who relies on riches
> And denies the good,
> We shall smooth the way to difficulty,
> And his wealth shall not profit him when he perishes.

The essence of generosity is not merely economic. It is allied to an inner purification, expressed by the verb *tazakka*. It is not necessary to be a rich benefactor to achieve this purity of heart.

Muhammad is rebuked in sura 80 for having paid less attention to a blind man, who may have been able to achieve purity, than to a rich man, who may not have been. This verb comes from the root that also gave *zakat*, which later became the technical term for charitable giving, another of the Five Pillars of the religion.

There is as yet no mention of murder, theft, adultery, false witness or the many other ethical topics that were to figure in the later passages of the Koran. These were no doubt already recognized as evils in the eyes of the Meccans; what they needed to be told before all else was the evil of tolerating a gulf between rich and poor.

The message was backed by the promise and threat of a day of reckoning, usually understood as the Last Day, the day when history shall come to an end, the dead shall be raised and Heaven and Hell filled. However, this has always been interpreted by some Muslims as a metaphorical description of a spiritual experience, for example in Koran 84:1–5, 7–13. This can be read as meaning that, having been spiritually transformed, a person can achieve a new and joyful life in society:

> When the sky is rent open,
> And hears her Lord as she must,
> And when the earth is flattened out,
> And throws out what is in her and is empty,
> And hears her Lord as she must,
>
> . . .
>
> Then he who is given his record in his right hand
> Shall have an easy reckoning
> And shall go back to his people rejoicing;
> But he who is given his record behind his back
> Shall call for oblivion,
> And shall burn in fire;
> He had been among his people rejoicing,
> He had thought he would not return [for judgement].

Trouble

It was not long before the message brought hostility and ridicule from many Meccans. What most alarmed them was the affirmation

53

that Allah was the only deity, and that the gods and goddesses who attracted the pilgrims did not exist. This was a new element in the teaching, not in the sense of being a contradiction of anything said before, but in that it is not explicit in the earliest parts of the Koran. However Muhammad was a constant visitor to the Kaaba, and even before his call to prophethood it may have been noticed that he was not impressed by the idols ranged all about it. The Meccans must have realized very early that he threatened the pilgrimage business. The Koran does not in fact contain any demand for the physical destruction of idols. Instead it repeatedly calls for a spiritual rejection of the error of associating partners with Allah. This is far wider than the Biblical commandment not to worship graven images, for it applies to setting up anything, however vast or however abstract, as being of the same majesty or nature as Allah.

It is difficult to know exactly how opposition developed, for the record is very sparse. The conflict is often presented as having been between clans, but that is probably more a reflection of the later rivalry for influence once Islam had triumphed. From the beginning, each clan had its own internal problem with its own Muslims, who were scattered all across the clan system. For example, within a year of beginning his public mission, the Prophet had been given space for his activities in the house of a member of Clan Makhzum, whose head was the leader of the opposition to Islam, nicknamed by the faithful 'Abu Jahl (Father of Ignorance)'. Another clan that later produced powerful opponents, Abd-Shams, had provided one of his earliest converts, Muhammad's son-in-law, the future caliph Uthman Ibn Affan.

Once opposition had begun to develop, it built up rapidly. The Prophet himself was comparatively safe, but there were incidents involving bodily harm to believers. The worst affected were slaves, who had no means of protecting themselves against their owners. Over the next few years, Abu Bakr is said to have bought the freedom of seven slaves to save them from persecution. One of these was Bilal, an African born into slavery, whose master used to take him out at the hottest time of day and pin him down with a rock on his chest in a vain effort to make him renounce Islam.

Within two years of the beginning of the public mission, this persecution produced a dramatic response; with the Prophet's encouragement, successive parties of his followers migrated to Axum in Abyssinia, four hundred miles away across the Red Sea. With its trade links and its sister language, it was the least foreign of foreign countries for the Meccans, but what is most interesting is that he felt confident that his followers would be safest under the protection of a Christian monarch, the Negus Armah.

Eighty-three men are listed as having gone to Abyssinia, many of them with wives and children. This must have been a substantial proportion of the community of believers. They included four of the Ten who later became leaders. It is of particular interest that the emigrants included the Prophet's daughter Ruqayya, with her husband Uthman. There were also seven of his cousins: Jaafar, Abu Salama, Abu Sabra, Abd-Allah, Ubayd-Allah, Zubayr and Amir. If Muhammad was willing to see such close relatives go, perhaps he considered following them himself.

Little is known about this stay in Abyssinia, beyond the bare lists of those who went and came back and those who were born or died there. Indeed these lists may have been preserved only because they became important in allocating pensions to veterans. When Jaafar returned he is said to have brought thirty-two African converts, who did not enter history as named individuals, and there may have been others who stayed in Abyssinia. The only Muslim reported as converting to Christianity was Ubayd-Allah, who died there. At any rate it can be said that, only two years after the beginning of the Prophet's public mission, the religion had already reached another continent.

CHAPTER SIX

PERSECUTION

Living with Idol Worshippers

The removal of more than eighty families of his supporters from Mecca left the Prophet's position greatly weakened. It provoked a change of policy in his opponents; instead of each clan trying to deal with its own Muslims, they now joined forces for an attack on the position of Muhammad himself. However, he was under the protection of the leader of his own clan, his uncle Abu Talib. The outcome was a boycott of his people, Clan Hashim together with the small allied Clan Muttalib. It took the form of an agreement between the other clans not to engage in trade or marriage relations with the Hashimites.

About this time, the Prophet was fortunate in acquiring a powerful ally in the person of Umar Ibn al-Khattab, a forceful and respected man in his thirties. The story of his conversion is reminiscent of that of St Paul. He was an active opponent of the new religion, and one day he became so angry that he picked up his sword and set off allegedly to kill Muhammad. On his way he met a friend and learned that his own sister Fatima and her husband Said (son of the Zayd who had been one of the original group of five monotheists) were believers. Deeply shocked, Umar went to their house and heard through the door the chanting of a Koranic passage. He burst in and, after a skirmish in which his sister's hand was injured, asked remorsefully to be shown the parchment on which the verses – from sura 20 – were written. He was so moved by what he read that he went to the Prophet to announce his submission.

This story is interesting not only because it sheds light on the personality of Umar – the tenth of the Ten who were to be the leading companions of the Prophet – but also because it confirms that the writing down of the Koran had already begun, as implied by an earlier passage, Koran 80:11–16:

> But no! Surely it is a Reminder,
> So let them that wish be in mind of it,
> On honoured parchments,
> Exalted, purified,
> In the hands of writers,
> Noble, virtuous.

The story of the 'Satanic Verses' is placed in this period by the historian Tabari. In his *History*, he preserves Ibn Ishaq's account of an alleged compromise between the Prophet and the polytheists. After Koran 53:19–20, which asks them whether they have ever seen their goddesses, Allat, Uzza and Manat, he is said to have received the continuation 'Those are the exalted cranes, and their intercession is approved.' The Meccans were delighted when they heard what they took to be an acknowledgment of those whom they regarded as the 'daughters of Allah', and for a while there was peace between them and the Muslims. However, the spurious verses were soon replaced by 53:21–22 and 24–25:

> Are you to have males and Allah females?
> That then is an unfair division.
>
> . . .
>
> Can man have what he desires,
> When Allah's is the Last and the First?

Tabari used the story to explain the following passage from the Koran, said to have been revealed to console the Prophet for his alleged mistake. This is made plausible because the Arabic word for 'signs' also came to mean Koranic verses. However, this comes in a sura that was mostly or entirely revealed after the Prophet's move to Medina, and the words in question can be interpreted simply as a general statement that prophets, Muhammad included, are not infallible:

Never did we send a messenger nor a prophet before you but that,
when he had a longing, Satan injected something into the longing;
but Allah cancels what Satan injects and establishes the signs
[verses] – Allah is knowing, wise –

To make what Satan injects a test for those in whose hearts is
sickness, the hard of heart. Indeed the oppressors are in schism
far away. (22:52–53)

Tabari also used the story to explain the return of thirty-three
of the men who had migrated to Abyssinia, with their families,
but this could simply have been the result of the collapse of the
boycott of Hashim. The initiative to end it was taken by two men
who were related to Hashim through their mothers, and it may
be that female opposition behind the scenes played an important
part in breaking down this blockade based on male lineages. In any
case, the boycott had failed in its object of making the Prophet's
clan withdraw its protection from him.

The main interest of the alleged incident lies in the theological
questions that it raises concerning the nature of revelation, but
these were to arise anyway, and indeed Muslims have debated
them repeatedly down the ages. Tabari did not see it as in any way
derogatory. The Prophet comes out of it very honourably; at no
point did he compromise his monotheism, and he soon recognized
what had happened. There is no justification for the demeaning
treatment that the story has received in recent decades.

There is no need for the story of the 'Satanic Verses' to show
the Prophet's readiness to live and let live without compromising
his beliefs. The Koran has many passages that carry this message,
for example:

Let him who will believe, and let him who will disbelieve. (18:29).

When you hear the signs of Allah disbelieved and ridiculed, do
not sit with them until they turn to other talk. (6:68).

In the Name of Allah, the Merciful, the Forgiving,
Say: 'You ungrateful ones,
I do not worship what you worship,

Nor do you worship what I worship,
And I shall not worship what you worship,
Nor will you worship what I worship.
For you your religion and for me my religion.' (109:1–6).

Surely the clearest and most uncompromising statement of Allah's uniqueness is sura 112, which may date from this time. It is one of the two shortest, but the Prophet is said to have declared it equivalent to a third of the Koran:

In the Name of Allah, the Merciful, the Forgiving,
Say: 'Allah, is One,
Allah the eternal,
Neither begetting nor begotten,
And no one and nothing is like Allah.'

The Only Miracle
Whether or not the Prophet was misled in this particular case, he never claimed infallibility. The Koran instructs him to: 'Say "I am just a human being like you, but to me is given the revelation that Allah is One."' (18:110 and 41:6). Throughout his life he impressed precisely by his refusal to raise himself up above his fellows or to claim any miraculous powers. With all his adoring followers, many of them very simple men and women, he could easily have allowed rumours of supernatural events to develop. Instead he insisted on sober realism. When he was asked for miracles the Koran instructed him to reply: 'Am I anything but a human being – a messenger?' (17:93), and 'The Unseen is only for Allah; so wait, and I shall be with you as one of those who wait.' (10:20). The only miracle that the Prophet claimed was his receipt of the Koran, as is attested by the book itself. For example, 10:37–38 declares:

This Koran is not such as can be produced by less than Allah, but it is the confirmation of what was before it and an exposition of the Scripture – there is no doubt in it – from the Lord of the worlds.

Or do they say: '[Muhammad] produced it.'? Say: 'Then bring a sura like it; and ask help, if you can, of anyone less than Allah, if you speak the truth.'

There is however one event from this period that is often understood as miraculous: that of the Prophet's Night Journey to Jerusalem and his Ascent into Paradise. Many versions of this exist, but the basic account must go back to Muhammad, as is proved by Koran 17:1: 'Glory be to Him who carried his servant by night from the Sacred Mosque to the Furthest Mosque (*al-aqsa*), whose precinct We have blessed, so that We might show him some of our Signs.' According to the *Sira*, he was sleeping in the vicinity of the Kaaba one night when the angel Gabriel came to him with a winged steed called Buraq, which transported him to the Temple of Jerusalem, where he met Abraham, Moses and Jesus. Then a ladder came down from Heaven and Gabriel led him up. In the First Heaven he saw Adam reviewing the souls of his descendants, and he was shown the torments of the damned. They went on up to the Seventh Heaven, where the Prophet found Abraham again, who took him into Paradise.

The Night Journey has been accepted literally by many Muslims as a miracle. However, Ibn Ishaq implies that he understands it as a vision, and he quotes Aisha as saying: 'The Prophet's body stayed where it was, but Allah transported his spirit by night.' This is confirmed by Koran 17:60, if it indeed refers to this experience, as most commentators suppose: 'We made the vision that We showed you only as a test for the people.' Either way, this event is part of the basis for the great reverence Muslims feel towards Jerusalem, the third most holy city of Islam.

One other event referred to in the Koran is understood by many Muslims as miraculous. Taken literally it would have been a cataclysm of literally astronomical proportions:

The Hour is near and the Moon is split apart.
And if they see a sign they say: 'Passing magic!' (54:1–2).

The first of these two verses could grammatically refer to the future and belong with the signs of the Day of Judgment, like those that open suras 81, 82, 84 and 99. However the second verse suggests that there may have been a striking optical illusion comparable to a mirage, such as is possible in Mecca, where very hot layers of air near the horizon may come in contact with cool layers. It is certainly not an article of faith that trillions of tons of moon-rock physically separated a quarter of a million miles away, unnoticed by the world's astronomers.

The relationship between the religion proclaimed by the Prophet and previous forms of monotheism was meanwhile becoming clearer. Throughout the latter part of his mission in Mecca, stories of biblical figures were being added to the Koran. The most frequently mentioned is Moses (Musa), with 136 references (taking all periods of the Koran together). He is followed by Abraham (Ibrahim), with 69, Noah, with 43, and Jesus, with 36. There are also references to – in order of frequency – Joseph, Lot, Adam, Aaron, Solomon, Isaac, David, Jacob, Ishmael, Mary the mother of Jesus, Zachariah, John the Baptist, Jonah, Job and Elijah. Two extended accounts each occupy much of a sura – that of Joseph (Yusuf), sura 12, and that of Mary (Maryam), sura 19. Alongside these stories of Biblical figures, there are accounts of warners sent in the past to Arabian peoples, and of the disaster that followed when their warnings were not heeded.

The stories of the prophets given in the Koran differ in many ways from those in the Bible. They concentrate on a few incidents, often adding lengthy dialogue and comment. Strangely, read literally, they include miraculous elements, in spite of the Prophet's refusal to claim miracles for himself. Jesus, for example, speaks in the cradle (3:46) and breathes life into a clay bird as well as raising the dead and curing the blind (3:50). The virgin birth, now doubted as a literal fact by many Christians, is accepted by the Koran (19:20), but Jesus' crucifixion is denied, as it was by many Gnostics; his death on the cross was simply made to appear to happen (4:157).

Muslims believe that the differences with the Bible result from inaccuracies introduced by Jews and Christians, either wilfully or carelessly; the Koranic version of the divine message is the only true one. To non-Muslims they are evidence that the material in the Koran comes from the sources available to the Prophet, perhaps through Khadija's cousin Waraqa, even if he did not consciously compose the revelations. The contradictions cease to be important if both Koran and Bible are understood as being concerned not with the literal truth of statements about history, but with symbolic meanings and deeper truths.

In the course of this period, many descriptions of Paradise and Hell were added to the Koran. A good example is sura 52:17–28. Paradise was portrayed as shady gardens with flowing streams, where the faithful would enjoy wonderful fruits and exhilarating drinks without intoxication. They would be attended by chaste companions, fair and dark-eyed (and, by the way, the Koran does not promise seventy of them nor any other number). Hell was depicted as an eternal fire, where the hunger of the wicked would find only bitter fruit, and their thirst only boiling water. These can be read as literal descriptions of life after death, but many Muslims down the ages have understood them metaphorically.

It is explicitly stated in many passages that Paradise is for both men and women (e.g. 4:124). The persistent Western myth that Islam offers Paradise only to men may have arisen from the promise of dark-eyed feminine companions. However, it is a crude misunderstanding of the metaphor to suppose that there is any sex in the 'gardens through which streams flow'. The dark-eyed ones are grammatically feminine to symbolize purity and refinement of beauty. Nouns, verbs and adjectives for the faithful in Paradise are masculine because that is the inclusive gender in Arabic (but note that the word for 'self' or 'soul' is feminine). The faithful and the dark-eyed ones are no more male and female than are Moon and Sun or water and fire, which likewise are masculine and feminine pairs in Arabic. Incidentally, although the Arabic word *Allah* is grammatically masculine, two of the most frequently used names of Allah, *al-Rahman*, 'the Merciful', and *al-Rahim*, 'the Forgiving', which stand at the head of every sura but one, derive from the Arabic root *RHM*, 'womb'.

New Perspectives

The ending of the boycott brought only a brief respite. Soon after came the death of the head of the clan, Muhammad's uncle Abu Talib, a loyal protector, though never a believer. His place was taken by Abu Lahab, who refused to protect his nephew, alleging that Islam consigned their polytheist forefathers to Hell. This enmity earned for Abu Lahab and his wife a unique personal damnation (Koran 111). It is possible that the Prophet's loss of protection was only partial. Abu Lahab had a Bedouin mother, and may not have stood much higher than Muhammad's believing uncle, Hamza, whose mother was from the Quraysh. His third surviving uncle, Abbas, also with a Bedouin mother, appears to have remained benevolent to his nephew, and as custodian of the holy well of Zamzam he had considerable weight. Still, the Prophet's position was uncomfortable and indeed dangerous.

Things were made worse for Muhammad personally by the death of his beloved Khadija, his first follower and his constant companion and supporter. However, he did not remain long a widower, marrying Sawda, a woman of about thirty, who had recently lost her husband after their return from Abyssinia. He also became engaged to Aisha, daughter of his close friend Abu Bakr. She was to be his only virgin bride, and her age is variously reported, but it seems clear that she was below the age of puberty when they became engaged. Given the interest of many men in later generations in justifying marriage with child brides, her age is likely to have been under-estimated.

The Prophet began to consider leaving Mecca and migrating to a new centre where the faithful could be organized in security as an autonomous community. It is interesting that he did not choose to go to Abyssinia. Perhaps he had received unfavourable reports of political developments there, or he may have been deterred by news of the conversion of his cousin Ubayd-Allah to Christianity. Anyway, the fact is that his first attempt to spread the religion outside Mecca took the form of a visit to the mountain oasis of Taif, where many of the Quraysh had properties. However, the leaders of the local tribe of Thaqif refused his message and a hostile crowd followed him as he retreated.

Having returned to Mecca, the Prophet began visiting all the annual fairs in the neighbourhood and preaching to the tribesmen who came to them. His greatest success was with men from the tribe of Khazraj in the oasis of Yathrib (Medina), whom he met in the year 620 CE at Aqaba, when they were making the old polytheist pilgrimage to Mount Arafat and the Valley of Mina. Their oasis had suffered a terrible war between rival groups of clans, culminating a couple of years earlier in the Battle of Buath, in which many lives had been lost. The population of the oasis included Jewish clans, so they were familiar with the concept of prophethood. Six of the Yathribis accepted Islam and went home to bring it to their people.

The following year a dozen believers came from Yathrib for the pilgrimage – five of the first converts plus seven new ones, including two from the rival tribe Aws. They swore allegiance to the Prophet in the First Convention of Aqaba, renouncing idolatry, stealing, fornication, infanticide, slander and disobedience to the Prophet, on pain of punishment from Allah. This set of prohibitions is interesting as an indication that there was already the outline of a code of ethics. It should be compared with the less complete list in Koran 6:151–2, which dates perhaps from a little earlier.

The year after that, 622, seventy-three men and two women came as believers from Yathrib for the pilgrimage. The Prophet held a secret night-time meeting with them, supposedly attended also by his uncle Abbas, who was concerned that his nephew should obtain proper protection. It was agreed that the Muslims of Yathrib should take over full responsibility for Muhammad, defending him if necessary with their lives. A solemn oath, the Second Convention of Aqaba, was sworn by nine representatives of Khazraj and three of Aws.

Two and a half weeks later, a new year began in the Arab calendar. It was to be fixed by the second caliph, Umar, as the beginning of the Muslim Era, AH 1 (where AH stands for *Anno Hegirae*, from *hijra*, 'emigration'). This threshold marks the final separation of Islam from the culture of the pre-Islamic age, which came to be known as 'the [Time of] Ignorance'. This new year's day is usually calculated as 16th July 622, backdating the abolition of the intercalary ('leap') months, which the Prophet announced ten years later. If up to four extra months had occurred in those ten years, as they should have done, the beginning of the era moves back perhaps as far as 21st March. There must have been agreement between Muslims and pagans on the calendar, because by all accounts they observed the same sacred months (Rajab, Dhu'l-Qaada, Dhu'l-Hijja and Muharram), when fighting was not permitted.

By this time, the essentials of the faith had already been laid down. Of the Five Pillars of Islam two were already established: Witness and Worship. A third, Charity, was implicit though not formalized, and a fourth, Pilgrimage, was already there in practice, as shown by the pilgrims from Yathrib, though not yet in its final form. Only one remained to be added – the fast of Ramadan. There was also already a basic code of ethical behaviour. As for the Koran, about two thirds had by now been revealed, in about ninety suras, which included most of the stories about former prophets, and much if not all had been written down, as will be made clear. If the Prophet had died at this time, and if Islam could have survived the attacks of its enemies without him, the religion would have been substantially the same as the Islam that we know.

CHAPTER SEVEN

IMMIGRANTS AND HELPERS

Settling into Medina

Now began the second emigration of Islam, and it is worth pointing out here that Islam encourages migration. It has always been considered praiseworthy for Muslims to move in search of security for themselves and their faith. The Koran says (4:97):

> To those who die submitting to oppression, the angels will say: 'What were you at?' They will reply: 'We were made powerless on earth.' They will say: 'Was Allah's Earth not big enough for you to migrate in?'

One family had in fact already left for Yathrib a year before the agreement at Aqaba – that of Muhammad's cousin Abu Salama, who had been one of the first to migrate to Abyssinia. They had suffered such treatment from the Quraysh since their return to Mecca that they made up their minds to leave once they knew that there were believers in Yathrib. Three other families, including those of Abd-Allah and Abu Ahmad, the sons of Jahsh by Muhammad's aunt Umayma, also went in advance. They all settled at Quba, the first hamlet in Yathrib on the trail from Mecca.

Once the agreement had been made, there began a steady stream of believers to Yathrib. On their arrival all were taken in by families living in various parts of the oasis. Ibn Ishaq records the names of more than fifty men who made the journey in the following weeks, most of them with their families. It was a difficult passage involving about twelve days' desert travel, requiring camels and a Bedouin guide. In reading the following history, one should always remember that a round trip between the two towns took the best part of a month.

Soon came the moment for Muhammad himself to leave Mecca, but not before an attempted assassination had been foiled.

The conspirators had agreed that one man from each clan should stab him simultaneously, so that no one clan could be saddled with the blame. They were to strike in the night as he slept. He learned what was coming and had a miraculous escape, with the help of his cousin Ali, by now in his early twenties. It was urgent to leave, and a secret departure was planned. Muhammad chose Abu Bakr to be his sole companion for the journey, and their wives and daughters were to follow later. Ali was to stay behind to return articles left for safe keeping with Muhammad, whom people treated like a sort of personal banker because of his reputation for honesty and confidentiality.

As soon as all was prepared, Muhammad and Abu Bakr left Mecca secretly. The two climbed out of Abu Bakr's rear window at dead of night and hid for three days in a cave near Mecca, where the Quraysh narrowly missed finding them. Their Bedouin guide then took them by a roundabout route to Yathrib, where they arrived at Quba on the 12th of the third month, First Rabi, three months after the Convention of Aqaba. It was the day conventionally taken to be the birthday of Muhammad, who was by now about fifty-two. It was also the date of his death. Depending on assumptions about intercalation, it was 30th May 622 or 24th September or the 12th day of a lunar month between those two.

Yathrib was an oasis spread over about fifty square kilometres (twenty square miles) of a partly volcanic plain, set apart from the surrounding plateau by rugged hills on all sides except the south-east. The site lies at altitudes ranging from 600 to 700 metres (more than 2000 feet) – not much lower than the mountains that ring it round – and temperatures can fall to freezing on winter nights. Three wadis run from south and east towards the north-west, the best land being along the central one, the Wadi Bathan and its tributaries. It is 340 kilometres (210 miles) north of Mecca, and just over 100 kilometres outside the tropics.

Yathrib was to become the 'city of the Prophet', *Madinat al-Nabi*, in English 'Medina'. The word *madina*, in the vocabulary of the Koran, is almost equivalent to *qarya* (e.g. 18:77–82; 36:13–20), which in later Arabic came to mean 'village'. However the Koran calls Mecca a *qarya* and never a *madina*, although it was certainly more urban than Yathrib. At the time of the Prophet's arrival, there was scarcely even a town. Where he built his mosque there were palm groves and wasteland nearby. The various clans lived in scattered settlements, each surrounded by its irrigated palm plantations, orchards and fields, and there was good land left fallow for want of people to cultivate it. To anyone arriving from the stifling heat of Mecca, this green and shady scene must have looked a paradise.

Following the long period of inter-clan warfare, the people of Medina were well armed, and many of their settlements were fortresses. The original inhabitants appear to have been various Jewish clans, the main ones being Bani Qaynuqa, Bani Nadir and Bani Qurayza, who lived on some of the best land, in the south-east of the oasis. It is not clear whether they were Arab converts to Judaism or immigrants from the north, nor is it known whether their first language was Arabic or Aramaic. The polytheist inhabitants were more recent immigrants from the south, tracing their ancestry back to two brothers, Aws and Khazraj. The Battle of Buath had pitted the Bani Qaynuqa and most of the Khazraj clans against an alliance of the other Jews with most of the Aws. The latter had come out of it with a marginally better position, but only at the cost of heavy losses.

The converts who had invited Muhammad as peacemaker came mainly from Khazraj clans, but there were several influential men from Aws, including the son of their leader killed in the battle. It was important for Muhammad to adopt a position in which he would not seem to favour either side, and the first visible sign of this would be his choice of a place to live. An easy solution would have been for him to go to his great-grandmother's people, the Bani Adi Ibn al-Najjar, of Khazraj, but that would have defeated his aim of standing above the clan system. His wonderfully diplomatic solution was to let it be known that his camel, Qaswa, would decide; where she finally knelt down, there would be his home. The admirable creature wandered around from clan to clan until she finally stopped by a date-depot on the land of the Bani Malik Ibn al-Najjar, a clan closely related to the Bani Adi. A better spot could not have been found; it was in the heart of the oasis, near the frontier that divided most of the Aws, to the east, from most of the Khazraj, to the west (see Figure 3).

The date-depot was duly purchased to serve as the site for the Prophet's Mosque, the building of which, in sun-baked brick, occupied the next ten months. Muhammad shared in the work, living meanwhile in the home of a nearby family. When the new building was completed, it served both as his home and as the community's principal mosque. The main feature was the courtyard, a rectangle aligned north–south, about 32 by 27 metres – the size of two tennis courts. There was a covered area, with a roof of palm branches, thatched and daubed, resting on palm trunks.

On to the outside of the eastern wall were built rooms for Muhammad's wife Sawda and his wife-to-be Aisha. New rooms were added for further wives until there were nine. The Prophet had no room of his own, apart from a small unfurnished attic reached by a ladder. The room furthest south was that of Aisha, which had a door on to the courtyard of the mosque. This doorway provided the passage between his private and his public life, and the presence of Aisha behind it was the guarantee that only he and close relatives could go through it. Those who had business with his household could approach through the oasis.

When he was in Medina, Muhammad spent much of his time in the courtyard of the mosque, discussing the affairs of the community, receiving delegations and leading worship. The word 'mosque' derives from Arabic *masjid*, which means literally 'place of prostration'. Any suitable place can be used as a mosque; the creation of dedicated buildings developed gradually. Following the example of the Prophet, mosques have always been used also for all kinds of meeting and discussion. With his mosque complete, his community was now focussed, and the terms 'Muslims' and 'Islam' came to be used for its members.

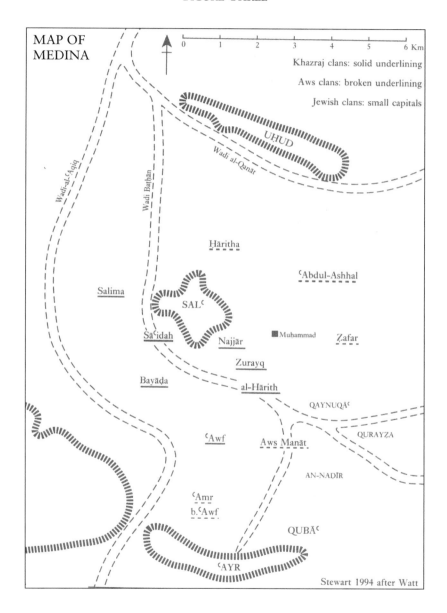

MAP OF
MEDINA

Khazraj clans: solid underlining
Aws clans: broken underlining
Jewish clans: small capitals

UHUD

Wadi al-Qanāt

Wadi al-ʿAqīq

Wadi Baṭḥān

Ḥāritha

ʿAbdul-Ashhal

Salima

SALʿ

Saʿidah   Najjār

Muhammad   Zafar

Zurayq

Bayāḍa   al-Ḥārith

QAYNUQĀʿ

ʿAwf   Aws Manāt

QURAYZA

AN-NADĪR

ʿAmr
b.ʿAwf

QUBĀʿ

ʿAYR

Stewart 1994 after Watt

Now that he was firmly established, the Prophet had a delicate political task as leader of the Immigrants. The other main groups in the oasis were the Medinan Muslims or 'Helpers', the Jews, and the polytheists, each divided into various clans. He was only one amongst several important leaders. As head of the Meccans, he was in much the same position as the heads of the various local clans. After the death of the leader of the Bani Najjar, he also acted as their head. The Helpers still belonged to their Medinan clans, and he had no authority over them other than religious. He had to use great diplomacy towards their clan heads, notably Saad Ibn Muadh of the Bani Abd-al-Ashhal (Aws), Saad Ibn Ubada of the Bani Saida, and Abd-Allah Ibn Ubay of the Bani Auf (both Khazraj). All three appeared to be Muslims, but the Islam of Abd-Allah was to prove skin deep.

Relations with the Jews

During his first year or two at Medina, Muhammad hoped that the Jewish clans would recognize him as a prophet, or at least that they would respect the Muslims and cooperate with them. Ibn Ishaq gives the text of an agreement known as the 'Constitution of Medina' (*Sira* pp. 231–233). This, which is generally agreed to be authentic, was drafted by Muhammad to regulate relations between the various groups present in the oasis. Its interpretation presents historians with many problems, partly no doubt because it is an amalgam of clauses drafted at different times, but what is important in the present context is its references to the Jews attached to nine different clans. They are said to form a community – *umma* – with the Muslims; 'to the Jews their religion and to the Muslims their religion'. Also: 'Whoever of the Jews follows us has the same help and support as the believers, not being oppressed and not having any helped against him.'

Islam at this time shared various features with Judaism. For example a formal weekly act of worship was instituted, like the Sabbath service in the synagogue. On this occasion a sermon was delivered, for the purpose of which Muhammad had a wooden pulpit made. However, for Muslims the special day was Friday, not Saturday, and there were no Sabbath regulations. All that the Koran prescribes is that Muslims leave off all business when the call to midday worship sounds (Koran 62:9–10). Friday was not made a day of rest; that is a modern practice, adopted by many Muslim-ruled countries on the pattern of the Western Sunday rather than the Jewish Sabbath.

Worship was led by the *imam* – literally the 'one in front' – normally the Prophet himself in his own mosque. At first worship was offered facing in the direction of Jerusalem, but five or six months after the completion of the Prophet's mosque came Koran 2:144, instructing the Muslims to turn towards Mecca: 'We shall turn you in a direction that will please you, so turn your face towards the Sacred Mosque, and wherever you may be, turn your faces in that direction.' The change was announced when Muhammad was about to worship in the mosque of the clan of Bani Saida, which became known as the Mosque of the Two Directions. This small detail gives us a picture of him going about the oasis and worshipping with different clans.

A small but interesting effect of the change of direction was to draw the Prophet's private and public realms even closer together. Previously, the door to Aisha's room had been behind the worshippers on their right; now it was in front of them on their left. This shortened Muhammad's path from his family to his station as leader of worship, but it made his comings and goings between the two roles very public. It was to become particularly important during his last illness, when the eyes of the faithful could not help straying to the place where he battled for life, and after his death, when that room became his tomb.

One problem that arose was how to announce the time of worship, both for those who were coming to the mosque and for those who worshipped elsewhere. At first the Prophet considered having a ram's horn blown on, like the Jewish shofar, but this was rejected in favour of a wooden clapper. However, before this had been used, one of the Medinans had a dream in which he was told that it would be best if someone with a powerful voice called people with a suitable form of words. Muhammad took up this idea with enthusiasm and chose Bilal, the African slave whose freedom had been bought by Abu Bakr when he was tormented by his polytheist master. He became the first muezzin of Islam. As yet there was no minaret, and the call to prayer was given from the roof of the tallest of the nearby houses, but the words are said to have been those that are heard today: 'Allah is most great. I bear witness that there is no god but Allah. I bear witness that Muhammad is the Messenger of Allah. Come to worship. Come to safety. Allah is most great. There is no god but Allah.'

Two things are especially interesting about this account. The first is that the words of the Call to Worship include the formula of Witness which is one of the Five Pillars of Islam. If this was the original form of the Call, it suggests that this was already the recognized way of declaring oneself a Muslim. The other point is that the idea of having a muezzin was attributed to an otherwise obscure person. No one took the credit from him and attributed it to the Prophet or one of his leading companions.

There were other features of Islam at this time that brought it closer to Judaism. A fast was prescribed for the day of *Ashura*, the tenth day of the first month, Muharram, corresponding to the Jewish Yom Kippur (though Muharram cannot by any reckoning have coincided with the Jewish month of Tishri). This ceased to be obligatory after the institution of the fast of Ramadan in the year 2 or 3. Even more significant was the provision made by the Koran for mutual recognition and mutual acceptability in food and marriage:

> Say: 'People of Scripture, come to fair terms between us and you: that we worship none but Allah, that we associate no partner with Allah, and that we do not some of us take others as lords beside Allah.' (3:64).

> The food of those who were given the Scripture is lawful for you, and yours is lawful for them, and chaste women from among the

believers and chaste women from among those who were given the Scripture before. (5:5).

The Jews of Medina did not take up these possibilities. The declaration that Muslim food was lawful for Jews seems to have referred to what Jewish opinion should have been rather than to what it was. The statement about women appears to mean that a Muslim woman could marry a Jewish or Christian man, which was not to be the case later. Marriages between Muslim men and Jewish women were to be commonplace in Medina and have always continued to be acceptable to Muslims, as have marriages with Christian women.

Unfortunately for both parties, the relations between the two religions could not be symmetric. Muhammad recognized the validity of the Jewish prophets, but the rabbis of Medina did not accept him as anything. Muslims respected the Bible, but Jews had no regard for the Koran. Islam would allow intermarriage and the sharing of food, but Judaism required its followers to keep to themselves. The situation was worse than a mere stand-off, for rejection by the Jews was a threat to the Muslims' faith in Muhammad; if the people of Moses and David did not recognize the man who came forward as their successor, might there not be something wrong with his claim?

Non-Muslim authors see such things as facing Jerusalem for worship and fasting at Ashura as instances of Muhammad trying to make Islam acceptable to the Jews, but Muslims cannot agree that the Prophet ever made any changes on his own initiative. At most they will accept that at this time it was appropriate to reveal an aspect of Islam that favoured agreement with the Jews of Medina. Some Jews did convert to Islam, most notably two rabbis, of whom one was the son of the head of the Bani Qaynuqa, but the general attitude of the Jewish clans varied between indifference and hostility. Their leaders had no desire to work with Muhammad; on the contrary, they hoped that they would soon be rid of him and his Immigrants.

In refusing the offer of a special relationship with the Muslims, the Jewish clans completely misjudged the situation, for the next few years were to see Muhammad's gradual transformation into the undisputed ruler of Medina, and indeed of most of Arabia. The factor that brought about this change was war with Mecca.

CHAPTER EIGHT

THE PROPHET AT WAR

For the last nine years of his life, the Prophet was at war – he who up to then had never struck a blow against anybody. On the face of it, it might seem that it was he who started it. However, it was the polytheists who had driven out the Muslims and who remained in possession of the Kaaba, the holiest shrine of Islam. The situation of the Immigrants was precarious. They were living on their savings and on the charity of the Helpers. They came from a town of financiers and traders, where cultivation was virtually unknown, and they lacked the skills that would have enabled them to make a living from the soil of the oasis. Many of them had left behind valuable property, which had been taken over by their enemies. Raiding offered a way to use their military skills to obtain restitution of some of what they had lost, and perhaps to do enough economic damage to Mecca to obtain a treaty from them.

The raids that began about a year after the Emigration may thus be regarded as ripostes rather than the start of something new. They took the form of the classic Arab *razzia*, which traditionally aimed at obtaining property rather than taking life. Seven expeditions are recorded as having been made before any booty was seized or blood shed. Four were led by the Prophet personally and three by close companions, and all the raiders were Immigrants. An eighth party of eight Immigrants was sent out in Rajab, the seventh month of AH 2 (January 623), under the leadership of Muhammad's cousin Abd-Allah Ibn Jahsh. At Nakhla, near the shrine of the 'goddess' Uzza, they intercepted a small caravan proceeding from Taif to Mecca, on the last day of the month. They killed one of the four Meccans accompanying it and brought two of the others back to Medina as prisoners, together with the camels and their cargo of raisins and leather.

The Meccans were very angry at this attack, particularly as it had taken place in the sacred month of Rajab, when Arab tradition forbade fighting. The Prophet was horrified, and he protested that his written instructions had been simply to spy on the Meccans and not to attack them. He refused to distribute the booty or take anything from the prisoners, until a Koranic verse authorized this (2:217):

> They ask you about fighting in the sacred month; say: 'Fighting in it is grave, but to block the path of Allah – being ungrateful to Allah – and of the Sacred Mosque, and to drive out its people is graver with Allah, and persecution is worse than killing.'

It was only a few weeks before a much bigger raid became possible. The Prophet got news of a very large caravan making its way from Syria to Mecca. To attack it required all the men he could muster, and for the first time the Medinan Helpers were invited to join the raid. He was well aware that this would be an act of war, but Koran 22:39–40 authorized this:

> Permission is given to those who are fought against, because they are oppressed – and Allah is powerful to help them;
>   Those who have been expelled from their homes without justification except that they say: 'Allah is Our Lord.'

This was clearly defensive warfare, and there is nothing in Muhammad's conduct that can be described as unprovoked aggression. Still less did he ever countenance using force to convert people to Islam. The Koran describes fighting in the service of Islam as jihad, the primary meaning of which is 'striving' or 'effort'. Anyone who died defending Islam was a martyr, *shahid* and would immediately enjoy Paradise.

The Koran makes it clear that the taking of life is a deeply serious action:

> 'Because of [the murder of Abel] we laid it upon the Children of Israel that whoever kills a person, except because of murder or creating havoc in the land, it is as if he had killed all the people;

and whoever saves a life, it is as if he had saved the whole people.'
(5:32).

Still more sternly condemned is the killing of a fellow Muslim:

'Whoever kills a believer intentionally, his recompense is everlasting
Hell, and the anger and the curse of Allah are on him, and Allah
has prepared a terrible punishment for him.' (4:93).

The Prophet imposed various restrictions on his warriors.
They were not to kill women or children (Bukhari 52:147–8).
Prisoners of war were to be treated humanely and provided
with what food, drink and clothing they needed, until they were
exchanged or ransomed (Bukhari 52:142, 171–2), the only exception
being a very small number who were executed for grave crimes.
Defeated parties who accepted Islam were allowed to retain their
liberty and their property (Bukhari 52:179–80). This was a positive
incentive to convert, but there were no threats of harsh treatment
for those who chose not to convert.

No one should be killed by burning, which was a punishment
reserved to Allah (Bukhari 52:149). The dead were not to be
mutilated (*Sira*, p. 388). When Mecca capitulated, the Prophet
ordered respect for all except those who resisted (*Sira*, pp. 550–553).
It is particularly important to note that there was not to be any
violence against any person not believed to be at war with Islam.
This was a complete break with the Arab tradition of exacting
vengeance from any member of the enemy's tribe.

Unlike the Geneva Conventions, which they anticipated by
thirteen centuries, and which in some respects they went beyond,
these restrictions were unilaterally adopted without any undertaking
of the other side to reciprocate. If the Islamic rules were followed
today, much of modern warfare would be impossible, and terrorism
would be unthinkable. There would be no attacks on civilians,
no retaliation against innocent parties, no taking hostage of non-
combatants, no incendiary devices. It has to be admitted that many
Muslims have failed to respect these limitations.

The main respect in which this warfare left room for improvement was in the treatment of women and children taken prisoner, who were enslaved if no one ransomed them. However, Islamic slavery was certainly not a fate worse than death, nor even, usually, a life-sentence. Indeed it was probably the only way, within the social conditions of the time, to care for widows and orphans instead of killing or abandoning them.

The Prophet recruited 314 volunteers to intercept the caravan. Ibn Ishaq gives the names of 83 Immigrants, 170 Khazraj and 61 Aws. They had only 70 camels between them, taking it in turns to ride. The man in charge of the caravan was Abu Sufyan, one of the leading Meccans, with thirty or forty men to help him. He got news of the Muslim ambush and appealed to Mecca to send out a relief force to fend off the attack. Abu Jahl of Clan Makhzum, the Prophet's most powerful opponent, set out with a large force consisting of almost all the able-bodied men left in Mecca, reportedly a total of nearly a thousand. It included a number of the Prophet's close relatives, among them his uncle Abbas, his cousin Aqil Ibn Abi Talib, and his son-in-law Abu 'l-As, husband of Zaynab. Aqil's brother Talib set out from Mecca but then turned back. Muhammad's uncle Abu Lahab did not join the rescue mission at all, preferring to send a representative.

In the event, Abu Sufyan managed to elude the Muslims by taking a coastal route. News of the caravan's escape reached Abu Jahl, and he could have gone straight back to Mecca, but he decided to take the risk of stopping at the watering place of Badr. The Muslims were there before him and took control of the wells. The Meccans attacked. They outnumbered the Muslims by more than two to one, despite the defection of two or three hundred. The clash took place in the third week of Ramadan. It was a crushing victory for the Muslims, who killed 50 Meccans and took more than 40 prisoners, including Abbas, Aqil and Abu 'l-As, for the loss of only 14 men.

Abu Jahl himself was killed, and leadership of Mecca passed to Abu Sufyan, the head of Clan Umayya, whose tactics had saved the caravan. He was to prove a formidable adversary, but he was a flexible man, and his personal qualities were to play an important part later in minimizing the cost of the Prophet's eventual victory to both sides. Abu Lahab died of wounds received in a quarrel after the return of the defeated force. His successor as head of Clan Hashim was Muhammad's uncle Abbas, who sooner or later became a Muslim.

Almost immediately after the Prophet's victorious return to Medina there occurred the first of a series of conflicts with Jewish clans. The Bani Qaynuqa, unlike the other Jews of Medina, were not cultivators but smiths, and they had a market in which they sold their products. A quarrel between them and some Muslims caused the Prophet to lead a siege of the clan, and they surrendered after two weeks. They were given three days to collect money owing to them and then expelled from Medina. There are said to have been seven hundred men, four hundred of them with chain-mail armour, but their position was isolated, as they had been on the opposite side to the other Jews in the Battle of Buath, and their Khazraj allies were not ready to protect them. Accounts of the affair are obscure, and it is not clear why the Muslim reaction was so strong, but the Prophet may have had information of secret contacts between them and the Meccans.

The Meccans were certainly trying to find allies in Medina. Abu Sufyan led a small expedition a few weeks later, in which he was secretly received by a leader of the Jewish clan of Bani Nadir. An important go-between was a desert Arab called Kaab Ibn al-Ashraf, whose mother belonged to the Bani Nadir. After Badr he composed satiric verses against the Muslims, then went to Mecca to rally opposition to them. After a while he returned to Medina and produced scurrilous verses on Muslim women. According to the *Sira*, Muhammad asked: 'Who will rid me of Ibn al-Ashraf?' Five volunteers, including Kaab's foster-brother, lured him out of his fortress and assassinated him in the night.

Several other killings are alleged by the *Sira*. If they really took place, they pose difficult questions: were they utterly exceptional acts, justified only by the destruction that, for the one time in its history, threatened the religion, or were they precedents that could legitimately be followed by later generations? Two things point to the former interpretation. Firstly, all were said to have taken place over a four-year period – the end of AH 2 to the end of AH 6, after which no more are reported to have happened during the last four and a half years of the Prophet's life, though warfare continued. Secondly, all the victims presented a real danger to Islam. Even where their only offence was to compose hostile verse, it must be remembered that for the Arabs, with their very verbal culture, poetry could be as powerful as physical action. Indeed, there was a veritable war of the poets going on in parallel with that of the warriors. The Prophet had his own 'court poet', a Medinan called Hassan Ibn Thabit, who composed a great deal of verse glorifying the Muslims and ridiculing their enemies.

The ensuing months saw a number of other raids, the most successful of which was the capture of a Meccan caravan carrying silver. Its defenders escaped under the leadership of Abu Sufyan. Finally, just over a year after the Battle of Badr, the Meccans responded with a direct attack on Medina, fielding 3000 men and 200 horses, led again by Abu Sufyan, accompanied by a party of women to cheer them on. They came round from the north and camped at the foot of Mount Uhud. Next day the Prophet brought out the Muslim defenders, after a disagreement with Abd-Allah Ibn Ubay, the Khazraj chief, who wanted them to stay in the heart of the oasis. Abd-Allah defected with about 300 of the Khazraj, leaving only 700 Muslims. They came across the shoulder of the mountain and commanded the high ground above the Meccans.

In a confused battle the Muslims suffered heavy losses after their archers abandoned the high ground to rush after booty. The Prophet himself was wounded and at one point was rumoured to have been killed. At the end of the day 65 Muslims lay dead. Only four of these were Immigrants, but these included Muhammad's beloved uncle Hamza and his cousin Abd-Allah Ibn Jahsh. On the other side only 22 had been killed. On the face of it, the Meccans had now avenged the disasters of Nakhla and Badr, for the combined totals of dead were 79 Muslims and 73 polytheists, but Abu Sufyan's decision to withdraw was in effect an admission of failure, for Islam represented as great a danger as ever. However, for the Muslims the near-defeat was a difficult test, throwing doubt on Allah's favour, and all the Prophet's qualities of leadership were needed to rebuild their morale. Sura 3:121–180 draws the painful lessons of the battle.

One effect of the experience of Uhud was to make the Muslims conscious of a new category of people, the hypocrites. Hitherto it had seemed that everyone was either a Muslim, a disbeliever or a polytheist. Abd-Allah Ibn Ubay and his supporters had appeared on the surface to be good Muslims, yet here in the test of a grave threat to the survival of Islam, they had withdrawn their help. It was a problem often alluded to in the later suras of the Koran, especially 4, 9, and 33, and it was destined to remain a key issue for later generations of Muslims. The Prophet was very patient with the hypocrites. When Abd-Allah eventually died, he gave his own shirt for him to be buried in and he personally officiated at the funeral.

The conflict with Mecca smouldered on for the next two years with a number of successful raids by the Muslims but without any major engagement. The most important development within Medina was the expulsion of another Jewish clan, the Bani Nadir, five months after Uhud. The pretext was an alleged attempt by their leader Huyay to kill the Prophet, but the deeper reason was clearly their contacts with Mecca and its Bedouin allies, and the risk that these might lead to further action. They were given an ultimatum: ten days to leave with their property, retaining rights to the produce of their date palms. When they refused this they were besieged, and when they surrendered they were expelled, leaving behind their arms and their fixed property, which was shared out between the poorer Immigrants, giving them for the first time in Medina a steady source of income. The Bani Nadir are said to have left with a caravan of six hundred camels, carrying great wealth and even taking their door-lintels. Some headed for Syria and others for the oasis of Khaybar, where they had relatives and land.

The Meccans meanwhile were busy forging an alliance of Bedouin tribes to help them defeat the Prophet. Eventually, two years after Uhud, they returned to Medina for their supreme effort with a confederate army of ten thousand, including six thousand Bedouin. Six hundred of them were on horseback. The Jews of Bani Nadir had promised the tribe of Ghatafan half the date harvest of their oasis, Khaybar, as the prize for victory. The attack came, as before, from the north. The Prophet had only about three thousand men, including only thirty-six on horseback, to defend the oasis – virtually all the adult male population except that of the Jewish clan of Bani Qurayza, who refused to take up arms, despite their pact with the Muslims.

The Prophet's strategy, suggested by a Persian convert, Salman, was to dig a trench across the path of the invaders – a technique never before seen in Arabia. The Bani Qurayza lent tools for the digging. When the Meccans arrived, they were unable to cross the trench. There were only a few skirmishes, in which four of the confederates were killed and none of the Muslims. Huyay, the chief of the Bani Nadir, offered to bring in the Bani Qurayza. He came secretly to their chief, Kaab Ibn Asad, an honourable man, who wanted to abide by his pact with the Prophet. However, Kaab was weak, and Huyay was persistent and persuaded him that the huge army of the confederates was invincible, and that it would be folly to be on the losing side. Eventually it was agreed that two thousand of the besiegers would join the Bani Qurayza in their fortresses to attack the Muslims from behind.

The Prophet's spies brought him news of the defection of the Bani Qurayza, and he succeeded in using a double agent to sow mistrust between the Jewish clan and the Meccans. Some of the Bedouin besiegers, too, were beginning to drift away. Low morale and appallingly cold and stormy weather eventually caused the remaining confederates to retreat one night. This incidentally suggests that the month is less likely to have been March/April, as conventionally reckoned, than December/January, as it would have been with intercalary months. Dawn broke, and the weary Muslims were overjoyed to find the plain beyond the trench deserted. However, the danger seemed only to have lessened a little. It was still possible that the confederation would re-form and join up with the Bani Qurayza. The Prophet led his army straight away against the Jewish clan.

The Muslims are said to have besieged the Bani Qurayza for twenty-five days until they surrendered. Because they were allies of the Aws clan of Abd-al-Ashhal, the Prophet turned them over to its chief, Saad Ibn Muadh, for judgement. Saad had been fatally wounded by an arrow fired across the trench, and he was brought out on a donkey from the hospital-tent that had been erected in the Prophet's Mosque. According to the account first written down over a century later in the *Sira*, he decreed that all the men should be killed, the women and children enslaved and their property distributed to the Muslims, pointing out that this was the punishment decreed by Moses (Deuteronomy 20:10–18). Different accounts give wildly different numbers of those executed, from 400 to 900.

This story is very suspect. The Koran says merely: '[Allah] brought those of the People of Scripture who helped them [the Meccans] out of their forts, and cast terror in their hearts. Some you killed, some you took prisoner.' (33:26) This hardly sounds like an account of a cataclysmic mass killing, which would have been so different from the Muslims' normal magnanimity as to require special comment. 'Some... some...' is awkward to take as meaning 'the men... the women and children...'. Ibn Ishaq was denounced as a liar by some of his contemporaries, notably Malik Ibn Anas, who accused him of getting the story from the descendants of Qurayza converts (which shows that there were survivors to become converts). Ibn Ishaq became so unpopular in Medina that he had to move to Iraq.

Whatever the number of those executed, it is important to emphasize that there was no element of ethnic hatred. Those who died were condemned not as Jews but as traitors in time of war.

Those of the women whose freedom was not bought by kindred Jewish tribes were taken into Muslim households and many became the mothers of Muslim children. Nor was this the end of Medina's Jews; several groups continued to live there in peace, and one of Muhammad's wives, Safiya, was a convert from Judaism. At the time of his death, his armour was in pawn to a Medinan Jew for a hundred kilos of barley (Bukhari 52:89).

A year later the Prophet astonished his followers by announcing that he would make the lesser pilgrimage, which was a visit to the Kaaba performed at any other time of year than the greater pilgrimage of the 12th month Dhu-'l-Hijja. This was in the sacred month of Dhu-'l-Qaada, so they would not be attacked. 700 Muslims set out with 70 sacrificial camels to make the two-week journey to Mecca. A Meccan force was sent out to block their path, but they took a rocky mountain path to get past and reached the Plain of Hudaybiya, just outside Mecca, for negotiations, which took place under the shade of a large tree. These led to an agreement for a ten-year truce, during which for three days each year, starting the following year, the Muslims would be allowed to make the pilgrimage. Each side would send back migrants who had gone to the other side without the agreement of their protectors. This last provision was very unpopular with the Prophet's men, but in practice few migrants had to be sent back, and the effect may have been to cause a rapid increase in the number of Muslims inside Mecca.

Strengthened by the truce, the Prophet now decided to put an end to the opposition from Khaybar. He led a large force to the oasis and besieged some of its fortresses. When these fell the remainder capitulated. Under the terms they were given, the land became Muslim property, but the mainly Jewish population could remain there and cultivate it, handing over half of the date crop to the victors. Another Jewish oasis, Fadak, soon after capitulated on the same terms and, because there had been no fighting, it became the personal property of the Prophet. It was virtually his only asset, and he used its revenue, like that of Khaybar, to help destitute Muslims.

It may have been at this time (early AH 7/628) that the Prophet received a delegation of Christians from Najran (just north of the modern border of Yemen). Ibn Ishaq places it much earlier in his *Sira,* but he indicates no date, and it could have been dangerous to make the journey while the war with Mecca lasted. In any case, he says there were sixty of them, headed by their ruler, a minister and their bishop. They stayed for several days and discussed theology, then parted amicably after having been allowed to say their Christian prayers in the Mosque.

The Koran accords a very lofty status to Jesus: 'the Messiah Jesus son of Mary was Allah's messenger, Allah's word bestowed on Mary, a spirit from Allah', but it rejects the Trinity (4:171–2). It denies that Jesus was killed by crucifixion, but says 'it was made to seem so to them' (4:157), which has been interpreted in different ways down the ages. Believing that Jesus had brought the Christians the same revelation that he was bringing, he hoped that they would submit to Allah, but if not he expected mutual respect. If Koran 5:82 is a reflection of this visit from Najran, it suggests that the Christians made a good impression:

> You will certainly find that the people fiercest in enmity towards the believers are the Jews and the idolaters. You will also certainly find the closest of them in affection towards the believers are those who call themselves Christians; that is because among them are scholars and monks, and because they are not proud.

This seemed to confirm what he had expected when he sent emigrants to Abyssinia. When the Persians overran Syria in 616 CE, the Koranic response was to prophesy that the Byzantines would retake it and to declare 'In that day shall the faithful rejoice' (sura 30:4). The Persians continued into Egypt in 618 and into Asia Minor in 620, but between 622 and 628 the Byzantines recovered all their lost territory, conquered Mesopotamia and destroyed the Sasanian capital in Ctesiphon. The Prophet began to fear that the triumphant Greeks might launch an expedition into Arabia. His expectation of a Christian alliance had gone, perhaps because of unreported mishaps in Abyssinia:

> You who believe, do not take the Jews and Christians for allies;
> they are allies to each other. Whoever of you becomes their ally is
> one of them. Allah does not guide an unjust people. (5:51).

The Prophet had reportedly already sent messages to five rulers: the Sasanian Emperor, the Governor of Bostra as representative of the Byzantine Emperor, the Muqawqis of Egypt, the Negus of Abyssinia, and the Prince of Ghassan – a north-Arabian Christian client-state of Byzantium. According to the traditional account, his message was a call to accept Islam, but it may have been more a request for diplomatic relations. It was one of the Prophet's reported instructions on his death-bed that his followers should treat diplomatic missions with the courtesy that he had shown (Bukhari 52:176). Two or three of these powers did respond, and the Muqawqis sent him a gift of four slaves, but the emissary to Bostra was beaten up and robbed on his way through Ghassan territory. A darker side of Christianity was becoming apparent:

> You who believe, many of the priests and monks devour people's
> wealth by false pretences and lead astray from the way of Allah;
> those who hoard gold and silver and do not spend it in the service
> of Allah – inform them of a painful punishment. (9:34).

An early consequence of the truce with Mecca was the return to Medina of the last of the emigrants from Abyssinia, led by Ali's brother Jaafar. One of them was Muhammad's wife, Abu Sufyan's daughter Umm Habiba, whom he had married by proxy when she lost her husband, Ubayd-Allah Ibn Jahsh, the convert to Christianity. Her father made a personal visit to Medina, hoping to use her good offices to get an audience with the Prophet or his Companions to arrange terms for capitulation, but none of them would receive him. He went back to Mecca realizing that surrender would have to be unconditional.

Following the abuse of his emissary to the north, the Prophet sent out a small punitive expedition under his formerly adopted son Zayd. Continuing fears of attack led to the sending out of a larger expedition led by Zayd and Jaafar. Both men were killed at Muta on the Syrian border in AH 8 (629). The impact of Zayd's death cannot be over-estimated. Muhammad had brought him up like a son, had given him his beloved nurse as wife, had enjoyed his support through the years of persecution, had entrusted him with the leadership of more expeditions than anyone else, and had rescued him from his marital difficulties with a favourite cousin. If Zayd had lived he would undoubtedly have played a leading role after the Prophet's death – and might well have become caliph. The fact that his beloved Zayd was killed and buried on the Byzantine frontier must have weighed very heavily.

A year after the Treaty of Hudaybia, at the end of AH 7, the Muslims successfully made the lesser pilgrimage in accordance with its terms. Its festive character was made clear by the Prophet's marrying Maymuna while in Mecca. She was a mature widow, sister-in-law of Abbas. Ten months later the opportunity came to conquer Mecca at little cost. Some Bedouin allies of the Meccans had broken the treaty by attacking Bedouin allies of the Muslims. The Meccan leaders were divided, and Abu Sufyan was advocating non-resistance. The Prophet managed to keep his plans secret until he was near to Mecca with a force of ten thousand, including many Bedouin allies. Abu Sufyan came out to treat with him and assured him that most of the clans would not resist. After a small engagement in which 24 were killed on the Meccan side for the loss of only two Muslims, resistance collapsed and the Prophet was able to enter his native city in triumph.

The Prophet was magnanimous in victory. He forbade all looting and issued a general amnesty, from which some ten people were excepted, of whom four were executed and six were pardoned. Those killed were two murderers and two who had persistently insulted Islam. Those spared included Abu Sufyan's wife Hind, who had chewed Hamza's liver after the Battle of Uhud, and Ibn Abi Sarh, who had become an apostate after having been Muhammad's secretary, and who was pardoned, reportedly at the request of his foster-brother Uthman. During the Prophet's two-week stay in Mecca, many people submitted to

Islam, but others remained polytheists, and no force was used to make them change their minds.

The most dramatic moment was the entry of the Prophet into the precinct of the Kaaba, where he cast down the idols and removed all the apparatus of idolatry. He also sent out missions to destroy the idols in shrines in the neighbourhood of Mecca. However, the Prophet showed mercy in this break with the past, and he allowed the clan of Abd-al-Dar to remain custodians of the keys of the Kaaba, while Abbas, in spite of the lateness of his conversion, was confirmed in his office of keeper of Zamzam.

The submission of Mecca did not mean the end of warfare. The Prophet had to set off directly with his victorious army of ten thousand, reinforced by two thousand Meccans, to face twenty thousand Bedouin led by his foster-mother's people, the Hawazin. The Muslims defeated this coalition in the Battle of Hunayn. After his victory, the Prophet returned to live in Medina. There he received so many delegations from tribes wishing to pledge allegiance to him that the year AH 9 (630) came to be called the Year of Deputations. The basis for agreement was that they should recognize that there was no god but Allah and that Muhammad was the Messenger of Allah, that they should destroy their idols and that they should pay zakat – the tax to charity.

By now, the Prophet had become more firmly convinced than ever that Byzantium, having all but annihilated the Sasanid Empire, was turning its attention to Arabia. In the middle of year 9, he led out the greatest of all his armies, said to have numbered thirty thousand, in a show of strength. They reached Tabuk in the territory of Ghassan. However, the only result was the conclusion of one or two local treaties.

The pilgrimage of the year 9 was led by Abu Bakr. After he had left, Ali was sent after him with the opening verses of sura 9. These included the famous Verse of the Sword (italics below), which every Christian preacher against Islam knows by heart. It needs to be seen in context:

A proclamation from Allah and Allah's Messenger to the people on the day of the greater pilgrimage, that Allah is free of obligations to the polytheists and so is the Messenger. If you repent it will be better for you, but if you turn away, know that you cannot incapacitate Allah. Give tidings of a painful punishment to those who disbelieve.

Except those polytheists with whom you have made a treaty and who did not then let you down nor aid anyone against you; fulfil with them their treaty until their term. Allah loves the virtuous.

And when the forbidden months have passed, kill the polytheists where you find them, and capture them and besiege them and wait for them in ambushes. But if they repent and observe prayer and give alms, then leave their way free. Allah is forgiving, merciful.

And if one of the polytheists asks you for asylum, grant it to him so that he may hear the word of Allah; then escort him to his secure refuge. This is because they are a people who do not know. (9:3–6).

This does not refer to Christians and Jews, who are in any case not usually called polytheists (*mushrikin* – those who associate [partners with Allah]), but only to specific Arab tribes who at that particular time were in breach of their treaty. They had four months to make their peace, and it is only after that that they were open to attack. Even then individuals have the option of seeking asylum with the Muslims and being informed about Islam. To find something relevant to the People of Scripture one must go to a later passage, which refers only to those Christians and Jews who do not truly practise their religion, the test being presumably whether they attack Muslims. The following, not the Verse of the Sword, was to become the basis for relations established with the People of Scripture after the Muslim conquests:

Fight those of the people who were given the Scripture who do not believe in Allah nor in the Last Day nor forbid what Allah and the Messenger of Allah have forbidden nor profess the religion of Truth, until they pay tribute [*jizya*] open-handedly, being humbled. (9:29).

A few weeks after his own Farewell Pilgrimage at the end of the year 10, the Prophet sent out his last ever expedition, again against Byzantium. It was placed under the leadership of Usama, the youthful son of Zayd – further evidence of the Prophet's special regard for Zayd. They had just left for Syria when news reached them that the Prophet was dying. They turned back, but one of Abu Bakr's first acts as caliph was to insist that the expedition should leave and that it should be led by Usama, despite complaints from Umar and other older companions. The historians are vague about its consequences, but claim that it was successful. It may thus be said that the conquest of Byzantine Syria was launched by the Prophet himself.

All these wars were defensive. Islam was still very vulnerable, and one defeat could have destroyed it. The object was simply to put an end to attacks or threats of attack by the enemies of Islam, it was never the intention to force anyone to become Muslim. This was to remain the essential character of subsequent wars between Muslims and non-Muslims. Of course, the danger is always that one side will see as aggression what the other sees as pre-emptive defence, and this is what rapidly came about in the conflicts with Christians. However, there is a basic asymmetry in that the Koran accepts the existence of the religions of the People of Scripture, whereas there is no room in Christianity for a later Prophet, and the Gospel tells Christians to go and 'make disciples of all nations' (Matthew 28:19).

CHAPTER NINE

ISLAM PERFECTED

After the move from Mecca to Medina, the Muslims were no longer scattered through a polytheistic society, but constituted a community, the *Umma*. Its organization became a major concern of the Prophet, and it was the object of many of the passages added to the Koran in Medina. At the centre of its life were the Five Pillars of Islam: Witness, Worship, giving to Charity, Fasting and Pilgrimage. As described in Chapter Four, these were already anticipated before the move to Medina.

Worship had been practised from the very beginning, but in Medina the number of cycles of movements in each act of worship and the number of acts in the day gradually increased to reach their definitive pattern. In Mecca there had been only two acts of worship, one in the morning and one in the evening, but an early Medinan verse (Koran 2:238) urges Muslims not to forget 'the middle act of worship', usually taken to be that of the afternoon. By the end of the Prophet's life there were five – dawn, noon, afternoon, sunset and night. The Koran does not mention all five in any one place, but they can be deduced by combining 11:114 with 30:17–18.

The regular giving of Charity started to be called *zakat* early in the Medinan period (Koran 2:43 etcetera, where it is always coupled with Worship). It came to be formally recognized as one of the Five Pillars. By the time the Bedouin tribes were submitting to Islam it had developed into a sort of tax. The exact rules for levying it and spending it became a matter of controversy, but the amounts due must have been clearly recorded, for it is reported that after the Prophet's death Abu Bakr swore to fight any tribe that tried to withhold even one kid that they had paid to the Prophet. The revenue from charity was used broadly in the same way as the fifth of the spoils of war that went to the Prophet (Koran 8:41, cf. 2:177):

> Know that, whatever booty you may acquire, for Allah is one fifth and for the Messenger and for his relations and orphans and the poor and travellers.

Fasting had been practised from the start, but it was only in AH 3 (625) that it occupied the whole of Ramadan, the ninth month in the Muslim calendar. It was observed then in the same way as it is today, with total abstinence from food, drink and sex between first light and sunset. It was associated with the coming down of the Koran, which first began in Ramadan, and the practice of reciting the whole Koran in the course of the 30 nights of Ramadan goes back to the Prophet himself.

Ramadan quickly proved one of the most powerful elements of Islam. Eating and drinking are such basic human activities that the experience of abstaining from them communally is a powerful cement for a group. As a shared discipline it may also have served as a form of 'training', contributing to the Muslims' success in war (though travelling and fighting, like sickness, pregnancy and breast-feeding, gave exemption from the obligation to fast). The feast at the end of the fasting month is in practice a bigger occasion than the one that comes at the time of the Pilgrimage, though in theory second to it.

The procedure for the Pilgrimage (*hajj*), the fifth and final Pillar of Islam, was not laid down in detail until the Prophet himself led the pilgrims from Medina three months before his death. On that occasion he combined into a single sequence the Visit (*umra*) to the Kaaba, the stay at Arafat (about twenty kilometres – twelve miles – east of Mecca) and the animal sacrifice in the Plain of Mina (about ten kilometres – six miles – east of Mecca). However, he had already observed all three separately. Visits to the Kaaba formed a regular part of his practice even before his mission, and his meeting with the first Medinan converts came in the course of a stay at Aqaba near Mina. As for the sacrifice, he had killed rams each year in Medina at the time of the sacrifice in Mina.

The elements of the Pilgrimage were part of pre-Islamic Arabian religion. Islam changed them in four ways: by cleansing them of their idolatrous associations; by combining them in a single act of devotion (though it is still possible to perform the Visit to the Kaaba on its own, at any time of year); by making it into the culminating spiritual aspiration of every Muslim; and by attaching its places and events to the roots of monotheism, seeing Mina as the spot where Abraham sacrificed a ram in place of his son Ishmael, and the Kaaba as the Sacred House founded by Adam and restored by Abraham and Ishmael, with the tombs of Hagar and Ishmael beside it.

References to Abraham in the Koran make him the focus of unity, the forefather of Jews, Christians and Muslims, the monotheist (*hanif*) whose pure message had not yet been distorted by faulty transmission by the 'People of Scripture'. The association of Abraham with Mecca has been a sticking point for Christians and Jews, since there is no evidence for it in the Bible. However, the Bible does not say that Abraham, the camel-owning nomad, did *not* go to Arabia, and it does say that Ishmael's descendants lived in Arabia, so there is room for the Muslim belief.

Forgetting its familiarity, the Kaaba is an extraordinary monument. It was astonishingly large and substantial for its original situation. Who would have taken the trouble to cut the stone and bring it to build a shrine in a barren valley far from urban centres, and why would they do it? Those who reject the Muslim explanation have never provided an alternative. At the same time, the Kaaba is remarkably small and simple to be the focus of a world religion. Its base measures about 11 by 13 metres (35 by 40 feet), and it is about 16 metres (50 feet) high – roughly the size of a narrow four-storied house. Inside, it is empty except for a few inscriptions, and no ceremonies are performed in it. It is the perfect symbol for the impossibility of imagining or describing Allah.

One aspect of the pilgrimage was to become important in the ecology of Islam. In the years that the Prophet was unable to make the sacrifice in Mina, he made it in Medina instead. It was his custom to slaughter two black and white rams. After his death this practice came to be followed all over the Muslim world, every household being expected to sacrifice a ram. This created a huge periodic demand for live rams, over and above any regular demand for mutton. It is one of the factors encouraging the spread of grazing lands at the expense of cropland and forests in Muslim countries. The peak demand for sacrificial rams does not always come at the same season, making herd management all the more difficult. Like all Islamic festivals it moves round the solar year, coming about eleven days earlier each year.

Arabia had never had a government, so prior to Islam the decision to add a thirteenth month had to be made by mutual agreement between the tribes. It appears that this was negotiated at the annual pilgrimage to Mecca, which was the biggest tribal gathering. When the Prophet announced on this very occasion that Allah prohibited the practice, it was made dramatically clear that a new order had been established. It seems very likely that this was just three weeks before an extra month would normally have begun.

If, as suggested in Chapter Six above, there had been intercalary months until they were abolished, then Ramadan would always have fallen in November or December and the Pilgrimage in February or March during the Prophet's lifetime. He would never have experienced either in the full heat of summer. As all the rest of the world calculates in solar or luni-solar years, it is the inconvenience of the Muslim calendar that is most frequently remarked. In its favour it may be pointed out that every part of the world, whatever its cycle of seasons, periodically enjoys the festivals at whatever happens locally to be the best time of year. Thirty-four Muslim years approximately equal 33 solar years, so that is the time it takes for the two cycles to come back into the same position relative to each other. An Islamic century is just 8 days more than 97 solar years, and a

Gregorian century is just 25 days more than 103 lunar years, so it is easy enough to do rough and ready conversions.

The Five Pillars sum up Islam in a form that is easy to grasp. It should be noted that four of them are concerned with actions; only one of them is verbal – a mere ten words. Islam is essentially a religion of practice rather than doctrine. It gives ordinary people things to do rather than forms of words to believe in. Later generations were to build a great structure of beliefs, but the simple acts of Worship, Fasting, Charity and Pilgrimage have remained the foundation for the whole religion.

There is of course much more to Islam than the Five Pillars. The religion is a whole way of life. The Koran covers especially marriage and divorce, the care of children and orphans, commerce and inheritance, and the punishment of serious offences. An enormous literature grew up over the next two centuries, purporting to fill out the basic scheme in elaborate detail with thousands of accounts of what the Prophet said or did in particular circumstances as the basis for Sharia. This word, which originally meant 'the path to water', came to mean Islamic Law. It occurs only once in the Koran: 'Then we put you [Muhammad] on a path of order, so follow it and do not follow the desires of those who do not know.' (45:18). However, the only document that *certainly* goes back to his lifetime is the Koran, and for the present chapter only those provisions that find an echo in its pages will be considered.

In the course of the Prophet's ten years in Medina, the Koran grew to completion. The suras reckoned as wholly or mainly revealed there make up about a third of its length. More than half of this material is concentrated in the four long suras 2–5. The revelations were more infrequent than in Mecca, but individually longer, and with lengthier verses. Much of their subject matter is concerned with regulating the life of the community   ~iled above, with its conduct of war and its relations w Christians.

Western critics have suggested that these l; the Koran are less elevated than the Meccan sur are too often convenient to the personal needs of the Prophet. A well-attested Hadith going back to Aisha tells how, when she heard the verse permitting the Prophet to vary the order in which he visited his wives (33:51), she said to him: 'I can only think your Lord hurries to your pleasure.' His reply is not recorded (Bukhari 60:240), but whatever one's theory of revelation, there is no reason to suppose that he consciously produced such verses.

The condition of survival for any society is to produce new members, since older ones are constantly being lost through death. Perhaps the greatest strength of Islam is the priority it gives to the family. In this respect, the religion stands midway between two extremes – the tribalism of ancient times and the individualism of the modern West. By exhortation and example, the Prophet encouraged all Muslims to involve themselves in family life. It is strongly recommended that all adult Muslims marry. Koran 24:32 begins: 'Marry the single ones among you.' Deliberate, lifelong celibacy is regarded as something peculiarly Christian (Koran 57:27). This does not imply any condemnation of monks; on the contrary, Koran 5:82, quoted above, praises their piety. It was not envisaged that there would be a category of people who classified themselves permanently as homosexuals (which is not to say that there were no homosexual feelings or behaviours). Unless 4:16 is taken to refer to homosexuality, the Koran mentions it only in telling the story of Lot and the men of Sodom (26:160–175; also 7:80–84 and 27:54–58).

The Koran permits up to four wives (4:3). This permission was introduced after the Battle of Uhud, when there were many war-widows and orphans in the community. Similar situations were to arise many times in the course of history, and polygamy made it possible for practically all women to find husbands. It is a matter of biological fact that more boy babies are born than girls. However, in most circumstances, a higher proportion of girls than boys survive to adulthood, which, together with the earlier puberty of girls and the greater life expectancy of women, means that in most any society adult women outnumber men, a disproportion that is increased when men are killed in war. If everyone is to marry, therefore, this can only be achieved with some polygamy.

The importance of polygamy should not be exaggerated; the majority of marriages will always have to be monogamous, since the excess of women is never enough to provide more than one wife for most men, not to mention the fact that many women will be unwilling to share a husband. There is nothing in the Koran to stop a woman from making a marriage contract that prevents the husband from taking a second wife. Nor was a woman obliged to be given away in marriage by a male relative; on the contrary, Koran 33:50 specifically refers to a believing woman giving herself in marriage.

The verse permitting polygamy (4:3) is preceded by an introduction of magnificent simplicity, which stresses the unity and equality of the sexes (4:1): 'You people, fear your Lord who created you from a single soul and created from it its partner and spread from them many men and women.' There follows a command not to abuse orphans by using up wealth left in trust for them, and – it is implied – making sexual demands on them; 'and if you fear that you will not deal justly with the orphans, then marry what women are pleasing to you, two, three or four; and if you fear that you will not deal fairly, then one or what your right hands own.' Understood literally, this means that extra wives should be married only by men who are exceptionally fair-minded.

Most commentators explained 'what your right hands own' as meaning slaves, but Ibn Abd al-Wahhab claimed it meant wives and that men should not take concubines. The grammar of the passage suggests that concubines are in principle a substitute for wives, not an addition to them. Given the understanding that a master should not have sex with his slave without her consent, that slaves should be offered the chance to earn their freedom, that a concubine who produced children must not be sold and must be freed if still a slave when her master died, should be offered the chance to earn their freedom, and slave-woman should be given the option, but not the of marrying her ex-master, it would seem that concubinage was originally intended as a transition to marriage. The abuse of it to establish large harems guarded by eunuchs was copied by medieval Muslim rulers from the courts of Byzantium and Persia, and was contrary to the spirit of Islam.

Medieval Christians regarded Islamic polygamy with a mixture of disgust and envy, and their attitudes have carried over into the post-Christian West. Anthropologists have found, however, that polygamous societies are commoner than monogamous ones, which suggests that polygamy is the more natural system. In practice, Westerners have approximated to it, accepting that prominent men take mistresses. In some European countries the kings gave an honourable example, acknowledging their mistresses publicly and endowing them handsomely, but too often Europeans have preferred a climate of hypocrisy in which men are disgraced if they get caught doing what many are known to do, and their women friends enjoy neither recognition nor security. Perhaps the choice is in fact between regulated polygamy of the Koranic kind and clandestine multiple unions.

The Koran obliges a man to pay a dowry to his bride, though she may waive part of it (4:4). This becomes the wife's personal property, though it can be held in trust for her by her parents. It is her economic security against the possibility of widowhood or divorce. The main Koranic passage regulating divorce (2:224–242) relates only to the repudiation of a wife by her husband. It leaves much detail to be filled in, but the main idea is clear: a man's wish to repudiate his wife must be expressed three times before it is irrevocable, and after each of the first two times he is encouraged to be reconciled equitably during a delay of three menstrual periods. After the third time he may not return to her until she has been married to another man.

From the wording it is clear that divorce was meant to be a slow and deliberate process, with recommendations for reconciliation, justice and compensation. The Koran provides no justification for the casual dismissal of wives that later came to be accepted. The prospect of having wasted the dowry is a deterrent to men seeking divorce. The Koran does not imply any social stigma for a divorced woman, for it is accepted that couples may simply not be compatible, and the Prophet set an example in that all but one of his wives were either divorcees or widows.

These Koranic rules on marriage and divorce do not imply an inferior status for women, but there are phrases that imply asymmetry within the relationship between man and wife. In 2:228 a statement of equal rights is followed by a suggestion of male primacy: 'Women hold rights like those held over them in fairness, but men have a degree above them.' The most difficult verse is 4:34: 'Men stand above women insofar as Allah has given the one more than the other and insofar as they [masculine] spend of their wealth; and virtuous women are devout and protective of the hidden as Allah protects, but those [women] whose uncooperativeness you [masculine] fear – admonish them and leave them alone in bed and chastise them; and if they comply with you, do not seek a way against them.'

This verse has attracted an enormous amount of commentary, and it may have been problematic for the Prophet himself, who is reported to have been unfailingly gentle and courteous with his wives; Tabari quotes a Hadith to the effect that he said 'I did not wish it, but Allah wished it.' The verse has never been considered by commentators as license for wife-beating. The degree of inequality implied is very much open to question, as may be seen by changing the above translation, taking *bima* as 'because' instead of 'insofar as', *nushuz* as 'disobedience' instead of 'uncooperativeness and *atana* as 'obey' instead of 'comply'. Muslim feminists argue that the verse makes any inequality the result of economic dependence, so that a change of economic circumstances means a change of relations. The very next verse recommends conciliation in cases of domestic dispute, with one arbiter drawn from the family of each side.

The measure that Westerners have made the symbol of women's inferior status is veiling. This has been traced back to two Koranic rules. Firstly, for the Prophet's wives and them alone, the Koran (33:53) specifies that men other than their close relatives should petition them 'from behind a curtain (*min wara hijab*)'. This verse is said to have been revealed when some of the guests at the wedding feast for the Prophet and Zaynab lingered in her room where it was held, until he was forced to draw a curtain to shut them out. The *hijab* was a fixture and not an article of clothing, and the ruling did not prevent the wives from going out, though it did mean petitioners must not accost them.

Secondly, for the Prophet's wives and daughters and for the wives of the faithful generally, Koran 33:59 says that they should 'pull close to themselves part of their dresses' when in the presence of men from outside their family. 24:31 words it differently, asking them to 'draw their head-dresses over their bosoms'. Inclusion of the Prophet's wives in this second injunction confirms the fact that 33:53 referred to something distinct from their dress. The general nature of the wording leaves it very much to women's discretion exactly how to satisfy this requirement for modesty.

Later Islam read into these recommendations the beginning of universal veiling for free-born Muslim women, combining the two cases and extending the meaning of *hijab* to include a veil in the sense of a style of dress. It is doubtful whether anything so radical happened in the time of the Prophet, even for his wives, and in the absence of any paintings or sculptures, we shall never know exactly how Muslim women dressed then. The Koran certainly does not spell out any general seclusion of women. It seems more likely that such practices were adopted from the Persians and Byzantines after the expansion of Islam.

Women continued to play a part in public affairs throughout this period and for several decades after it, as will be seen in a later chapter. The Prophet is reported to have consulted his wives on every aspect of the life of the community, as witness the many Hadiths that were attributed to them. Indeed, some of his companions, most notably Umar, complained that he was allowing Muslim women to become too forward. Some of them were involved in warfare, mostly urging their men on and helping with the wounded and dead, a few of them even wielding arms. In economic matters women could acquire, own and dispose of property, though Koran 2:282 makes two female witnesses equivalent to one male for contracts (other kinds of evidence not being specified).

Most important of all, in spiritual matters women and men are completely equal. The first to accept Islam was Khadija, and throughout the Prophet's mission women became Muslims in roughly equal numbers with men. No great significance should be read into the fact that the Koran usually refers to believers in the masculine plural, for this is also the grammatical form used for mixed company. However, some women, led by one of the Prophet's wives, Umm Salama, are said to have complained that there was not enough specific reference to women, and in response Koran 33:35 was revealed, spelling out the spiritual equality of the sexes with great emphasis.

There is a widespread myth that Muslims prefer sons to daughters. Where this is true, it is by secular tradition and not by religious teaching. The fact that the dowry is provided by the groom and not by the bride's family removes the burden that causes many parents to prefer sons to daughters in traditional Christian or Hindu society. On the contrary, the Koran fiercely condemns the evil of preferring boys:

> When one of them is given news of a girl, his face becomes dark as he grieves; he hides himself from the people because of his "bad" news: "Should he keep it in spite of shame or bury it in the dust?" How evil is their judgement! (16:57–59).

The Islamic emphasis on family life gives both sexes their value, and it confers a high status on the woman who devotes herself to raising children. However, the Koran nowhere implies that this is the only role for women in life. On the contrary, for those who are not blessed with children, there is the comfort of believing that all earthly satisfactions are as nothing beside spiritual fulfilment, and the Prophet himself set an example by his esteem for his own childless wives:

> Know that the life of this world is only a game and a distraction and a trinket, out-boasting each other and competing to have much wealth and many children. (57:20).

The importance of family life also explains the Koran's attention to inheritance. In Medina, guidance was given on this (Koran 4:11–12 and 4:176). The exact implications of these verses for all possible cases were to take many years to work out in detail, but the essential principles are: that all dependents of the deceased should receive their share, that the share of a male is in general twice that of a female (because a man is expected to provide for his family), and that the heritage of orphaned minors must be held in trust and given to them when they reach adulthood. These rules represented a great advance over pre-Islamic custom, which guaranteed nothing to women or orphans, and which indeed made them part of the property inherited by men.

A side-effect of the inheritance and dowry laws was the preference for first-cousin marriages, preferably with fathers' brothers' daughters, which later became the norm in many Islamic societies, and which has begun to break down only in modern times. This cannot be attributed to the example of the Prophet, who married only one cousin – an aunt's daughter. By marrying paternal cousins, it was possible for men to keep more resources in the extended family. The unfortunate effect of this has been to weaken the intermixing of families, clans and tribes.

Another important innovation was the forbidding of adoption (Koran 33:4–5) – a feature shared with traditional Christianity (and maintained in, for example, English law until 1923). Henceforth there could be only fostering. People remained the children of their real parents, where these were known, and were otherwise brothers or sisters in the Faith. This measure served to strengthen the link between sex and childbirth, making the responsibilities engendered by biological parenthood inalienable.

The other major aspect of everyday life to which the Koran gives special attention is eating and drinking. Food laws similar to those of Judaism but much simpler were laid down in Medina. Certain foods are prohibited: pigs, carrion, blood, and animals not killed in the prescribed manner (Koran 5:3), to which Hadith adds carnivores and donkeys (Bukhari 67:27). Animals are to be slaughtered humanely, and the proper purpose of hunting is to obtain food (Koran 5:4). In the matter of drinking, Islam breaks with Judaism and Christianity and joins Buddhism and the Hinduism of the higher castes in discouraging the drinking of wine, and by implication any intoxicant. However, the Koran does accept that alcohol has uses, presumably medicinal:

> They ask you about wine and divination. Say: "In both there is great harm and usefulness for people, but the harm is greater than the use". (2:219).

With hundreds and soon thousands of Muslims in his charge, the Prophet was obliged to concern himself with crime and public order. The essentials of a criminal justice system were laid down, with the Prophet acting in effect as the judge for disputed cases. Severe punishments, known as *hudud* ('limits'), were laid down for serious crimes: murder, highway robbery, theft, illicit sex, false accusation of illicit sex, and drunkenness.

Murder is treated as essentially a matter for the victim's family, and the Koran sets limits on what they can demand: 'the free for the free, the slave for the slave, the woman for the woman' (2:178), but the verse goes on to recommend mercy and the acceptance of compensation, as is the case with all these hudud.

For theft, the Koran uses a phrase that means literally 'the cutting off of the hand' (5:38), but tradition gives no well-attested or detailed account of any actual instance of this punishment being inflicted in Medina, and some commentators have compared the phrase to one that means literally 'the cutting of the tongue', which means simply 'hold your tongue', 'be quiet'. They conclude that the phrase means imprisonment, not amputation. The next verse promises Allah's forgiveness for the thief who repents; as with murder, the threat seems more important than the execution.

Illicit sex – *zina* (which covers both adultery and fornication) – was treated as an offence. The Koran has no double standard for men and women; for both parties it prescribes a hundred lashes (24:2). Again there are commentators who take it figuratively. This punishment was rarely administered. In the first place, there was little reason to seek illicitly what could be had licitly in a society that accepted divorce and remarriage. Secondly, it was difficult to prove; four witnesses were required – something that was rarely possible – and an accusation brought without them rendered the accuser liable to flogging. A husband could condemn his wife without witnesses by swearing five solemn oaths, but she could establish her innocence by herself swearing five oaths.

Attitudes to sex are perhaps the most powerful causes of misunderstanding between peoples. Modern Westerners tend to see the Muslim attitude in terms of the anti-sexual element in Christian tradition. Islam, on the contrary, teaches that sex is good and should be enjoyed by everyone, but only in the context of marriage, which is not a sacrament or an indissoluble bond but a civil contract designed above all in the interests of any children that it produces. Sexual display in public is discouraged not because there is anything wrong in sex, but because indiscriminate sexual arousal is socially disruptive. Illicit sex is condemned not because sex is base, but because extra-marital sex undermines the family. Whether it should be criminalized is keenly debated among Muslims today, but none doubts that it is a grave social evil.

In economic matters, Islam generally accepted existing institutions, recommending honesty and moderation. Ownership and commerce, wages and rent were largely unaffected, except that Muslims were required to make witnessed, written contracts for deals affecting the future. However, usury (*riba*) was categorically prohibited (Koran 2:275–278), as it was by medieval Christianity, and it has usually been understood to include both the taking of interest and the making of excess profits.

The owning of slaves continued, as it did in Christianity, but measures were introduced to improve the lot of slaves, who were regarded in spiritual terms as the complete equals of free people. Indeed, a Muslim slave was superior to a free polytheist (Koran 2:221). As already noted, one of the earliest passages in the Koran recommends the freeing of slaves. A Medinan passage, 24:33, lays down a procedure for this: if a slave requests a contract of manumission, the owner should agree. The contract was an agreement to free the slave on completion of a payment in instalments, and the owner was to provide suitable and legal ways for the slave to earn the necessary money. Koran 24:32 exhorts owners to arrange marriage for worthy slaves, male or female. Alternatively, a master could take his female slave as a concubine, but it was understood that this must be with her consent.

The very last passage of the Koran, revealed on the Farewell Pilgrimage, is said to have been the one inserted into the middle of the food laws in 5:3:

> Today those who disbelieve have despaired at your religion, so do not fear them, but fear Me. Today I have perfected your religion for you, completed My favour upon you and approved for you Islam as religion.

There can be no doubt that this is true: Islam was perfected in the lifetime of its Prophet, who was quite clearly a Muslim in the sense that we recognize today, and all the important elements of the religion were firmly established by the time he died.

CHAPTER TEN

THE KORAN COMPLETED

Islam is unique among the world's great religions in that its scripture remains just as its founder left it. This view has been contested by orientalists. In the nineteenth century, European and American scholars applied to the Koran the techniques that were so successfully prising apart the Bible. Some may have hoped to discredit the book, but others had purely scientific motivation. They pored over thousands of codices and fragments of text, looking for discrepancies that would show how the received version had been put together. The effort continued in the twentieth century, fortified by new techniques such as carbon-14 dating, infra-red and ultra-violet photography and the chemical analysis of inks and parchments. The outcome of this huge labour was that the consonant text was virtually identical in all these Korans, apart from a few trivial scribal errors, and that slight variations in the pointing and vowelling made no significant difference.

Since the 1970s, a school of so-called 'new historians' has developed, initially in the University of London's School of Oriental and African Studies. Its members have attempted to show that the universally accepted text of the Koran was nevertheless put together long after the death of Muhammad, perhaps as late as the third century AH, largely by Jewish converts (though one wonders what they could have converted to, if Islam had still lacked its founding text). In the atmosphere of growing tension between Westerners and Muslims, these historians have understandably kept their heads down, but their ideas have been publicized by journalists writing under inflammatory titles such as 'The Great Koran Con trick' (*New Statesman*, 10 December 2001).

The argument put forward for questioning the authenticity of the Koran is the supposed absence of contemporary evidence. The earliest surviving biography, Ibn Ishaq's *Sira*, was not written until over a century after the death of the Prophet, and it is known only in the revised version made a couple of generations later. The oldest law book, Malik's *Muwatta*, dates from the end of the second century. The collections of Hadith were not produced until the beginning of the third century AH. If these were the only sources, then the beginnings of Islam would indeed be as obscure as those of Judaism and Christianity.

However, the most important source of all, the Koran itself, is unquestionably ancient, as is proved by one simple truth, which Western textual examination has helped to establish: the very fact that there is in effect only one consonantal text. As the civil war between Sunnis, Shiites and Kharijites started twenty-four years after the death of the Prophet, in AH 36 (656), this universally accepted document must have existed by then in copies all over the Muslim world. Otherwise the warring factions would undoubtedly have produced rival versions to justify themselves. In any case, it is now generally accepted that the oldest surviving Korans date back to the first century AH.

There remains the question of whether the document universally accepted two decades after the Prophet's death existed during his lifetime. The essential evidence for this is to be found in the Koran itself. For some details, such as the names of the scribes and the preparation of the definitive edition, we have to depend on much later documents, but even without this supplementary information, the essential fact would still be clear: the Koran was written down in the lifetime of the Prophet.

As described earlier, the sura most widely thought to have been the first, number 98, begins with an instruction to read or recite (*iqra*). Taken with verse 4 which speaks of teaching 'by the pen', this shows that the idea of written revelation was present from the beginning. Subsequent passages suggest that, whether or not the Prophet could write, he was able to read. Koran 29:48 says: 'You were not reading before it from a scripture, nor writing it with your right hand; if so, the prattlers would have doubted'. Koran 98:2 refers to Muhammad as 'a messenger of Allah reading parchments (*suhuf*) made pure in which are clear writings'. The verb in both these passages, *tala*, can mean recite, but reciting from parchments would in any case require reading. Parchments are mentioned also in an early Meccan sura 80, which calls itself a reminder 'in honoured parchments, exalted and pure, in the hands of scribes, honourable and just' (verses 13–16). In three Meccan passages, 20:133, 53:36 and 87:18–19, the Jewish scriptures are referred to by the same term.

Other words for parchments or scrolls occur in Meccan suras. *Qirtas*, from Greek *khartes,* is used in 6:7: 'Even if we sent down on you a writing in a parchment and they touched it with their hands, the doubters would say "This is just plain sorcery".' The meaning of this is clearly that, even if a text dropped out of the sky (instead of being written by the Prophet's secretaries), the doubters would still refuse it. The same word in the plural is used in 6:91 for scrolls of the Book of Moses. Another word, *raqq*, occurs in 52:2–3: 'a writing inscribed, on a parchment spread out'. The word *sijill* (from Latin, via Greek *sigillon,* 'a seal or sealed document') is used in 21:104: 'The day that we roll up the heavens like the rolling up of a scroll for writings'.

A Medinan passage, 62:5, describes those who were charged with the Torah and did not discharge it as being like 'a donkey carrying scrolls' – the one Koranic use of the word *asfar* (singular *sifr*, Hebrew and Aramaic *sefer*), a general word for documents, which in Arabic came to mean especially the Torah scrolls. If the Prophet ever saw such a load, it would have been when Jewish clans left Medina for exile.

The Koranic word usually translated as 'book' is *kitab*, plural *kutub*, which it applies to itself (e.g. sura 2:1) as well as to the Jewish and Christian scriptures. This is simply a verbal noun meaning 'a writing', and there is nowhere in the Koran that it has to be understood as 'book' in the modern sense. Indeed it is highly unlikely that the Prophet ever saw a bound book in his life. The binding of pages into a codex was a Christian invention of about the second century CE, but it had not yet been adopted by Jews.

111

It is most unlikely to have reached Arabia, where there were no texts to bind and few if any buyers who would import one of these costly items in a foreign language.

It thus seems that the Prophet saw the Koran as physically embodied in a set of parchments, possibly as a future scroll or scrolls. There is good evidence that he organized the material much as it has come down to us. He certainly put the suras into their present form. The occurrence of the word *sura* in the text (10:38, 11:13) shows that this structure was already a fact in the Meccan period. One Medinan sura announces itself at the beginning as 'A sura that We have sent down...' (24:1). But were all the suras of the completed Koran as the Prophet left them? One detail suggests that they were: there is a single exception – sura 9, the last revealed – to the rule that each sura begins with the Invocation, 'In the Name of Allah, the Merciful, the Forgiving.' Only the Prophet himself could have had the authority to make such an exception, or only in his absence could there have been insufficient authority to remove the anomaly, so it must have been he who put the Invocation at the head of the other 113 suras.

There is also evidence that the Prophet may have grouped some suras together in sets, each perhaps tied together as a roll or bundle of parchments. Each set is characterized by having the same or a very similar combination of letters at the beginning of each member: 2–3 and 29–32 have ALM, 10–15 have AL[M]R, 26–28 have TS[M], and 40–46 have HM. No one has ever given a satisfactory explanation of these letters, but there can be no doubt that they form an integral part of the text, for they follow the Invocation, and in all except three cases they introduce a reference to the Koran or Scripture or its revelation or writing, such as is found in only three or four other opening verses. These continuations include 8 of the 11 occurrences of the phrase 'Those are the signs... (*tilka ayat...*)', and 5 of the 11 occurrences of the word 'revelation (*tanzil*)' – something that could not conceivably have happened by coincidence. Also, in 20 of the 29 suras that begin with such letters, the last letter of the group rhymes with the following verses.

It is unimaginable that anyone but the Prophet could have put these striking openings on to so many suras without provoking protests. It therefore seems certain that he put the letters there, and very probable that he intended suras with the same combination of letters to form a set. All except two of the suras in question (2 and 3) are from his time in Mecca, so he was already organizing the Koran at an early date. He may well have put together other sets, for example the ten short Medinan suras, 57–66, and the very short suras, 67–114, which are distinguished by many recurring features from the rest of the Koran.

The one respect in which the Prophet may not have finalized the Koran is the order of the suras, apart from the possible groupings. He does not seem to have given them titles, let alone numbers, which are missing from the oldest Korans. Tradition does tell of recitations in different orders, but no text of the complete Koran uses a different order from the received version, which was therefore fixed at latest by the time the authorized text was prepared. Even if it was not he who fixed the order, it would in no way detract from the authenticity of the Koran, for each sura is a self-contained unit, and there is neither a logical nor a chronological reason for any particular order.

This much can be deduced from the internal evidence of the Koran; for the rest we must rely on much later sources. For example, there is nothing in the text to tell us who did the actual writing, though Koran 25:5 implies that the writing down of the revelations was not done by the Prophet himself; his enemies are described as saying 'Tales of the ancients, which he has caused to be written! They are dictated to him morning and evening.' Tradition claims that he was unable to write, which is held to enhance the miraculous nature of his receipt of the divine Book. The proof is supposed to be in the Koran's reference to him as 'the *ummi* prophet' (Koran 7:157–8). However, the word *ummi*, which later came to mean 'illiterate', is derived from *ummah*, 'community' or 'people', and originally meant 'of the people' or 'indigenous'. Even if he was illiterate, like any Meccan businessman he would certainly have appreciated the importance of written documents. Tradition supplies the names of more than sixty people who took down passages to his dictation at one time or another, but most of these probably did so only occasionally, and some accounts may have been fabricated by people wishing to improve the reputation of an ancestor.

Four men can with some confidence be described as having been the Prophet's secretaries. One of the earliest and longest serving was a Meccan, Abd-Allah Ibn Masud. Another Meccan, Ibn Abi Sarh, became an apostate and returned to Mecca after having emigrated. He allegedly lost his faith when the Prophet failed to notice a discrepancy from what he had dictated. The story is obscure and may have been invented by enemies who resented the fact that his apostasy was pardoned after the Conquest of Mecca and that he was eventually appointed Governor of Egypt by the third caliph, Uthman, who was his foster brother. Early in his time in Medina, the Prophet started dictating to a local man, Ubay Ibn Kaab. He was later joined by another Medinan, Zayd Ibn Thabit, a brilliant youth still in his teens (no relation of the poet, Hassan Ibn Thabit).

According to Hadith, the Prophet's angelic Presence reviewed the whole Koran with him once a year, and twice in the last year of his life. Zayd, Ubay and Ibn Masud are all mentioned as witnesses to these recitations of the whole Koran. However, Zayd appears to have become the most frequently employed secretary, and his name comes up in accounts of every stage in the finalization of the Koranic text. He cannot have been much older than forty when authorized copies were being spread all over the Islamic territories.

It is inconceivable that the precious rolls or bundles of parchments were stored anywhere other than where the Prophet lived, and for security and privacy this would have been alongside the rooms occupied by him and his family. It seems reasonable to suppose that there was a small office where the secretaries could work and keep documents and writing materials. It would be here that Zayd Ibn Thabit and perhaps Ubay and Ibn Masud organized the files of suras, keeping them open for the frequent additions that had to be made. When new verses came to him, the Prophet would say where they were to be placed, and Zayd or the others would write them down, sometimes perhaps in the margin, sometimes on a partly filled parchment, sometimes on a new parchment.

This would explain the mystery of 'the parchments of Hafsa' or 'of Aisha', from which the definitive copies of the Koran are said to have been made. If the Koran was there in its original form, in a room next to the apartments of his widows, it would be natural that they became its guardians. In that case, the consonantal text of the Koran that we have in our hands today is the selfsame text that was written down in the lifetime of the Prophet.

CHAPTER ELEVEN

THE PERSON OF THE PROPHET

We know hardly anything about Muhammad's orphan childhood. Of his adult life in the time of his obscurity, before he began his public mission, we can say little, only imagining the tension between his busy family and working life and his solitary wanderings in the mountains around Mecca. However, in Medina he lived under the eyes of thousands of Muslims, and some of what was recounted of his life there must surely be true. Between the affectionate portrait given by Ibn Saad and details culled from the Hadith literature, we can build up a plausible picture.

The situation was the more difficult in that his home was attached to the mosque. Unfortunately for historians, the original buildings were destroyed a century later to make room for enlargement of the mosque, and we have only inadequate descriptions, but it is clear that Muhammad and his family lived in the simplest conditions. Each wife had her own premises, the words for which (*buyut* – Koran 33:53 – or *hujurat* – 49:4) have been variously translated as 'houses', 'rooms' or 'apartments', but in modern terms they were 'bed-sits', each measuring about 3½ by 4 metres (12 by 14 feet). The walls of some were in stone, those of others in palm-fronds daubed with clay, and the ceilings were so low under the roofs of palm thatch that a standing man could touch them. The furniture was minimal – some rugs, a leather mattress stuffed with straw, and cushions for sitting on. There was no privy, and calls of nature by day or by night involved a walk to nearby wasteland.

The courtyard of the mosque was rarely empty of people. Besides those who came to worship or pray, or in the hope of an audience with the Prophet, there were usually newly arrived immigrants who had nowhere else to go, and for whom a bench had been provided near the gateway. Muhammad and his family

117

did all that they could to help these people, giving them clothes and blankets and sharing their food with them. After the battles of Uhud and the Trench, a hospital tent was set up in the courtyard to care for the wounded.

Muhammad slept in his wives' rooms, each in turn in rotation, and his only refuge during the day was his attic. According to Ibn Saad, Aisha once asked him what he did when he was alone there, and he replied that like any other man he mended his shoes and patched his clothes; but the most important thing he found there must certainly have been the solitude necessary for his inner life, away from the business that always waited for him down below.

Muhammad's need for solitude was matched only by his need for feminine company. Westerners have made the number of his wives an excuse for disrespect, but if one lays aside any prejudice in favour of monogamy, it is impossible to find any ground for criticism. Each of his wives gave her free adult consent to marry him, with the possible exception of Aisha, whose age at marriage is disputed. With his great energy and generosity, he had much to give to all of them, and although they suspected that he had a favourite, he never acknowledged the fact. They regarded themselves as privileged people, being closer to the Messenger of Allah than any man could ever be, and he saw in them precious companions, to whom he could unburden himself and from whom he could count on hearing frank opinions and wise advice.

Muhammad was very honest and open about the reason for his marriages; according to one Hadith, he used to say that the three loveliest things in this life are prayer, women and perfume. In fact it was only in his last years that he enjoyed more wives than the most favoured of his companions. Until his early fifties he had only one – first Khadija and then Sawda. He added a second, third and fourth during his early years at Medina: Aisha daughter of Abu Bakr, his only virgin bride; Hafsa daughter of Umar, widowed by the Battle of Badr; and Zaynab bint Khuzayma, of his foster-tribe, the Bani Hawazin who predominated east of Mecca, widow of a third cousin of Muhammad's, known for her great generosity to the poor. This Zaynab died a few months later and was succeeded by Umm Salama, widow of Muhammad's first cousin Abu Salama, who died of wounds received at Uhud.

It was only in his last five years that Muhammad went beyond the usual maximum of four wives, adding a further five, as specially authorized by Koran 33:50. The marriage that took him over the limit has often been misrepresented. As senior surviving male relative of his cousin Zaynab, daughter of his aunt Umayama, the Prophet had married her to his adopted son, Zayd Ibn Haritha. It was not a happy marriage, and Muhammad himself was attracted to her. Zayd offered to divorce her but he said: 'Keep your wife and fear Allah!' Eventually the couple divorced by mutual consent, but the Prophet was still reluctant to marry the ex-wife of his adopted son (though 4:23 only prohibits 'the ex-wives of your sons that are from your loins', and 33:4 had declared that all adoption was only fostering). The marriage was finally permitted 'in order that the believers be not in difficulty over marriage with the divorced wives of their foster sons' (Koran 33:37).

This marriage, contracted early in AH 6 (627), some months after the Battle of the Trench, was the occasion for a wider change in Muhammad's dealings with his people. From now on he was no longer available to all comers; visitors should come by invitation, and if they were invited to a meal they should not arrive before it was ready, nor linger after it was finished. His wives were to be treated with special respect as the 'Mothers of the Faithful', and should never remarry after his death (33:53). They were given the option of an honourable divorce if they did not wish to accept this condition. The rule that men from outside their family should speak to them from behind a curtain dates from this time, as distinct from the general requirement for modesty in women's dress.

Muhammad's next marriage was with Juwayriya, daughter of the chief of a Bedouin tribe, the Bani Mustaliq, who had been conniving with the Meccans and who were defeated in a raid later that year. She had been allotted to one of the Muslims and came to Muhammad for help in buying back her freedom; instead, he offered to marry her and she accepted. This alliance apparently won over her tribe and their confederates to Islam.

The raid on the Bani Mustaliq produced a distressing incident. Muhammad had, as usual, taken one of his wives, chosen by lot, on the expedition. On this occasion his companion was Aisha. On the return journey through the desert to Medina, she went aside from the encampment for a call of nature, and her necklace broke. In her anxiety to pick up all the beads, she missed the departure of the caravan. She was found by a man who had lagged behind, and he brought her back to the main party on his camel. Tongues began to wag, and Muhammad himself became greatly distressed, but she protested her innocence. The incident was closed only when Koran 24:11–21 condemned those who had spread the rumour.

Muhammad's further marriages were with Safiya, Umm Habiba and Maymuna. Safiya was a Jewish woman of the Bani al-Nadir, captured at Khaybar. Aged seventeen, she was the youngest wife next to Aisha. Her father had been Huyay, the leader who had so disastrously persuaded the Bani Qurayza to change sides. Umm Habiba was the daughter of Abu Sufyan, the Meccan leader, and the widow of Muhammad's cousin Ubayd-Allah Ibn Jahsh, who had become a Christian in Abyssinia, so she was the sister-in-law of Zaynab. Muhammad married her by proxy through the good offices of the Negus, and she was brought back with the other remaining Abyssinian emigrants after the capture of Khaybar. Maymuna was another Bedouin of the Bani Hawazin. She was the widowed sister of Umm al-Fadl, the wife of Muhammad's uncle Abbas. He married her on his way back from his performance of the lesser pilgrimage in the year AH 7 (629).

Koran 33:52 forbade Muhammad from making any further marriages, allowing only concubines. There seems to have been only one: Mariya, who was one of two Coptic girls given by the Governor of Egypt in response to Muhammad's sending of an envoy. She lived on the edge of Medina, to avoid provoking the jealousy of the Prophet's wives, and bore him a son, Ibrahim, his only child after those of Khadija. She was given her freedom, but the baby died in his second year.

Having so many wives brought problems, and there appears to have been a rift between a group of four – Sawda, Aisha, Hafsa and Safiya – and the rest. On one occasion a breach of confidence led Muhammad to withdraw from all his wives for a month (Koran 66:1–5), which he spent in his attic, in such Spartan conditions that Umar wept (Bukhari 60:316). Eventually Muhammad returned to his wives after they had been offered – and had all refused – an honourable divorce (Koran 33:28–9):

> O Prophet, say to your wives: 'If you seek the life of this world and its adornment, then come; I shall provide for your enjoyment and release you handsomely.
> But if you desire Allah and His Messenger and the home of the Ultimate, Allah has prepared for those of you who do good a great reward.'

Muhammad's experience of fatherhood was full of sorrow. All his baby sons, his adopted son and three of his four grown-up daughters died before him – Ruqayya during his absence at Badr, Umm Kulthum soon after the submission of Mecca and Zaynab soon after her husband, Abu 'l-As, a polytheist nephew of Khadija's, had become a Muslim and rejoined her. He had been one of the captives of Badr, and with his ransom Zaynab had sent her father a necklace that had belonged to Khadija. He was so moved that he freed her husband without accepting the ransom, on condition that she be sent to Medina.

Zaynab eventually reached Medina, but only after an incident in which she was captured and suffered a miscarriage as the result of rough treatment. This roused Muhammad to a rare state of fury, and he is said to have asked that the men responsible be burnt alive if caught. Next day he repented of his anger and declared that it was wrong to burn a person, however wicked, 'as fire is Allah's way of punishment'. In the event, the culprit became a Muslim, and Muhammad accepted his homage before he realized who he was, after which he forgave him. Six years later, Zaynab's husband was captured by Muslims on his way back from Syria. He was allowed to return to Mecca, where he wound up his affairs, declared himself a Muslim and left at last to rejoin his wife, but she died soon afterwards, as did her son Ali, leaving only her daughter Umama.

Fatima alone survived her father – but only by a few months. Fortunately Muhammad was compensated for the loss of his children by having several grandchildren. There were the children born in Medina to his daughter Fatima and her husband, his cousin Ali: Hasan, Husayn, Umm Kulthum and Zaynab. There was also Umama, for whom he had special tenderness after she had lost her mother. Later generations of Muslims remembered mainly the two grandsons, but there is no evidence that Muhammad attached any less importance to his three granddaughters.

Many anecdotes bear witness to Muhammad's great affection for children. For example, he once had Umama on his shoulders at the time of worship, and he kept her there, putting her down when he bowed or prostrated, then picking her up again. When Aisha came into his household as his betrothed, she brought her toys with her, and he enjoyed watching her play with 'Solomon's horses'. Incidentally his tolerance of her dolls shows that he did not condemn all images of living things. A story that became very dear to the partisans of Ali described how Muhammad sheltered Ali and Fatima and their two little sons Hasan and Husayn under his cloak, and the five became known as 'the People of the Cloak.

Muhammad had many close male friends. It was said that when he talked to people, he always gave them such complete attention that each would seem to be the most important person in the world. Ten friends were to be of particular importance for the part they were to play in the development of Islam after his death, and these will be described in detail in the next chapter. One of the greatest personal blows to him was the death of Zayd Ibn Haritha, for whom he still felt a fatherly tenderness, although no longer legally his adoptive father. Few men were as close to

Muhammad as Zayd, and he was entrusted with the leadership of nine expeditions – far more than anyone else except the Prophet. He died leading an expedition to Muta on the borders of Byzantine Syria in AH 8 (629).

Hadith gives many examples of Muhammad's fondness for animals, with which he had close dealings all through his life. An often repeated story is that he took off – or even cut – his cloak to avoid waking a cat that was asleep on it. Even the dog, despite its uncleanness, could arouse his tenderness, and when his army passed a bitch with puppies on their way to the conquest of Mecca, he is said to have placed a guard over them, with orders that no man should molest them. He also respected trees, and when the army entered Mecca he prohibited the cutting of any. In the account of the conversion of Salman the Persian, Ibn Ishaq describes how Muhammad himself planted the palm trees required as part-payment for Salman's freedom.

Muhammad was a man of great physical courage and endurance. Between the approximate ages of fifty and sixty he led the Muslims in twenty-seven of their eighty-odd expeditions and engagements. Various authors describe how he had chain-mail armour and was skilled with sword, spear and bow and arrow. Even while on campaign, he was careful of his personal appearance, according to Ibn Saad, taking with him mirror, comb and hair-oil. But he was no dandy; his clothes were few and simple, and he made them last till they were very old.

A great deal of property passed through Muhammad's hands during his last few years, including all the Charity payments and a fifth of the booty from all the expeditions, but he continued to have few personal possessions and to live very simply. Ibn Saad describes how he had a copper bath, in which he used to bathe using four pints – two or three litres – of water. In his last three years he had a glass drinking vessel, a gift from the Governor of Egypt. He wore a signet ring, made of silver-plated iron, engraved with the words 'Muhammad Ibn Abd-Allah, Messenger of Allah'. He had been given a gold ring but refused to keep it, saying that it was inappropriate for a prophet. His only valuable assets when he died were his chain-mail armour, which was in pawn to one of the Jews of Medina, his white mule and the oasis of Fadak.

Aisha is reported as remarking that besides women and perfume he liked food, especially sweet things, but that while he had been blessed with the first two, he had not had much of the third. He took two meals a day, sitting on the ground, usually either barley-bread or dates or a little meat, and he milked his own goats and drank their milk, but he fasted every Monday and Thursday. On one occasion he was presented with a pumpkin, which he enjoyed so much that he continued to speak of it long after.

The missing element from our image of Muhammad is his portrait. The early Muslims refrained from creating any image that might be taken as an idol, and even the Persian miniaturists left a blank in place of his face. In modern times, the same reticence has prevented the making of films portraying his life, with the one exception of *The Message*. Again, Ibn Saad offers the most information. He is said to have been of a little more than medium height, broad-chested and sturdily built, and he walked quickly, like a man going downhill. He had a large head with a prominent forehead, dark, wavy hair, which he wore down to his shoulders, and a thick beard. His eyes were large and dark, his nose hooked and his mouth wide. He was often grave and silent, but never idle. When he spoke, it was always rapidly and to the point. His voice was gentle, and he scarcely ever raised it.

Muhammad's last illness came when he was about sixty-two, two months after returning from his Farewell Pilgrimage. His thoughts had been on death, and he had spent the night before the first symptoms praying in the cemetery of al-Baqi, where so many of his family and friends lay buried. With his usual tact, he asked permission of his other wives to be moved to Aisha's room for her to nurse him. Some thought this was acknowledgment that she was his favourite, but it could just have been because her room had a door into the mosque. His condition grew rapidly worse. On Monday the 12th of First Rabi, AH 11 (8th June 632),

Muhammad Ibn Abd-Allah died. It was the day said to be the tenth anniversary of his arrival in Medina and conventionally taken to be his birthday. Worn out by his exertions and his privations, he was ready to die, having completed his life's work.

The last two verses of sura 9, the last sura to be revealed, are a fitting epitaph (though there is a problem with these verses, whose authenticity has been questioned, as discussed in a later chapter):

> There has come to you a prophet from among yourselves, on whom it weighs heavy when you go wrong, who is concerned over you, who is merciful and forgiving to the believers.
>
> But if they turn away [from you, Muhammad], say: 'Sufficient for me is Allah. There is no god but Allah. In Allah I trust, the Lord of the Throne, the Mighty.'

It seems astonishing that anyone could ever have maligned this admirable man. In the last twenty years of his life he gave up most of life's comforts and subjected himself to great hardships, all in the selfless pursuit of the mission that had been thrust upon him. Starting with no followers except his family, he acquired the affection and confidence of countless men and women of all ages. His success required a unique combination of qualities: deep inwardness with great social gifts, high idealism with unfailing practical sense, personal humility with towering authority. When asked for miracles, he quietly answered that he was only a man. Yes, but no ordinary man!

CHAPTER TWELVE

THE FIRST CALIPHS

Inventing the Caliphate

The death of Muhammad threw the Muslim community into deep crisis. He had been not only Prophet, but also head of state, legislator, chief justice, treasurer, and commander-in-chief of the armed forces, not to mention his role as incomparable friend and guide. Arabia was still a tribal society, and the loyalty of the sovereign tribes was to him personally. The daunting question for Muslims was what institution or which person should and could succeed to as many of these functions as possible.

Ten men held the fate of Islam in their hands. Sunni tradition calls them the 'the Ten given Good News' because the Prophet is said to have declared that they were sure to go straight to Paradise. The list in its final form must date from after the death of Zayd Ibn Haritha in AH 8 (629), as there is no other way to explain his exclusion. On the other hand, no one selecting ten names after Muhammad's death would have included Said Ibn Zayd, who played hardly any significant part in the further history of Islam. Perhaps they were originally the Twelve, including Zayd and, say, Jaafar Ibn Abi Talib.

Five of the Ten were older men, in their fifties or early sixties; Abu Bakr, Umar and Abu Ubayda, who together created the office of caliph, Uthman who was the third to fill it, and Abdul-Rahman, whose support for Uthman was decisive. The three last named had all been in Ethiopia together. There were five men in their thirties – Ali, Zubayr, Saad, Talha and Said. The first three of these were all cousins of the Prophet. The last two were kinsmen of Abu Bakr and Umar respectively.

The Ten all came from seven clans of the Quraysh, and all except Uthman and Abu Ubayda from the five clans of the old Confederation of Honour. All except Umar were listed by Ibn

Ishaq among the earliest converts to Islam; no Medinan had been Muslim long enough to attain comparable influence. They were all bound to each other and to the Prophet in a complex network of marriage ties – the consequence, not the cause of their closeness – and relations between their womenfolk account for some of the interactions between them. Only human frailty can explain, and nothing can excuse, the fact that within twenty-five years three of the four survivors would be at war with each other.

Probably the oldest and certainly the most senior of the Ten was Abu Bakr Ibn Abi Quhafa, of clan Taym, father of Aisha. He was aged about fifty-eight when the Prophet died. He had been the first man to accept Islam after the two in Muhammad's household, and had been his companion in the migration to Medina. He had been chosen to head the pilgrimage of the year 9, and to lead worship during the Prophet's last illness. He was known as '*al-Siddiq*, the Witness to the Truth', a man who combined cool judgement with passionate faith.

Umar Ibn al-Khattab, of clan Adi, was the other father-in-law of the Prophet among the Ten, being the father of Hafsa. He was younger than Abu Bakr – in his late forties – but his great friend. Umar later married the Prophet's granddaughter Umm Kulthum, daughter of Ali, though Shia Muslims claim this was another woman of the same name. He was a tall man with piercing eyes, forceful and impulsive, as seen already in the story of his conversion.

Beside these ten men there were ten illustrious women: the nine widows of the Prophet and, until her early death, his surviving daughter Fatima, whom Shia Muslims rank above all other women. The most influential widow was the youngest, Aisha, to whom much Hadith is ascribed. Umm Salama and Hafsa were also very authoritative, and like Aisha they are reported to have known the Koran by heart. Zaynab too was often quoted as a source of information. The nine widows continued to live in their homes along the eastern wall of the Mosque – Aisha sharing hers with the Prophet's tomb. They formed a small celibate community, bound together by a unique experience. The subsequent history of Islam might have been different if they had been allowed to advise on the decisions that followed their husband's death as they had on those of his lifetime.

A few hours before he died, the Prophet appeared at Aisha's door while Abu Bakr was leading the dawn worship, and raised his hand to the worshippers. Believing him to be getting better, Abu Bakr thought he could safely go home to the Medinan wife he had recently married, near the edge of the oasis. In fact Muhammad died in the heat of noon, his head in Aisha's lap. Abu Bakr hurried back and arrived hot and breathless to find Umar addressing the crowd and saying that the Prophet was not really dead and would outlive them all. Overcoming his fatigue, Abu Bakr took charge of the situation, asked Umar to stand aside, and quoted a Koranic verse (3:144):

> Muhammad is only a messenger, and the messengers before him have passed away. If he dies or is killed, will you turn on your heels?

This was a historic moment: the first use of the Koran to settle a disagreement between Muslims in the absence of the Prophet. Now that the news was accepted as true, people began to look at the implications while Abu Bakr, Umar and Abu Ubayda and the other Immigrants debated in the Prophet's Mosque. News then arrived that the Medinan Muslims were meeting in the Barn of the Bani Saida, on the other side of the oasis, with the object of choosing their own separate leadership. Abu Bakr, Umar and Abu Ubayda hurried across to prevent this division. In the course of a heated debate, Abu Bakr proposed that the people choose between Umar and Abu Ubayda. Umar was shocked at the suggestion that he should be set over Abu Bakr, and he went down on his knees, grasped Abu Bakr's hand and swore allegiance to him. In a wave of enthusiasm the rest of the company followed his example.

And so was invented the office of caliph. The Arabic *khalifa* occurs in the Koran twice in the singular, referring respectively to Adam and David as 'viceregent' on earth, and seven times in its plurals to express people who are 'successors' of previous people. This was the first important feature of Islam not established by the Prophet. Ali seems to have objected to Abu Bakr's elevation, and the Shia movement, which developed some twenty-five years later, regarded Ali as the divinely appointed immediate successor, the First Imam, and did not recognize the caliphate. However, so young a man could not realistically have expected to have his rule accepted by men twice his age, in a society that traditionally attached much importance to seniority.

There seems also to have been a wider lack of understanding between the older and younger members of the Ten. While their seniors were investing Abu Bakr, Ali, Zubayr and Talha were consulting privately in Fatima's house. These three played a very modest part in affairs as long as the older companions dominated. Said was briefly prominent in the Syrian campaign, but refused a governorship and thereafter retired almost completely from public life. Saad was a general in Iraq and was made Governor of Kufa, but Umar later dismissed him from the post.

Ali became involved in Fatima's conflict with Abu Bakr. As Muhammad's only surviving child, she claimed inheritance of his property, notably the oasis of Fadak. It was a valuable possession, bringing in an annual income of forty thousand dirhams (for comparison, a male slave cost four hundred). However, she was as abstemious as her father and wanted it not for its value but to respect the principle of a daughter's right to inherit. Abu Bakr steadfastly refused to consider her claim, holding that prophets do not have heirs, and that the oasis was the property of the community, to be administered by himself in the interests of all. Fatima outlived her father by only a few months, but when she died, Ali took over her claim.

After Abu Bakr's investiture, the men of the Prophet's family went to Aisha's room to make preparations for the burial. They were his cousin Ali and his uncle Abbas with two of his sons, also Usama Ibn Zayd, and Shuqran, Muhammad's freedman. On Monday evening they washed the body and shrouded it in three cloaks. In the middle of the night of Tuesday to Wednesday they buried him under the floor of Aisha's room. They got a Medinan grave-digger as they had not managed to find Abu Ubayda to dig a Meccan-style grave. Aisha, who was staying with a fellow widow, is reported to have said that the first they knew of it was when they heard the pick-axes in the middle of the night. She was also critical of the way the men had washed the body, and regretted that it had not been done by the Prophet's widows.

There is some mystery about these events. The people are reported to have filed through the tiny room on Tuesday to pay their last respects. Somehow, the Hashemite group who had prepared the body on Monday evening seems to have regained possession of the room on Tuesday evening. They had had a whole day to find Abu Ubayda, yet neither he nor Abu Bakr nor Umar was present for the funeral. The three men who had just established the caliphate were thus excluded from its first major event. It has to be said that the new era was not beginning well. Abu Bakr seems to have tried to be conciliatory, quoting the Prophet as having said: 'No prophet died but was buried where he died.'

The caliphate of Abu Bakr was dominated by what were called the Wars of Apostasy. Many of the Bedouin tribes that had sworn allegiance to the Prophet claimed that this had only been personal homage to him, and that they were now free to break with his successor. Some of them seem to have proposed to remain independent Muslims. The decision to fight against these was definitely that of the sober Abu Bakr, and it is interesting to note that the impetuous Umar tried to restrain him, pointing out that the Prophet had said 'The property and life of anyone who says "There is no god but Allah" are safe from me, unless in righting (*haqq*) [an injustice]; his reckoning is with Allah.' To this Abu Bakr replied: 'I shall fight anyone who separates worship from payment of Charity (*zakat*), for Charity is the right (*haqq*) due from property. By Allah! If they refused me even one kid that they used to pay to Allah's Messenger, I would fight them for refusing.' (Bukhari 84:3).

This was a crucial decision. Islam could have evolved in a quite different way, as a network of communities, each with its own leader, coming together freely for common causes, with the Koran as their shared foundation. This indeed was the vision that was adopted a generation later by the Kharijite faction of Islam. There was no inherent necessity for a centralized structure, and mainstream Islam did eventually contain great diversity in its unity. The Companions of the Prophet derived a certain authority from their life with him, but there was no priesthood and no religious hierarchy, so they could have adopted a form of collective leadership.

Other tribes truly wanted to break with Islam altogether, and some of these were led by men or women claiming to be prophets. The most prominent was the man nicknamed by the Muslims 'Musaylima' – roughly 'Muslimette' – who led a confederation of tribes in Central Arabia, grouped round the Bani Hanifa. He had already been active in the Prophet's lifetime, and had proposed to him that they divide Arabia between them. The greatest battle of the Wars of Apostasy was that of Yamama, early in AH 12 (633), in which Musaylima was killed.

An important consequence of this battle is said to have been that Abu Bakr decided to commission an official copy of the Koran, in view of the danger of relying on perishable human memories. Many Muslims had learned passages of the Koran by heart under the Prophet's guidance, and some had learned all of it, adding each new passage as it came. This was the beginning of a tradition that has lasted unbroken to this day. Given its central place in Islam, there was clearly great advantage in having all of it available for instant recall.

There is much mystery over this alleged edition. For a start, it is doubtful whether the Battle of Yamama made it necessary, as few Koran reciters were lost; most of those killed were new converts. There are also conflicting accounts of which of the two men – Abu Bakr or Umar – had the idea; indeed virtually every detail is variously reported. If the edition was made, it is hard to explain why it was not immediately propagated, making unnecessary the work carried out some twenty years later. It is not even clear what became of it, unless it is identified with the parchments that Hafsa or Aisha lent to Uthman, but it would have been strange in such a patriarchal society that such an important official document was handed over to a woman, however distinguished. On the other hand, if the widows had become custodians of the parchments written to the Prophet's dictation, there is no need for an explanation.

The task of making this edition of the Koran is said to have been entrusted to Zayd Ibn Thabit, the Prophet's youngest secretary and the one most familiar with the final state of the revelation. According to the traditional accounts, people brought him fragments of the Koran written on parchments, slates, the midribs of palm-leaves, shoulder-blades, ribs, bits of leather, boards, wooden pack-saddles, and 'in human hearts'; each author has a different version of this extraordinary catalogue. It is difficult to believe that any such painful search was necessary, in view of the evidence presented in Chapter 10 that Zayd and others had already written the Koran on parchments to the Prophet's dictation.

It has been suggested that this process of calling in all these fragments of the Koran was necessary in order that every verse could be confirmed by witnesses. However, Zayd, Ubay and Ibn Masud are all said to have been present for the Prophet's annual recital of the whole Koran with his angelic Presence, in which case there were already three witnesses to the original parchments. It seems more probable that all these stories with their improbable and contradictory details were invented either to make the survival of the Holy Book seem as miraculous as its original delivery or to explain away differences between Koran and Hadith.

There is a story that after the inauguration of Abu Bakr, Ali stayed at home. Abu Bakr sent for him and asked whether he was unwilling to swear allegiance. Ali said it was not that, but 'I think something has been added to the Book of Allah. So I said to myself that I will not put on my street clothes except for the

Friday prayer until it has been resolved.' This cannot be true, since it confuses the aftermath of the inauguration in the middle of year 11 and a supposed collection of the Koran made in year 12, after Ali had played a prominent part in the Wars of Apostasy. It is also told of Uthman's authorized version of twenty years later.

One curious detail is that the last two verses of sura 9, quoted above at the end of Chapter 11, were said to have been found by Zayd with only one man, an obscure Medinan. Another story has them supplied by Ubay Ibn Kaab, the Prophet's other Medinan secretary. Some sources claim that these verses were Meccan, leaving the mystery of why only a Medinan could supply written confirmation of them. No internal evidence suggests a date; without this story, one would be inclined to say that they came at the end of the last sura because they were among the last verses revealed.

The sombre legacy of the Wars of Apostasy was the doctrine that to give up Islam was a crime punishable by death. There is no Koranic justification for killing those who have quit Islam either individually or collectively. The most severe reference is Koran 3:86–90:

> How shall Allah guide a people who have disbelieved after believing and who had borne witness that the Messenger was true and to whom clear proofs had come? Allah guides not the wrongdoing people. Of such the reward is that on them shall be the curse of Allah and of the angels and of men together, abiding there under. Their punishment shall not be lightened, nor shall they be reprieved, except those who repent afterwards and amend.

Koran 4:137 refers to those who abandon Islam more than once, clearly meaning that they survive to repeat their error:

> Those who believe, then disbelieve, then believe, then disbelieve, then increase in disbelief, Allah will not forgive them nor lead them in the right path.

There are a number of Koranic texts that exclude any violence against apostates. The strongest of these are 2:256: 'Let there be no compulsion in religion' and 18:29: 'Let him who will believe, and let him who will disbelieve.' Koran 4:140 (cf. 6:68) prescribes simple avoidance of those who mock Islam: 'When you hear the signs of Allah disbelieved and ridiculed, do not sit with them until they turn to other talk.' Koran 3:144 proclaims 'He who turns back on his heels shall not harm Allah at all.'

The only Koranic text said to justify killing apostates is 5:33 (italics below), which needs to be seen in context:

> Because of [the murder of Abel] we laid it upon the Children of Israel that whoever kills a person, except because of murder or creating havoc in the land, it is as if he had killed all the people; and whoever saves a life, it is as if he had saved the whole people. And our messengers came to them with clear signs, then many of them went on committing excesses in the land.
>
> *The recompense of those who wage war against Allah and Allah's messenger and who strive to create havoc in the land is to be killed or crucified or have their hands and feet cut off on opposite sides or be exiled from the land. That is their disgrace in this world and a severe torment for them at the last.*
>
> Except for those who repent before you have power over them; know that Allah is forgiving, merciful. (5:32–34).

However, this relates to waging war or spreading havoc, not apostasy. In any case, it is not the prescription of a punishment, since it mentions four different recompenses, two of them certainly fatal, one possibly fatal and one not fatal. The incident to which it is said to refer describes horrible cruelty quite out of character for the Prophet.

There are no well substantiated cases in Hadith of the Prophet killing anyone for apostasy. On the contrary, in the one recorded case when an apostate was brought for judgement – Ibn Abi Sarh after the conquest of Mecca – the Prophet pardoned him (though some said that he implied by the long silence with which he greeted him that he wished him killed). There is one report that amounts to hearsay: 'Some Magians were brought to Ali and he had them burnt. News of this event reached Ibn Abbas who said: "If I had been in his place, I would not have had them burnt, because of the prohibition by Allah's Messenger:

"Do not punish with Allah's punishment [fire]." I would have killed them according to the saying of Allah's Messenger "Whoever changes his religion, kill him".' (Bukhari 84:2). This story is questionable both because of its apparent aim of discrediting Ali in favour of the family of Abbas, and because it fails to cite any context for the Prophet's alleged remark.

After victory in the Wars of Apostasy, Abu Bakr launched Arab armies against Syria and Iraq, and he lived to see the first great triumph: the defeat of the Byzantine army at the Battle of Ajnadayn in Syria. This expansion outside Arabia was not really an innovation, given the history of the expeditions of the Prophet's last years. The action may be regarded as defensive rather than aggressive; Arabia by itself could never have the resources to be strong (until oil became valuable), and it would have been always at the mercy of strong powers on its frontier. If neighbouring provinces were not to be a threat, it seemed necessary that they be Arab provinces. In any case, the rural population of Syria and Iraq were Aramaic-speaking cousins, much closer to the Arabs than to the Greeks and Persians, and they had long suffered oppression for their heretical brand of Christianity.

The Caliphate of Umar

The rule of Abu Bakr lasted only a little over two years. Like his friend and master, he died at about the age of sixty, and he was buried next to the Prophet in the room of his daughter Aisha. On his deathbed, after secret individual consultations with various men, he nominated Umar to succeed him. Ali is said to have been discontented again, and in a conciliatory gesture, Umar reversed his predecessor's decision and assigned the oasis of Fadak jointly to Ali and Abbas, as the two male relatives closest to the Prophet. Sunni Muslims claim that Ali made his peace with Umar, who used to consult him about points of belief or practice, but Shiites deny that there was any reconciliation. However that may be, Ali continued to be without any responsibilities. Zubayr and Talha also remained apart, and Umar's closest associates were Abd-al-Rahman and Abu Ubayda, who was sent to be governor of Syria and died there in an epidemic.

Umar remained caliph – or Commander of the Faithful, as he preferred to be called – for ten years, which were among the most remarkable periods in world history. Arab armies completed the occupation of Syria and Iraq and began the conquest of Egypt and Iran, and Umar laid the foundations of a multinational Islamic state. He organized its administration, set up a system of taxation, and created a welfare system that assigned revenues to the Muslims out of the proceeds of conquest, the amounts corresponding to services rendered. The lists of pensioners later provided invaluable material for historians. He appointed the first judge (*qadi*), setting in motion the development of an Islamic judicial system. He also marked history by adopting the Islamic Era, counting dates from the year in which the Prophet had migrated to Medina.

Abu Ubayda's rapid occupation of Syria was assisted by two brilliant generals: Amr Ibn al-As and Khalid Ibn al-Walid. In a series of battles against superior numbers, they routed the Byzantine forces and put an end to seven centuries of almost continuous Greek and Roman rule. Meanwhile, under Saad, Arab armies removed the remaining Sasanid presence in Iraq. He founded the garrison towns of Basra and Kufa, which were to become leading centres of Islamic culture until they were eclipsed by Baghdad. Kufa became the capital of the province, and soon also the leading centre for opposition to rule from Medina. Saad built a palace there in the imperial Persian style, which displeased Umar, who practised what he preached and lived very frugally like the Prophet. Indeed, Umar is even said to have once walked beside a donkey while his servant rode on it.

It is important to stress that Islam was not 'spread by the sword' at this or any other time, with the exception of Abu Bakr's conquest of apostate tribes. As 'People of Scripture', Jews and Christians were '*dhimmis*' (from *dhimma*, 'covenant'), protected by Arab armies in which they did not have to serve, in exchange for a special tax, *jizya*. They enjoyed considerable autonomy as long as they respected the Islamic authorities. Far from trying to convert them, the early Muslim government made it difficult to become a Muslim; converts had to find an Arab tribe that would accept them as clients. It was only in Arabia that Umar was intolerant towards the People of Scripture. He expelled the Christians from Najran and the remaining Jews from Khaybar and other oases. Hadith claims that this was the will of the Prophet, who is held to have said 'Let there not be two religions in Arabia.'

Umar himself set up the system of relations with the People of Scripture outside Arabia. He made the journey to Jerusalem in AH 17 (638) to receive its surrender in person. To the Christians he guaranteed continued ownership of their churches and property, freedom of worship and the right to judge themselves by their own laws. He also granted their request for Jews not to be allowed back into Jerusalem, but later extended the same freedoms to Jews, allowing them to restore open practice of their religion, which had been suppressed by the Byzantines. It should be noted that they were also given access to the cave of Abraham at Hebron, which they continued to enjoy until it was taken over by the crusaders in AH 493 (1099). For Muslim worship Umar selected the ancient Temple Mount, which had to be cleared of centuries of accumulated debris.

When Umar visited Palestine, Amr Ibn al-As asked his permission to continue into Egypt. Umar is said to have been reluctant in giving his consent, but by AH 21 (642) the whole of Lower Egypt was in Arab hands. The garrison town of Fustat, later absorbed into Cairo, replaced Alexandria as capital. A persistent myth claims that Umar ordered the contents of the Library of Alexandria to be burnt, but in fact it had been destroyed in 389 CE by Archbishop Theophilus. Like those of Syria, the Coptic Christians welcomed the departure of the Byzantines, who had tried to suppress their Monophysite Christianity.

In domestic policy Umar was no liberal. He reduced the influence of women, separating them from men in the mosque and giving them a male imam where before they had a woman. He restricted the movements of the Prophet's widows and stopped them from making the pilgrimage to Mecca, until he relented in his last year. His harsh attitude to sex found particular expression in the introduction – according to him the reintroduction – of stoning for adultery. Near the end of his life, he became worried that sexual misbehaviour was not being severely enough punished, and he called upon Muslims to stone adulterers, claiming that the Prophet had done so. According to some Hadiths he made a solemn declaration that he remembered a verse of the Koran that decreed death by stoning as the proper penalty: 'Do not turn away from your fathers, for that is disbelief. If a mature man and a mature woman have illicit sex, stone them definitely as a punishment from Allah. Allah is mighty, wise.' This incidentally was the Law of Moses (Deuteronomy 22:22).

No one else remembered this verse, nor was it written down anywhere, which casts doubt on the notion of the official copy supposedly made at Umar's suggestion under Abu Bakr. Nor could its meaning be comfortably fitted into any appropriate context, nor does the wording sound Koranic: the only references in the Koran to 'your fathers' are warnings not to revere them at the expense of religion; the word translated as 'mature man' occurs there only with the meaning 'old man', and the words translated as 'mature woman' and 'definitely' do not occur at all. Worse, the universally agreed text of the Koran says that sexual offenders should only marry sexual offenders, which they could hardly do if they had been stoned (24:3).

If Umar did indeed speak as reported, he doubtless believed the verse to be genuine, but it seems he must have been mistaken; yet such was his prestige that his word was accepted, and stoning became the statutory Sunni punishment for adultery. The Koranic punishment of 100 lashes came to be reserved for fornication, in spite of the sheer unlikelihood of the one meaning of the word *zina* having been intended without the other. In due course the strange doctrine was put forward that the words of the 'Verse of Stoning' had been cancelled from the Koran but their force remained.

One day in the year 23 of the era that he had established, while in the mosque at Medina, Umar was fatally injured by a Christian Persian slave. He was buried alongside Muhammad and Abu Bakr, the last person to be honoured with a tomb in the Prophet's Mosque. His death was the consequence of a personal grievance and not the outcome of any conspiracy or disaffection, but it opened again the question of how to choose a successor. The replacement of Umar was almost as great a problem as the replacement of the Prophet, for he had proved one of the greatest statesmen in world history.

Under Umar's leadership, the Muslims had destroyed the powers that had ruled the Middle East for the best part of a thousand years, and they had laid the foundations of a new order that was to persist, recognizably itself, into modern times. The bulk of the victorious armies had been provided by Bedouin tribesman, yet their propensity to loot and destroy had been kept in check by outstanding generals and governors, mainly provided by the great families of Mecca and Medina. Existing administrative structures and personnel had been maintained intact as far as possible to manage the transition in a way that latter day occupiers would have been wise to emulate.

CHAPTER THIRTEEN

CIVIL WAR

The Caliphate of Uthman

At the end of his life Umar decreed that the next Commander of the Faithful should be chosen by an electoral committee (*shura*, cf. Koran 42:38). Accounts differ; some say that he did this on his death bed, others earlier. Some say that he nominated the members, but there is some doubt about who they were. All agree that the two eldest survivors of the Ten were present – Abd-al-Rahman Ibn Awf (the chairman) and Uthman Ibn Affan, both in their sixties. Of the five younger survivors, Ali and Zubayr were certainly present. Talha, however, though invited, returned to Medina too late to attend. Opinions differ as to whether Saad or Said or both or neither took part. It appears that Umar's son Abd-Allah was also present, though he may not have had a vote. They met in the home of Usama Ibn Zayd, and he too may have joined in the discussions, though as a very junior partner.

No account of their meeting has survived, but it is clear that they could not agree even on a compromise candidate. In the end it was left to Abd-al-Rahman to decide, and he chose the other man of his own age, Uthman, once his companion in Ethiopia. Through his mother, the new caliph was the Prophet's cousin and his son-in-law by two marriages. He was of the Umayyad Clan, which under Abu Sufyan had led the Meccan opposition to Islam. He had been one of the first Muslims and was known for his piety and his knowledge of the Koran, but he had never taken a very active part in affairs. He is said to have been an exceptionally beautiful man in his youth, and he was exceedingly rich, but he had none of Umar's administrative genius.

It is impossible to give an account of the subsequent events that is acceptable to all Muslims. For the Sunni majority, Uthman and Ali are both revered figures who made unfortunate but pardonable mistakes, and Uthman was rightly chosen caliph before Ali. For the party (*shia*) of Ali, Uthman was a usurper and Ali was the saintly victim of other men's mistakes. For one small faction, neither was a worthy leader. The following version attempts to stick to agreed facts, without apportioning blame.

In some respects Uthman's tenure of the caliphate was successful. The conquest of the Persian Empire continued, though more slowly than before, reaching Armenia, and some administrative improvements were made. However, his most important contribution was his sending out of authorized copies of the Koran. According to some accounts, this was made necessary by quarrels over rival versions of the Koran (some say codices, others say recitations), claiming the authority of two of the Prophet's secretaries, Ubay in Damascus and Ibn Masud in Kufa. Others said that disputes over wording had broken out between speakers of different Arabic dialects in the Iranian garrisons. However, it is clear that Uthman took a close personal interest in the Koran, and he seems to have acted as final arbiter over points of detail. He was probably just acting to anticipate possible disputes.

After consulting the other leading companions, Uthman is said to have set up a commission to make the copies. There is no unanimity over who they were, and twelve names are mentioned in different accounts. Some give various lists of four, and one author combines all the versions and claims it was a commission of twelve. The one member on whom all agree is the Prophet's principal secretary Zayd Ibn Thabit, but some say that another secretary, Ubay, participated. The third, Ibn Masud, had recently died. What is remarkable is that none of the survivors of the Ten was included, though the sons of Zubayr are mentioned. The omission of Ali is particularly noteworthy, as he is credited with having been an outstanding calligrapher. A particularly beautiful codex is attributed to him, but it shows no significant difference from the version produced by Uthman's commission.

One story told to explain the need for a commission is that the work of Zayd, who was a Medinan, had to be checked by

Meccans for conformity to the dialect of Mecca. This seems unlikely; the main idiosyncrasy of Meccan pronunciation was the absence of the glottal stop, but there was no sign for it anyway. Other peculiarities of Meccan Arabic would have required the substitution of one word for another, and it is inconceivable that Zayd would have changed the wording dictated by Muhammad. The other commissioners were surely there simply because of their skill in writing.

There are conflicting versions of what was done. Some say that Uthman borrowed the parchments held by Hafsa and asked Zayd and his team to make copies. Others say that Zayd first went through the whole business of compiling a text from all available sources – in effect repeating the work he was claimed to have done under Abu Bakr – and that this was then checked against Hafsa's parchments before being copied. Another version says that Uthman sent someone to Aisha to 'fetch the parchments on which the Prophet had dictated the Koran in its entirety', and that Zayd's copies were checked against this.

The simplest harmonization of all these accounts is that there was just one authoritative copy of the whole Koran, that it was the one dictated by the Prophet to Zayd and others, that it had remained in the custody of his widows, and that Uthman borrowed it to serve as the template for Zayd's copyists. Since no other version of any part of the Koran could compare with the Prophet's own, there was never any need for Zayd to compile a text from scattered sources. The only innovations were the making of multiple copies and binding each as a codex (*mushaf*) of the kind that had become familiar to the Arabs in their northern dominions.

The one major editorial decision that may have been necessary was fixing the order of the suras. A number of short suras may have been on the same parchment, and medium length suras may have been on parchments kept together in a roll. Zayd may well have remembered perfectly in what order the Prophet recited the whole Koran. Anyway, the order in all existing Korans starts with the Fatiha or Opening – a prayer, of only seven verses – then ranges the other 113 suras roughly in order of decreasing length. As the later suras were generally longer than the earlier ones, this meant that the order also tended to be the reverse of chronological. This was not a mechanical rule; in fact there are 51 cases out of 113 in which a sura is longer than the previous one. Some of these exceptions could have been made to keep intact the various sets put together by the Prophet, as argued in Chapter 10. It must be added that the order of the suras matters very little, as each is a self-contained unit. Muslims usually refer to them not by number but by title, mostly taken from an unusual or notable word in the sura. However, no titles were written into the earliest Korans.

The completed copies were sent to the main provincial centres in AH 32 (653). Some limit the list to Damascus, Basra, Kufa and Medina, with an extra copy being retained by Uthman. Others add Mecca, Egypt and Yemen. Differences over the number of centres may help to explain differences over the number of copyists. At any rate, copies were soon being made of the copies, and quite a number of very early Korans or fragments of them still exist. It is claimed for three codices – in Tashkent, Istanbul and Cairo – that they are Uthmanic originals.

Tradition claims that Uthman had all other copies of the Koran destroyed, which is said to have angered the reciters of Kufa in particular. Even if such an order was given, it is hard to believe that it could have been carried out all over a state that stretched from Armenia to Egypt and which was about to be plunged into civil war. Either there were very few such documents, in which case their value would have been huge and the incentive to hide them very great, or there were many copies of individual suras or groups of suras, in which case enforcement on large numbers of owners would have been impossible. One way or the other, one would have expected lost variants to have been found by now. Once again, the story has been used to allege that significant variants were destroyed.

Such variants as are actually found in the consonantal text are few and insignificant. A few variant readings had crept in by the end of the first century of Islam (early seventh century CE). For example initial 'F' and 'W', similar in shape and both meaning 'and', were occasionally confused; the letter alif, 'A', a single upright stroke, was particularly liable to get added or dropped, almost always with negligible effect on meaning.

A small number of 'mistakes' are present in the authorized version – for example changes of subject in consecutive verbs (e.g. 25:45), abrupt changes in the person addressed (e.g. 65:1), omission of the word 'Say' when words are clearly to be spoken by the Prophet (e.g. 27:91), and so on. It is a general principle of textual criticism that a hard reading is more likely to be valid than an easy one. The presence of such roughness of language, which many a scribe must have itched to correct, adds to the impression of authenticity.

As for the widows' precious parchments, they disappeared from view. One story claims that Marwan, as Umayyad Governor of Medina, kept sending to Hafsa and demanding them, but that she refused to release them. As soon as she was dead and buried, Marwan seized them and had them destroyed because he was 'afraid that after a time people will be suspicious of this copy or they will say there is something in it that was not written'. This is doubly dubious, both because of its evident anti-Umayyad intention and because Aisha lived on for more than ten years to guard the parchments. In any case, it would have been very much out of character for Marwan to take a close interest in the sacred text. This sounds like yet another story aimed at weakening the authority of the standard Koran.

In a closely argued thesis, John Burton has suggested a plausible reason why later generations of Muslims were ready to believe that the Koran as we have it was not compiled until after the Prophet's death. In the course of time, contradictions developed between the Holy Book and Hadith. If the compilation had been delayed, that left open the possibility that the community had lost verses, such as Umar's Verse of Stoning, which would have removed the contradictions. This would have happened in accordance with the divine plan: 'We shall teach you to recite so that you do not forget / Except what Allah wills.' (87:6–7). It came to be widely accepted that there was a distinction between the 'Mother of the Book' (Koran 13:39) – the complete original with Allah 'in a Tablet Preserved' (85:22) – and the written version in the hands of Muslims. This made it much easier to build up a consistent body of law.

The conclusion drawn here from this textual history is that, in the Uthmanic edition, the Koran is virtually as the Prophet had left it. He had thus been granted what had been denied to every previous prophet: the message had been passed on intact. This implies that nothing important is missing from the text; if there is no mention of the stoning of adulterers or the killing of apostates, that is because there is not meant to be any mention of them, with important consequences for the present day.

The establishment of the authorized text only twenty years after the Prophet's death was a colossal achievement, and one that can certainly be credited to Uthman, because it is recognized by all of the three major factions in Islam, although they went to war with each other within a couple of years of the distribution of the codices. With the small differences mentioned above, the same consonant text is used all over the world by Sunnis, Shiites and Ibadis, even by those whose ancestors complained about some aspects of Uthman's editorial work.

War

Uthman's great failing was political. Impending trouble was visible from the beginning in the lack of cooperation of the younger members of the electoral committee, though it was popularly believed that Uthman only began to go wrong half way through his time as caliph. Saad was willing to work with him and was reinstated for a while as Governor of Kufa, and Talha at first cooperated with him but soon became his fierce critic. Ali and Zubayr were hostile from the beginning, though Uthman regularly made a point of consulting them.

Uthman gave key appointments to members of his clan, the Bani Umayya, most of whom had fought against Islam and converted only after the conquest of Mecca. They were still the wealthiest clan in Mecca and enjoyed luxurious living. He gave control of the public treasury to his first cousin Marwan, the man who was later blamed for destroying the widows' parchments and who eventually became the fourth Umayyad caliph. He sent his foster-brother Ibn Abi Sarh, the Prophet's disgraced apostate secretary, to be Governor of Egypt. He appointed his half-brother Walid, who is said to have spat in the Prophet's face, as Governor of Kufa. He accepted extravagant gifts from those who sought his favour.

The centres of active discontent were in Kufa and still more in Egypt, from which a party of rebels set out towards the end of AH 35 (656). They entered Medina and besieged Uthman in his house. He negotiated with them and agreed to all their demands. They left to return to Egypt but captured an emissary allegedly carrying a letter from Uthman to Ibn Abi Sarh, telling him to kill them all. It is generally thought that this was a fraudulent message, sent by Uthman's enemies to discredit him. Anyway, they returned to Medina, renewed the siege, broke into Uthman's house and assassinated him, allegedly as he sought guidance in the Koran, reading 2:137, which speaks of schism.

The fratricidal nature of this conflict may be seen in the fact that one of the leaders of the siege was Muhammad, the son of Abu Bakr by Asma, the widow of Ali's brother Jaafar, He was born on the Farewell Pilgrimage and as a baby had no doubt been admired by the Prophet. After Abu Bakr's death, Asma married Ali, so this Muhammad grew up as Ali's stepson, step-brother to Hasan and Husayn. His grand-daughter married the grandson of Husayn and was mother of Jaafar al-Sadiq, the Sixth Shia Imam. One of the defenders of Uthman's house was Abd-Allah Ibn Zubayr, son of a different Asma, Abu Bakr's daughter and Aisha's sister. He had been one of the scribes of the Uthmanic Koran, and he later led the disastrous rebellion against the second Umayyad caliph, Yazid.

These events threw Medina into a state of turmoil. Of the survivors of the Ten, Ali, Talha and Zubayr were all contenders to succeed Uthman, while Saad kept out of the conflict, and Said had withdrawn from public affairs. Aisha, who had been on pilgrimage to Mecca at the time of the assassination, got up in the mosque and called for the punishment of the culprits. The rebels from Egypt favoured Talha, but they were outnumbered by the partisans of Ali. For several days, Uthman's family were prevented from organizing his funeral, and when it did finally take place they were not allowed to bury him in the Muslim cemetery of Baqi (though the boundary was later moved to include his tomb), let alone beside the Prophet, Abu Bakr and Umar in the Mosque.

At the end of a week of chaos, Ali accepted homage as caliph from all who were prepared to recognize him. He had no experience of government, but he had grown up in the Prophet's household, married his daughter Fatima, fathered his only grandsons and fought valiantly in the battles against the polytheists. After the death of the Prophet, and more especially after the investiture of Umar, he is reputed to have occupied himself with piety and scholarship, having an unrivalled knowledge of the Prophet's life, and being, according to Shiites and Sufis, the transmitter of the inner meaning of the Prophet's message. He is also said to have been the father of Arabic calligraphy, the supreme Islamic art. However, his inauguration came at the worst possible moment for a man of retiring disposition. In his anxiety to calm the people, he made conciliatory moves towards the rebels.

The shedding of Muslim blood by Muslims was absolutely condemned by the Koran (4:92), and nothing had prepared the community to face such shocking events. Since Uthman had committed no crime, his death could be nothing other than murder, requiring punishment of the guilty, but no one dared to arrest or try them. Within days, Aisha set off for Basra with her brothers-in-law Zubayr and Talha to raise an army against Ali. Zubayr was son of Khadija's brother and of the Prophet's favourite aunt, Safiya, and he had been the other one of the Ten in Ethiopia. Talha came like Abu Bakr from Clan Taym and had married the Prophet's cousin and sister-in-law Hamna Bint Jahsh.

Ali set off to join his supporters in Kufa. His troops were victorious six months later near Basra, and Zubayr and Talha were both killed in the Battle of the Camel, so called because the camel on which Aisha was riding was killed under her. Ali was a reluctant victor and treated the losers magnanimously. However, he angered the supporters of Uthman by assigning one of the assassins, Aisha's half-brother Muhammad, to escort her back to Medina, where she lived out her remaining twenty years as the 'First Lady' of Islam. The respect and influence that she continued to enjoy suggest that many inhabitants of the Prophet's city shared her view of Ali's accession. However, her defeat was made into an argument against giving women a leading role in public life, and a questionably reliable Hadith attributes to the Prophet the saying that 'a people that entrusts its affairs to a woman shall not prosper'. (Bukhari 88:18).

Ali had no time to consolidate his position, for he had to prepare immediately for war with Muawiya, son of Abu Sufyan and Governor of Syria. Far from trying to satisfy his opponents by punishing the murderers of Uthman, Ali provoked them further by promoting them. He appointed Muhammad Ibn Abi Bakr Governor of Egypt. He moved the capital to Kufa, which had rebelled against Uthman, relegating Medina and Mecca to provincial status. The conflict between Ali and Muawiya thus became a war between Iraq and Syria, aggravated by differences between the Arab tribes that had occupied the two countries.

Ali raised an army of fifty thousand and set off for Syria, where battle was joined at Siffin, near the Euphrates. Fighting was spread out over many days. Eventually, early in AH 37 (July 657), just when it seemed that Ali's forces were winning, Muawiya's general instructed some of his front-line soldiers to attach pages of the Koran to their lances to signify that judgement belonged to Allah and not to force of arms. This shows that by now the Koran-as-document was coming to be as important as the Koran-as-recitation.

Fighting stopped immediately, and Ali agreed to submit to arbitration. This lost him the support of a large part of his following. Some twelve thousand deserted to become a new enemy for him to fight. Their slogan was 'No arbitration save Allah's (cf. Koran 6:57)'. They became known as the Kharijites, which means 'those who walked out'. Ali's army faced them a year later at Nahrawan, near the future site of Baghdad. The Kharijites were nearly annihilated, but they were able to revive sufficiently to play an important part in the history of the next century, and one offshoot of their movement survives to this day.

The arbitration between Ali and Muawiya finally took place in AH 38 (January 659). It agreed to depose both men, but failed to say who should be caliph, so in fact nothing was settled. It was in effect a victory for Muawiya, who was required only to renounce a governorship, while Ali would cease to be caliph. In the event, both leaders remained in place, each seeking to strengthen his position for the inevitable renewal of war. This period of false peace was brought to a sudden end by the assassination of Ali in AH 40 (January 661). On his way to the mosque in Kufa, he was stabbed in the eye by a Kharijite. So died the last of the four recognized by the main body of Muslims as the 'Rightly-guided Caliphs'. A Kharijite attempt to assassinate Muawiya at the same time failed, and he declared himself caliph in Jerusalem.

The Aftermath
The conflict was not yet at an end. Ali's elder son Hasan, the Second Imam, according to the Shia, prepared to resist, but he agreed to renounce his claim, allegedly in exchange for a large lump-sum and a handsome pension. He retired to live quietly in Medina. His brother Husayn retired there too for twenty years, until Muawiya was succeeded by his son Yazid. At this, Husayn, by now the Shiite Third Imam, set off to raise a rebellion in Iraq.

With a small party of followers he was encircled at Karbala, north of Kufa, and killed on the 10th Muharram – the day of the old Ashura fast – in AH 61 (October 680). This, even more than the death of Ali, became the martyrdom that consolidated the schism. By an unkind twist of fate, this grandson of the Prophet was killed by a force commanded by Umar, whose father, Saad Ibn Abi Waqqas, had so wisely kept out of the conflict between Uthman and Ali. The tragic event is commemorated every year by the partisans of Ali and his sons, in great public outpourings of grief.

This second round of civil war was again triangular, with the places of Ali, Muawiya and Zubayr taken by their three sons, for rebellion had also been raised by Abd-Allah Ibn Zubayr, with his headquarters in Mecca. This led to two sieges of the holy city. The first, in AH 64 (683), caused the burning down of the Kaaba. The second, in AH 72–3 (692), ended with the death of Ibn Zubayr. The Umayyads even tried to replace the pilgrimage to Mecca with one to Jerusalem, where they built the great al-Aqsa Mosque (cf. Koran 17:1).

The readiness of the Prophet's companions and their children to go to war against each other was the great tragedy of Islam. Its legacy has been a three-way split, which has never been healed and which has repeatedly led to further wars between Muslims. The majority revered all the first four caliphs, advocating submission to their established successors in spite of their moral failings, regarding peace and unity as more important than the impossible search for the ideal leader. They found support in the Koran: 'Guard against civil war (*fitna*), which hurts not only those of you who do wrong' (8:25). It was several centuries before these people even gave themselves a label: they simply thought of themselves as *the* Muslims, as opposed to small bands of extremists. It was only when dissidence had persisted for several centuries that they came to define themselves as 'Sunni' Muslims (followers of the *sunna* – a word whose meaning will be discussed below).

The party (*shia*) of Ali, eventually called *the* Shia, held that Ali was the only rightful successor of the Prophet, and that thereafter leadership remained in his family. It was more than a century before this elect family was exactly defined. For a long time any rebellious descendant of Abu Talib could raise a following. These leaders took the title of 'Imam' by which they meant much more than the usual sense of 'leader in an act of worship' or 'religious leader in general'. This special sense is indicated in this book by use of a capital letter.

The Kharijites accepted the first three caliphs up to the end of Uthman's sixth year, and Ali until the Battle of Siffin, but beyond that they rejected both caliphs and Imams. With their readiness to denounce other Muslims as infidels and their alleged belief in jihad as the Sixth Pillar of Islam, they made life very uncomfortable for their neighbours until the militant form of their movement gave way to versions that allowed them to live in peace under a non-Kharijite government.

In fact the caliphate was already becoming an irrelevance during the first century of Islam, which is why the religion was able to survive the early series of civil wars intact. As the essentials of the religion had been laid down by the Prophet and the Koran, there was little that could happen subsequently to alter them. In religious practice, Sunnis, Shiites and Kharijites differ in such small details that in times of peace they can share the same mosques, and to the outsider there is usually no detectable difference.

Even the developments that had followed the death of the Prophet were generally accepted. For example, while rejecting the legitimacy of the first three caliphs, the Shiites accepted the policy on apostasy, the ruling on adultery, and Uthman's edition of the Koran. The Kharijites, however, despite their respect for Umar, never accepted the stoning of adulterers. Influence flowed in the opposite direction too: some of the men revered as leaders by Shiites or Kharijites are respected authorities for Sunnis.

At a deeper lever, the conflict opposed three radically different conceptions of authority. For Sunnis, there was no religious authority other than that of the Prophet. The first four caliphs shared some of this by virtue of having been his companions, but subsequent caliphs were essentially civil leaders, and if they were bad rulers, it was better to put up with injustice for a while than to plunge society into civil war. Religious leadership fell to those who were acknowledged for their piety and knowledge, and if different leaders led in different directions there was room in Islam for all people of good will. It is often said that Islam does not separate Church and State, but for Sunni Muslims there is no equivalent of the Church. Later Sunni thought distinguished between caliph (religious figurehead) and sultan (civil power), or between imam (religious leader) and emir (political and military leader).

In contrast, Shia Islam looked to a leader who was both a civil and a religious authority. Leadership was hereditary, and, except for Hasan and Husayn, there could not be two Imams in the same generation. Different factions recognized different lines of descent, but after an early period in which various claimants came forward, descendants of Ali and Fatima came to be seen as the only valid line. The Imam was truly head of both 'Church' and 'State', and when the last ones disappeared, those who spoke for them fulfilled much the same role. For Sunnis, Shiite rulers claim a religious authority that is illegitimate. For Shiites, Sunni leaders have no proper authority.

The Kharijites did not see the need for a unitary state. They believed that different Muslim communities should be autonomous and that each should elect its own leader, who should be the best Muslim among them. After the death of the Prophet, the Koran was the only continuing religious authority, and every Muslim must read it and make it the basis for life, though they later developed their own body of Hadith. It was in the nature of their ideology that they never created a large-scale state.

It is a weakness of Islam that it never developed an agreed way to change governments. Each of the first four caliphs was chosen by a different method: Abu Bakr by acclamation, Umar by nomination, Uthman (in theory) by electoral committee and Ali by popular pressure. Without believing in the hereditary principle,

Sunnis repeatedly accepted dynasties, which lasted until they were overthrown. Shiites did the same when they did eventually control the state. There is nothing in the Koran to prevent the adoption of some procedure for electing governments; it just has not yet become the norm.

For ordinary Muslims, the civil strife that marred the middle third of the first Muslim century, and which has so often recurred, was not really about anything so abstract as concepts of religious authority. The Prophet's reaching out across boundaries of clan and tribe was rapidly being forgotten. However faithful the caliphs and Imams themselves may have been to the vision of the Prophet, many of those around them had reverted to the old way of seeking power and wealth for themselves and their relations. Tribalism and its offspring nationalism are still very much with us today, and the lessons of those terrible years are as relevant now as ever.

The Koran should have the last word:

People: we created you from male and female, and we made you into nations and tribes so that you might recognize each other. The noblest of you in the sight of Allah is the most virtuous. Allah is knowing, aware. (49:13).

CHAPTER FOURTEEN

THE LAW AND THE PROPHET

Political Developments

The Umayyad family ruled for ninety years (more than a hundred, if you include Uthman), producing some very good administrators and some disastrously bad ones. Under them, the caliphal state expanded to include the Indus Valley in the east, and North Africa and most of Spain in the west, but expansion northwards was blocked by Constantinople, which withstood attempts to take it. In general these caliphs lived like kings instead of adopting the simple lifestyle of the Prophet and the first caliphs, and they showed no deep interest in religion.

The one Umayyad caliph who sought to play an active part in the development of Islam was Umar Ibn Abd-al-Aziz, or Umar II, whose death at the age of forty-three cut short his tenure after only two and a half years, in AH 101 (720). He came to be seen as Renewer (*mujaddid*) of the Religion – the first in a series of men predicted to appear at each turn of century, according to a saying attributed to the Prophet. More generally, Umar can be seen as the first of many Muslim leaders who have tried to restore the purity of Islam by returning to the example of the Prophet and his companions.

Umar dressed like a pauper and spurned luxury, preferring the company of the religious to that of notables. He took part with enthusiasm in theological debates, and he may have contributed to the development of signs to be added to the Koranic text to aid in correct recitation. He used political means to encourage conversion to Islam, exempting non–Arab Muslims from taxes, and discriminating against Christians, Jews, Zoroastrians and Manichaeans, with confiscation of property and disqualification from office. This was one of the very few departures from religious tolerance in the history of the caliphate, though it does not merit the name of 'persecution'.

Ironically, it was the austere Umar who, as Governor of Medina, caused the premises of the Prophet's family to be razed, to make room for an enlargement of the Mosque, destroying for ever the physical evidence of the simplicity of their way of life. It must be pointed out, however, that strict Muslims are very wary of anything that might seem to be worship of relics – an admirable determination from the religious point of view, but one that has often allowed valuable historical evidence to be destroyed.

The last thirty years of Ummayad rule, following the death of Umar, were a time of increasing political agitation. The Islamic state had in effect become an Arab kingdom, and the grievances of non-Arab subjects came together with those of discontented Arabs to produce a succession of revolts. These took the form of religious challenges to the authority of the Umayyad caliphs. Leaders arose from various branches of the clan of Hashim (Figure 4), and there were failed rebellions, including one led by Zayd Ibn Ali, grandson of the martyred Husayn, and his son Yahya. The Umayyads were eventually overthrown by great-great-grandsons of Abbas, who founded the Abbasid dynasty of caliphs in AH 133 (750).

Support for the Abbasid revolution, like that for the failed rebellions, came mostly from Iraq and Iran – the former Sasanian Empire. The caliphs therefore moved the capital to Iraq, and soon to a new city that they founded: Baghdad, which rapidly became the most magnificent city west of China. Their realm was never as large as that of the Umayyads, as they never controlled Spain and the Maghreb, nor Sind; but they ruled over a vast multi-national society, whose lingua franca was Arabic. Under the Abbasids, intellectual life flourished, with the meeting and development of Greek philosophy, medicine and geometry, Egyptian alchemy, Indian arithmetic and Mesopotamian astronomy. There were wonderful achievements in architecture, horticulture, music and abstract visual art, and even recreation became a source of new ideas, with the first scientific study of the Indian game of chess.

FIGURE FOUR

HASHIMITE CLAIMANTS AND SHI'ITE IMAMS

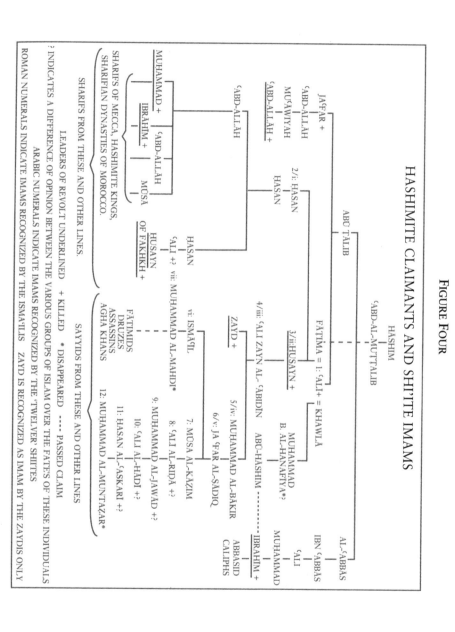

However, in matters of religion the Abbasids soon showed themselves to be at least as worldly as the Umayyads, most of them being neither able nor inclined to provide either leadership or personal example. Paradoxically, they may be said to have strengthened Islam by weakening the caliphate, for Muslims came to realize increasingly that religious questions were best answered not by an unattainable ideal caliph, but by the learned and the saintly. Umar II had been able to contribute not because he was caliph but because he was a scholar and a holy man. Islam was increasingly understood as submission to divine laws, and the essential task seemed to be to salvage as much knowledge as possible of the words and deeds of the Prophet, who still ruled from beyond the grave.

Developing the Sharia

Generations were necessary for the work of collecting and organizing knowledge about the Prophet and his contemporaries. In the first Islamic century, scholars appeared who made it their business to gather information from the Prophet's Companions, and from those in the next generation who had known them – the Followers. Some of these early scholars were themselves relatives of the central figures, for example Urwa, a son of Zubayr, who was about thirteen when his father was killed and who came to be regarded as the founder of Islamic history. He lived in Medina till his death in AH 94 (713). Other children of the Ten important for their religious knowledge were Abd-Allah, son of Abu Bakr, and Abd-Allah and Asim, sons of Umar. The Prophet's cousin Abd-Allah Ibn Abbas became specially known for interpretation of the Koran. Some of these men had known the Prophet themselves in their youth, and all of them had access to those who had been close to him, including Aisha herself, who lived till about AH 58 (678).

Two of this generation became particularly important by virtue of a long life that enabled their influence to reach into the next century. Ata Ibn Abi Rabah, who lived from about AH 21

(642) to 114 (733) was a Meccan of Nubian origin. He was later credited with having been the founder of the study of Islamic jurisprudence. Hasan al-Basri, a Medinan born at about the same time, migrated to Basra at the age of sixteen, remaining there to radiate a saintly influence until he died in 110 (728). He was a noted scholar, but his greatest contribution was to maintain and enhance the tradition of ascetic piety (*zuhd*). His reputation was such that most later movements claimed him as a forerunner.

Urwa Ibn al-Zubayr had a pupil called Ibn Shihab al-Zuhri who was a chief source for virtually all subsequent scholarship. He moved to Damascus in AH 81 (700) and enjoyed the patronage of the Umayyad caliphs until his death in AH 124 (742). His most important contribution was the practice of always quoting the chain of sources (*isnad*) for each Hadith that he passed on, for example 'I heard from 'Urwa, who had it from Aisha, that Allah's Messenger said...' Thanks to this more than to any other single feature, the record of the Prophet's life is better authenticated than that of any other religious founder.

The first person to write a biography of the Prophet was a Medinan, Muhammad Ibn Ishaq. His grandfather had been brought to Medina as a Christian captive in the caliphate of Abu Bakr, and both his father and his uncle had been scholars. He was born about the year 85 (704), and was able to gather his material from Zuhri and others who had known the children or grandchildren of the Prophet's generation. His massive book, 'The Life of Allah's Messenger (*Sirat Rasul Allah*)', usually referred to simply as 'the *Sira*' and often quoted above, was to remain unrivalled. However, it is known only from quotations in later histories and especially from the edition prepared some decades later by Ibn Hisham, which amounts to several hundred thousand words, comparable with the largest modern biographies. Ibn Hisham seems to have been a fairly faithful editor.

Ibn Ishaq's work was usefully supplemented by al-Waqidi's history of the Prophet's campaigns, written later in the second century. Al-Waqidi's assistant, Ibn Saad, went on to produce eight

volumes of invaluable biographies of the Prophet, his contemporaries and their children and grandchildren. His final
volume is devoted to the women of early Islam, throwing light on
an important group who had received too little attention.

Ibn Ishaq and his successors aimed mainly at inspiring
Muslims by giving them an account of the life of the Prophet.
However, among his contemporaries it was jurisprudence (*fiqh*), the
study of Islamic law, that was emerging as the central intellectual
discipline. This was born of the reaction of the pious against
the pragmatic and almost secular system of law that had grown
up under the Umayyads. With the advent of the Abbasids, the
conditions were created for the flowering of a specifically Islamic
system of law, the Sharia. The task of jurisprudence was to work
out its details – a process called in Arabic *ijtihad*, which means
'making an effort', and practised by a *mujtahid*. These terms will
be translated here as 'elaboration' and 'elaborator'.

It is important to stress that the Sharia was essentially an
idealized system, solving legal problems one by one on the basis
of what scholars believed to have been the example of the Prophet.
It did not grow like English law out of the practical experience of
the courts, nor was it like Roman law based on the application of
fundamental legal principles. It was specially concerned with matters
that had been mentioned in the Koran – the Five Pillars, marriage,
divorce, inheritance and bequests, and warfare, and with seven
particular crimes: murder, highway robbery, theft, drunkenness,
illicit sex, uncorroborated allegations of illicit sex, and apostasy.

The intellectual task of building this structure involved
establishing everything possible about the Prophet, the Koran
and the early history of Islam. This was achieved by generations of
scholars in a variety of disciplines: reciters, commentators, linguists,
historians and genealogists, and even 'proto-anthropologists' –
students of the tribes and customs of Arabia in the time of the
Prophet – and scholars in 'comparative religion', who examined
Jewish and Christian literature for any light it could throw on the
previous prophets.

The Koran by itself gave only certain elements of a legal system and there were important questions on which it was silent. If Islam was to have a detailed body of law, many details needed to be worked out. The majority agreed that the basis for completing the body of Sharia should be *Sunna*. This word originally meant 'the beaten path', hence 'the way' in general. At first it was understood as meaning the practice followed by good Muslims in the various centres. There were several ancient schools (singular *madhhab*) of jurisprudence, but two dominated: that of Medina, which drew its prestige from its continuity of descent from the city of the Prophet, and that of Kufa, which shared in the general intellectual pre-eminence of the city.

Foremost among the Medinan jurists was Malik Ibn Anas, a contemporary and stern critic of Ibn Ishaq. He lived to a great age, from AH 90 (709) to 179 (795), and thus stood, like Ata and Hasan al-Basri, as a bridge across time; through his father and grandfather, both scholars, and through his teacher Ata, he reached back into the first century of Islam, while some of his pupils were still active in the third. His reputation was enhanced when the caliph Mansur had him flogged for his Shiite sympathies. He came to be the unrivalled leader of the Medinan School, which later came to be called after him 'Maliki'. His book *Al-Muwatta* – another word meaning 'the Beaten Path' – is the oldest work of Islamic jurisprudence to have survived complete in its original form. It gives a fascinating insight into early legal thinking as it existed before the relationship between the various sources of the Sharia was formalized. What Malik presents is essentially the Sunna of Medina as interpreted by him, using the Koran and Hadiths to support his views, applying the principle of the public interest in cases of doubt. His system is conservative, but that does not mean it is illiberal.

Despite the prestige of Medina, the intellectual centre of gravity was shifting northward to Iraq, even before the fall of the Umayyads. Ibn Ishaq himself migrated there to escape the hostility of Malik. The reputation of the Medinan School soon came to be rivalled by that of the Kufan, whose earliest prominent leader was Abu Hanifa, another pupil of Ata, who lived from about AH 81 (700) to 150 (767). He was not a professional man of law, but a cloth merchant who commanded respect by his immense learning. Like Malik he got into trouble with the Abbasids for his Shiite sympathies and he died either in prison or soon after his release. Abu Hanifa's ideas are known from the writings of his disciples, but the School came to be known after him as Hanafi. Like Malik, he made use of the Sunna of his community, and the more cosmopolitan nature of Kufa produced a less conservative, but not always more liberal system. Hanafis made great use of reasoning to support their views, applying the principle of equity.

These ancient schools of jurisprudence, the 'Sunna Party' were criticized by the 'Hadith Party' for making too much use of current practice and personal opinion, instead of relying on Hadith going back to the Prophet and his companions. A radical solution to this conflict was proposed by Muhammad al-Shafii – of all the legists the one with the most structured view. He was born in Mecca in the year that Abu Hanifa died, and he studied with the aged Malik and with the successors of Abu Hanifa. Like his two great predecessors he got into trouble with the Abbasid caliph, for obscure activities in Yemen, and he moved to Fustat in Egypt, where he died in 204 (820), and where his tomb is still a place of pilgrimage on the edge of Cairo. He is generally regarded as the Renewer for the Third Century.

Shafii held that the Sunna of the different communities was valid only insofar as it represented the Sunna of the Prophet, who was divinely inspired and who therefore had a unique role in completing the Koran through his words and deeds. Shafii supported this by quoting the Koranic statement that 'whoever obeys the Messenger indeed obeys Allah' (4:80). References to 'the Scripture and the Wisdom (*hikma*)' (e.g. 2:129) were taken to mean Koran and Sunna, *HKM* being a root with the meaning of 'judgement'. Understood in this way, there could be only one Sunna and it was not in conflict with Hadith. On the contrary, it could be known only through Hadith going back through a reliable chain of authorities to the Prophet himself.

Sunna was thus ranked as equal in authenticity to the Koran, and the great mass of oral Hadith literature was put on a par with the Koranic text. This was made more acceptable by the belief that the Holy Book had been collected together only after the death of the Prophet, so that knowledge of it depended on the testimony of his Companions, in the same way as knowledge of the Sunna. The twenty-odd years that separated Uthman's edition of the Koran from the Prophet's death were thus treated as comparable in importance to the century and a half of oral transmission of Hadith.

Equipped with this doctrine, Shafii proposed a new solution to the problem of abrogation. It was well known that there were contradictions within the Koran, and the accepted solution was that Allah had included different rules, one to be followed earlier and another later in the course of the Prophet's mission, the latter abrogating the former (a process to which Koran 2:106 and 16:101 are traditionally said to refer). Similarly one Hadith could abrogate another. The problem was to know whether the Koran could abrogate Sunna, or vice versa. Where there was conflict, the old schools of jurisprudence had allowed that the Koran could override Hadith. Shafii maintained that this could not happen; the Koran could be abrogated only by the Koran, Hadith only by Hadith.

Alongside these two divinely revealed 'Roots of Jurisprudence', Shafii recognized two others. One of these was reasoning by analogy – a more restricted and supposedly objective process than the formation of opinion by the older jurists. The final source, consensus, was the general agreement of the whole Muslim community. It was based on a Hadith: 'My people shall never agree on an error'. This meant in effect that the community was infallible. However, this last principle was conceived in a negative sense, to override the claims of the local consensus of Medina or Kufa. It was in practice impossible to have any universal agreement subsequent to the break with the Shiites and Kharijites.

The Four Sunni Schools

Shafii failed in his attempt to absorb the old schools of jurisprudence into his new system. What happened was that a new school grew up in his name and took root in Egypt and southern Arabia. The Hijazis and North Africans remained faithful to Malik, and the caliphs adopted Abu Hanifa's as the official school of the Abbasid state. However, the old schools adopted Shafii's theory of the Roots of Jurisprudence, though maintaining their own under-standing of reasoning and consensus. Some of the Hadith Party still believed that Shafii was giving too much weight to reason, and they continued to work for a Sharia based only on Koran and Sunna. One of these men, Ahmad Ibn Hanbal, founded a school of jurisprudence that was eventually accepted on a par with the other three. He was equally important for his place in theological controversy, which will be dealt with in the next chapter.

There thus came to be several rival versions of Sharia, and for a time the controversy between them was bitter. In due course, however, their followers learned to accept their differences. The doctrine grew up that they were all part of the one Sharia. In the precinct of the Kaaba a place was provided for the imam of each of the schools, to enable its members to observe the Pilgrimage in their own slightly different way. To get a feel of the significance of this, the reader might try to imagine St Peter's Church in Rome with chapels for Anglican, Protestant and Orthodox Christians, as well as Roman Catholics.

In spite of their differences, the various schools were in broad agreement on the most important topics – the observance of the Five Pillars, and many of the laws applicable to all the main aspects of life. They classified actions on a fivefold scale, ranging from obligatory and recommended through neutral to discouraged and prohibited, with recognized punishments for the latter. All the essential features were attributed to the Koran or to the Sunna of the Prophet.

With the passage of time, the idealistic character of the Sharia came to be somewhat eroded by the development of legal fictions to avoid certain inconvenient requirements without breaking the letter of the law. Although the creation of the religious trust (*waqf*) was not strictly such a device, it had similar effects, allowing the wealthy to avoid the break-up of large estates under inheritance law. Property could be settled in perpetuity in the form of a trust, the income of which was to be used for a named purpose. Many of these trusts had laudable objectives, providing for a mosque or a school or for the poor, but others were set up simply to keep money in one branch of a family. Because they were perpetual, the effect was cumulative, and in the course of time an enormous amount of property came to be held in trusts.

The Sharia is today a controversial subject, and one of the aspects most often criticised is the position of women. It will be useful to take this as the subject for one or two examples of how the Four Schools differ in practice. As regards getting married, the Hanafis were the most liberal, allowing a mature woman to arrange her own marriage. The other schools required a woman to be given in marriage by a man, though requiring her consent.

As regards getting divorced, it was the Malikis who were the most liberal, recognizing a wide variety of grounds on which a woman could petition for divorce, including the husband having become impotent, his desertion, failure to maintain, cruelty, affliction with a disease that threatened her health, or even his bad breath. The Hanafis were the most restrictive, recognizing only a woman's right to obtain annulment of her marriage by reason of the husband's inability to consummate it, or to obtain dissolution on the grounds of his being a missing person aged more than ninety. On the other hand, all four schools allowed the husband to repudiate his wife with minimum safeguards other than the Koranic waiting period.

All the schools agreed on a rule that assumed the ascendancy of the male in the family: the prohibition of marriage between a Muslim woman and a non-Muslim man, on the grounds that the religion of a child is that of its father; for her to produce non-Muslim children would amount to apostasy. Incidentally, this is the reverse of the Jewish principle which judges the religion of a child by that of its mother. Technically, this means that the child of a Muslim father and a Jewish mother belongs to both religions – an interesting possibility that has never been built on.

One contentious subject is female genital ablation. Male circumcision is an ancient Middle Eastern custom that became obligatory in Islam, though not mentioned in the Koran. Unlike the Jewish practice, which was to circumcise boy babies on their eighth day (Genesis 17:12), the Arab tradition was to perform the operation when the boy was about six to eight years old, avoiding the tissue damage of the Jewish *periah*, but with greater psychological impact. Some jurists even recommended female 'circumcision', though only Shafii, pursuing to the limit his principle of reasoning by analogy, made it obligatory like male circumcision. In practice this operation never became widespread. Even in Shafiite countries it occurs only in parts of Egypt, Sudan, East Africa, Arabia and Indonesia. Unlike the circumcision of boys it is not an occasion for popular celebration but is done without ceremony. Some protection against its spread may have been given by the fact that it is known by a different Arabic term from male circumcision.

By combining the most favourable elements from all the schools, it would be possible to achieve a status for women that would be less unequal than that of any one school. However, as long as the schools remained separate, the women under the jurisdiction of each had cause for complaint. This can be accounted for by the social context in which the elaboration of the Sharia took place. The expansion of the caliphal state had given immense wealth to the Muslims, particularly the ruling class. This had brought a great influx of slaves. Among these, women predominated, because it was troublesome to break adult men in to slavery. The surplus of women over sexually available men was further increased by the transformation of a proportion of male slaves into eunuchs. The abundance of female slaves devalued free women by the ethical equivalent of the law of supply and demand. The position of women in Abbasid society was worse than at any other time in Islamic history, before or since. Although the authors of the Sharia were devout and fair-minded men, often in conflict with the luxury-loving rulers, they could not help being influenced by the society of their times – and by the fact that they were all men. Out of the range of possibilities that did not contradict the Koran, they tended to opt for those that most favoured their own sex.

A topic of burning relevance to the present is that of jihad. The word means simply striving, and it is frequently used to mean simply the individual's striving to become a better Muslim. It also acquired the technical sense of fighting 'in the way of Allah' – fighting war for Islam. The consensus was that such war was a last resort, to be fought only in self-defence, not for aggrandizement or material gain. Later jurists defined two territories, *Dar al-Islam*, the Home of Islam, where Muslims were free to practise their religion, and *Dar al-Harb*, the Home of War, from which attack was to be feared. Neither category figures in the Koran or Hadith. Still later, it was recognized that such a division was too simple and a third category was introduced, *Dar al-Sulh*, the Home of Treaty, in which Muslims, though a minority, were protected.

It was never the doctrine of classical jurists that there must be constant jihad against the *Dar al-Harb*, and the historical fact was that there were long periods of peace with non–Muslim neighbours. The death of fighters was regarded as martyrdom, but no one was encouraged to court death deliberately, and a suicidal attack on civilians would have been doubly wrong, both as suicide and as a breach of the rules of war.

Hadith

The most pressing need, now that Shafii had established the principle that knowledge of the Prophet's Sunna must be based on sound Hadiths, was to sort out the Hadith. This was accomplished by a whole generation of scholars, who travelled all over the Muslim world and interviewed thousands of people in search of every last scrap of information about the Prophet. In fact they were acting a hundred years too late, for they had to sift through a vast mass of spurious reports created to give support in all the arguments that had been raging.

The guiding principle of the collectors of Hadith was the soundness of the chain of authorities reaching back to the time of the Prophet; each transmitter had to be of sound mind and good character, and each pair of successive transmitters had to have had the opportunity to meet. Analysis of these chains involved an enormous labour studying the lives of the many transmitters. Needless to say, the method could not detect changes that had crept into genuine stories in the course of transmission; still less could it root out pure inventions whose authors had been clever enough to forge a passable chain. Experts classified Hadiths according to the quality of the chain and the number of different chains through which a given Hadith had come down. Nothing in the Hadiths has the rock-firm reliability of the Koranic text. Nevertheless there is no reason to accept the conclusion of some Western scholars that most of them are spurious; many seem inherently plausible and probably do go back to the time of the Prophet, even if they have changed slowly in the course of being relayed down the generations.

Of the many collections of Hadiths that were made, six were eventually accepted as authoritative. Two of the six books are prized above the rest: those of Bukhari – died 256 (870) – and of Muslim – died 261 (875). Bukhari claimed to have sifted through six hundred thousand reports to select the seven thousand that he accepted as valid. A seventh collection was not given the same authority, partly because it was a 'musnad', that is to say it was inconveniently arranged under the names of the first transmitters and not under subject heads. This enormous collection of eighty thousand Hadiths remains important because of the reputation and influence of its author Ahmad Ibn Hanbal, founder of the Hanbali school of law.

The overwhelming bulk of Hadith is concerned with or bears on legal questions. The outcome of all this work was a very legalistic conception of Islam, illustrated by the fact that Sunni Islam divided itself along the fault lines between the schools of law. Such a development was not inevitable. Only about 150 verses of the Koran, out of over 6200, are concerned with matters of law. Even allowing for their greater than average length, they do not amount to more than about three percent of the total. Muslims could have decided to leave it at that and to allow secular legal systems to develop and change flexibly in different places and times, on condition that they did not contradict the spirit of the Koran. This is exactly what happened under the Umayyad caliphate and was to happen again during much of the twentieth century CE.

Koranic Studies

The other major body of scholarship required by jurisprudence was knowledge of the Koran. There was no problem with the basic text, which had been fixed from the beginning, but it was in fact only a skeleton. In Uthman's edition there were no dots to distinguish different consonants with the same shape (seven pairs, one triplet and one set of five), no signs for short vowels, no punctuation, no indication of the break between verses, no verse numbers. Even the beginning of each sura was not indicated by any more that a blank line, and the suras had neither titles nor numbers. It was, so to speak, a 'performer's prompt', needing the voice of an experienced reciter to give it sense.

By the end of the first century AH, more than a dozen variant recitations had developed. Each of these is known from two disciples who passed them on until they were fixed in writing by the addition of dots and vowels and punctuation to the Uthmanic text. Ibn Mujahid, who died in AH 324 (936), put forward the doctrine that there were seven canonical readings of the Koran, based on the authority of three reciters from Kufa, and one each from Basra, Medina, Mecca and Damascus. Other authorities produced lists of ten or fourteen readings. It is noticeable that Kufa produced more variant readings than any other centre, so

Uthman's alleged destruction of alternative Korans did not prevent the reciters there from developing different traditions. There were also seven slightly different systems of verse numbering, two from Medina and one each from Kufa, Basra, Mecca, Damascus and Homs. Eventually most of this variety died out, and most modern printed Korans use Asim's reading from Kufa, as conveyed by Hafs, using the Kufan verse numbering. In Maliki north and west Africa, the reading of Nafi from Medina is preferred, as conveyed by Warsh, with the later of the two Medinan numberings. Other readings survive locally.

Ibn Mujahid relied on a Hadith in which the Prophet said he had taught the Koran in seven dialects. This seems highly unlikely as the effort involved would have been immense and the gains minute. The slight differences in vowelling make virtually no difference to the meaning and they do not correspond to any known dialectal differences. Most are no more significant than the difference between replacing 'while' by 'whilst' or making English 'ate' rhyme with 'gate' or 'get'. It seems unnecessary to refuse the obvious explanation that slight differences in pronunciation developed over time in the different centres, as happens with all oral traditions. The fact that so little variety developed before the readings were written down proves that there was already broad consensus on recitation when the Prophet died.

Once the readings had been written on to the consonantal outline, the text was permanently fixed. Only the styles of calligraphy and ornamentation evolved. The Koran continues to be written in the traditional way, without breaks, filling the whole of every page and interrupted only by sura titles in ornamental frames. It is not normally typeset, but is printed from a handwritten original with a decorative border round each page. Signs in the margin indicate its division for purposes of recitation into 30 parts for the 30 days of Ramadan, each divided into two portions, each of which is further divided into quarters or sometimes eighths.

More important than establishment of the canonical readings was the exegesis of the Koran. This had existed as part of the Hadith literature from the earliest times, and one of its main sources was the Prophet's cousin Ibn Abbas. The special feature of Koranic commentaries has always been their close and detailed attention to the circumstances in which each passage of the Holy Book was revealed. Indeed, they contain so much biographical and historical material that it would be virtually possible to reconstruct the life of the Prophet out of the commentaries.

Elements of commentary were scattered over a vast literature until they were painstakingly extracted and compiled in a monumental work by Muhammad al-Tabari, who lived from 224 to 310 (839 to 923). This was to be the main quarry for all subsequent commentators on the Koran. Not content with this, al-Tabari also wrote a history which remains the main source on the first three centuries of Islam. He was a most scrupulous scholar, and always reproduced all the alternative versions of a tradition that had reached him, leaving it to the reader to judge which was preferable.

Al-Tabari also founded a school of jurisprudence, one of several that failed to establish themselves. Eventually four schools were to be accepted as orthodox: those of Malik, Abu Hanifa, Shafii and of Ibn Hanbal. There is a common tendency in the designation of the Four Schools of Law, the Six Books of Hadith, the Seven Readings, the Seven Verse-Numberings; whenever Sunni Muslims were faced with rival versions of some aspect of their religion, their instinct was to be tolerant and accept them as equally valid. There was not the same passion for rooting out heresy that one finds in the history of Christianity. Nor was there the readiness for debate that might have established which was the better opinion in each particular case.

After the third century of Islam, it came to be accepted by most Sunni Muslims that the working out of the Sharia was complete, and that 'the gate of elaboration was closed'. From now on, all that was needed was adherence to what had been elaborated. It was of course still open to the judges to adapt the law to particular cases, and a *mufti* (decision-maker) could be asked for a *fatwa* (decision) to clarify a difficult instance, but the overall structure of the Sharia was thought to be permanently fixed.

CHAPTER FIFTEEN

REASON AND BELIEF

Greek Influence

The debates about the role of reasoning in the elaboration of the Sharia were part of a wider movement to reconcile Islam with Greek philosophy and science, which the Arabs had encountered among their formerly Byzantine subjects. The influence had been close; for example St John of Damascus (676–760?), a rationalist Christian philosopher and theologian, played as a child with the children of the Umayyad court, for which his father worked. He himself worked for the later Umayyad caliphs and, after his retirement to a monastery, wrote the last considerable work of Greek philosophy. His abusive account of Islam became the chief source of information on the religion for centuries of Christians.

Inevitably, as Greek culture was in the hands of Christians, it was the Christian interpretation of Plato and Aristotle that most influenced Muslim scholars. These two philosophers had been accepted by Christian theologians, who believed that Aristotelian logic could prove the existence of God, and that the Platonic theory of forms could account for the relations between the eternal and the temporal, soul and body.

Out of this encounter with Greek thought grew a school of rational theology (*kalam* – literally 'discourse'), which had steadily matured through the second Islamic century. This was a completely new element in Islam, for the Prophet had not been concerned with logic or abstraction, and the early scholars had sought only to pass on his legacy. It differed from the Christian encounter of Greek thought with Semitic religion, which had taken place in the Greek language. The encounter with Islam took place in Arabic.

It was the Abbasid caliph al–Mamun who placed theological questions at the centre of interest of Muslims for a generation. He was the last caliph to see himself as having an important contribution to make to the development of the religion. Indeed, he probably saw himself as the Renewer for the Third Century. He had won the throne in AH 198 (813), after a civil war in which he defeated his half-brother al-Amin. He had won this war thanks to his ascendancy in the Iranian provinces, particularly Khorasan, in the east of Iran, where speculative approaches to Islam were popular.

Al-Mamun was deeply interested in rationalist theology and set out to reform Islam and make it compatible with philosophy. He adopted the Mutazilite school of theologians as the official interpreters of Islam and set out to eradicate rival schools of thought. He founded an institute, the Bayt al-Hikma (House of Wisdom), to translate philosophical and scientific texts from Greek into Arabic.

The Mutazilites ('those who set themselves apart') attempted to combine the solutions of the main theological problems of Islam in a rational synthesis. Three questions in particular had been debated from the time of the Civil War: was the Koran eternal or created, did human beings have free will, and were Muslims who sinned gravely still Muslims? To these the rationalists had more recently added the problem of the Qualities of Allah.

The problem of the eternity of the Koran stemmed from the fact that the sacred Book is taken to be the discourse of Allah, much of it uttered in the first person plural. Indeed quotations from it are always introduced by 'the Almighty has said: ...'. If it is literally what it sounds like, then it must have existed for all eternity, since Allah is eternal and unchanging and therefore cannot express an idea at one time and not have it at another. In popular belief, earthly Korans were copies of the eternal original preserved in Heaven.

For the philosophically minded, to regard the Koran as eternal was idolatry, the error of associating a partner with Allah. If the Koran were eternal then there would be two eternal entities, Allah and the Word (*kalam*) of Allah. Logically this was the same as the problem that Christians had run into when they decided

174

that the Son was the eternal Word, and Muslims had to avoid any solution that resembled the doctrine of the Trinity. The Koran itself said that Jesus was a word (*kalima*) from Allah and linked this statement with rejection of the Trinity (4:171).

In any case, the Koran nowhere calls itself eternal, as it should do if this belief formed part of Islam. The nearest that the partisans of the eternal Koran could find was 85:21–22: 'It is a glorious Koran / In a Tablet preserved.' (This incidentally is one of the few cases where there is a significant difference between canonical readings; the last vowel determines whether it is the Koran or the Tablet that is preserved.) They also claimed that the eternal original of the Koran was the 'Mother of the Book' referred to in 43:4 and elsewhere.

Against this, the Mutazilites could produce a passage in which the Koran implies that it was produced (*iftara*), i.e. created, by Allah, and describes itself as confirming or explaining previous scripture, which must therefore have the same status (10:37):

> This Koran is not such as can be produced by less than Allah, but it is the confirmation of that which was before it, and the explanation of the Scripture – in it there is no doubt – from the Lord of the worlds.

The problem of free will was closely related to that of the eternity of the Koran, for the Holy Book speaks in Arabic and assumes the existence of an Arabia; worse, it refers specifically to many events in the lives of the Prophet and his companions; if the Koran were eternal, then it must have been predestined from eternity that these events should happen. To this, the believers in predestination added the argument that if human beings were free then Allah would not be almighty. The proponents of free will, the Qadarites, countered by pointing out that if Allah decided people's acts, then Allah was responsible for the evil that they did, and could not justly punish them. The argument had a political aspect: if sinful caliphs were responsible for their wickedness then it was right to rebel against them, but if Allah had predestined it, then the faithful should bear it patiently. Those who rebelled against bad caliphs had to be Qadarites.

The question of grave sinners too was bound up with politics. If the Muslim leader who had committed grave sins had thereby ceased to be a Muslim, then again rebellion was not merely a right but a duty. Those who defended the status quo held that the decision was postponed to the Day of Judgement. They were called Murjites, from Koran 9:106: 'There are others held in suspense (*murjawna*) for Allah's decree; either Allah will punish them or will turn back to them.' This approach also allowed judgement between Uthman and Ali to be put off indefinitely. The Mutazilites traced their origin to Wasil the son of the great Ata, who broke with Hasan al-Basri over this question, holding that grave sinners were neither true Muslims nor disbelievers, but something in between.

The problem of the Qualities of Allah is a scholastic one, arrived at through the attempt to apply the Aristotelian theory of 'accidents' to theology. If Allah is merciful, for example, then the eternal quality of Mercy becomes a second eternal entity, and so on for each other quality; logically one would end up with a large number of eternal entities – again idolatry, associating partners with Allah. The philosophers concluded that Allah can be defined only by negatives; if we say that Allah is merciful, for example, all that we can know is that Allah is not unmerciful. The popular position was to say that we know Allah is merciful because the Koran says so – and never mind about the philosophical consequences.

A particular difficulty arose from the Koran's application of physical attributes to Allah, where it speaks for example of the face (2:115), the eyes (11:37) and the hands of Allah (3:73), or Allah's sitting on a throne (7:54). To the rationalist it was clear that these were metaphors; to take them literally was anthropomorphism rejected by Koran 112:4: 'No one and nothing is like Allah'. Their opponents cleverly turned things round, accusing the rationalists of anthropomorphizing by trying to make Allah fit into the categories of human reason. They said that we know that Allah has a face and eyes and hands and sits on a throne, because the Koran says so, but our puny human minds cannot understand; we must just accept, 'without [asking] how (*bi-la kayf*)'.

The Mutazilite solutions to these problems formed part of a comprehensive account of an Islam in harmony with philosophy. It was summed up in five doctrines:

- *The Oneness of Allah* allowed no existence of any other eternal entity, neither Allah's Qualities nor the Koran nor Heaven and Hell nor anything else.
- *The Justice of Allah* meant that evil was the work of human free will.
- *The Threat and the Promise* meant that evil would certainly be punished and good rewarded.
- *The Intermediate Position* meant that grave sinners were neither Muslims nor unbelievers but something in between.
- *The Promotion of Good and Forbidding of Evil* (Koran 3:104) meant that Mutazilites were obliged to promote their beliefs by every means available.

The Mutazilites took the last of these doctrines as justifying the use of force to impose their beliefs. They persuaded al–Mamun to require all religious authorities to subscribe to their doctrines under oath. An inquisition, the *Mihna*, was set up to root out heretical beliefs. To be fair to al–Mamun it must be said that the inquisitors did not begin their work until a few months before his death, aged only forty-seven, in AH 218 (833), so that he cannot be held personally responsible for their excesses. Perhaps if he had lived he would have found politic ways of completing his life's work of making Islam compatible with philosophy.

This was the only inquisition in the history of Islam, and it is interesting to reflect that it was set up under the influence of Greek philosophy, which lay at the root of the recurrent Christian concern with doctrine and heresy. Precise rational definitions are foreign to the Muslim religion, the true spirit of which expresses itself in practice rather than theory. The Mutazilites had reduced religion to a system of logical propositions, and in so doing they had lost the quality of mercy. If they had focused on making philosophy acceptable to Muslims, instead of trying to make Islam acceptable to philosophers, perhaps the Renaissance would have happened in Baghdad instead of waiting six centuries to happen in Europe.

The Reaction

The Mutazilites met their match in Ahmad Ibn Hanbal, a popular preacher widely respected for his piety. He was a collector of Hadiths and expert in jurisprudence, who adopted a literalist interpretation of Koran and Sunna and mistrusted reasoning as a source of Sharia. He was in his early fifties when he was imprisoned for two years and flogged by the inquisition under the caliph al-Mutasim. After his release he was the hero of the Baghdad masses, even though he no longer dared preach his ideas publicly. The caliph and his official theologians were so unpopular that the court had to be moved to a new capital, Samarra, where it remained for more than fifty years before returning to Baghdad.

Eventually, in AH 234 (848), the caliph al-Mutawakkil bowed to popular pressure and abandoned the Mutazilites. He banned discussion of the eternity of the Koran, and sought popular favour by a fierce policy of Islamic orthodoxy. It was the end of the last attempt to give the caliphate a role in the religious development of Islam. The great debates were over. All that was left to do was to tidy up the legacy of the preceding centuries. The clear victor was Ibn Hanbal, and when he died in 241 (855) his funeral in Baghdad was attended by an estimated eight hundred thousand men and sixty thousand women.

Al-Mutawakkil's reign saw a new persecution of Christians, Jews and Zoroastrians, who were banned from office, burdened with extra taxes, made to wear distinctive clothes and harassed with petty restrictions. Churches and synagogues were pulled down and property confiscated. Similar harsh measures were extended to Shiites, and the shrine of Husayn at Karbala was destroyed. This was the only time in the five centuries of Abbasid rule that such un-Islamic policies of religious intolerance were followed.

The Mutazilite movement survived the oppression of al-Mutawakkil, but their decline was accelerated when Abu 'l-Hasan al-Ashari broke with his fellow Mutazilites, who had considered him a future leader. He made this move in the year 300 (912), thus bidding to be considered the Renewer for the Fourth Century. He left Basra for Baghdad and set about constructing a rational defence of orthodoxy. He managed to envelop such views as predestination and the eternity of the Koran in such a subtle web of argument that few people could find anything to object to. However, even this use of reasoning was too much for the followers of Ibn Hanbal, some of whom eventually destroyed al-Ashari's tomb. The physical monument to al-Ashari was easily enough destroyed, but the intellectual monument built by him and his followers was destined to last virtually unchanged for a thousand years. Even today it forms the core of Sunni theology.

Mutazilite ideas were not extinguished, however, but lived on in the thought of the great Muslim philosophers, Al-Farabi (AH 256–339; 870–950) and Ibn Sina ('Avicenna'; AH 370–428; 980–1037). Both were polymaths, as accomplished in mathematics, science and medicine as in philosophy. However, they were at odds with the prevailing Asharite orthodoxy, and their influence was countered by that of Abu Hamid al-Ghazali, who was born at Tus, near Meshhed in Iran, in AH 450 (1058). He proved such a brilliant scholar that at the age of thirty-four he was appointed by the Seljuq chief vizier, Nizam al-Mulk, to the principal professorship in his foundation, the Nizamiya College in Baghdad. Here Ghazali lectured in philosophy and theology.

Al-Ghazali wrote *The Confounding of the Philosophers*, in which he adopted a radically sceptical view, according to which all causality was denied. If cotton burnt, for example 'it is Allah that

179

made the cotton burn and made it ashes either through the intermediation of angels or without intermediation. For fire is a dead body which has no action, and what is the proof that it is the agent? Indeed, the philosophers have no other proof than the observation of the occurrence of burning when there is contact with fire, but observation proves only simultaneity, not causation, and, in reality, there is no other cause but Allah.' Such an approach effectively made impossible the development of science, which is founded on the discovery of causal relationships.

Al-Ghazali's book was answered half a century later by the Andalusian philosopher, physician and scientist Ibn Rushd ('Averroes'; AH 520–595; 1126–1198). He wrote *The Confounding of the Confounding*, but the damage was already done, and Islamic philosophy was to find its keenest audience in Europe, where Latin translations of Avicenna and Averroes were eagerly read by Aquinas and others.

CHAPTER SIXTEEN

DISSIDENTS

The Shia Mainstream

The labours of the scholars had come perilously close to creating an Islam so learned that ordinary people would not have access to it. If a proper knowledge of the religion required one to memorize the Koran, to study an exegesis of the Koran, to read the *Sira*, to be familiar with at least one of the Six Books of Hadith, to know the teachings of at least one school of jurisprudence, and to be at ease with arguments about such things as free will, the createdness of the Koran, the position of grave sinners and the status of the Qualities of Allah, then there could be very few proper Muslims. The Koran itself denounces this kind of bookish religion (62:5):

> Those who are charged with the Torah, and who do not discharge it, are like a donkey charged with Torah scrolls.

Ordinary Muslims believed it was enough to carry out the duties of the Five Pillars of the religion, to know a few passages from the Koran and to lead decent lives. They wanted to be led by people whose superior knowledge of Islam shone out in lives of great virtue and simplicity. Instead they saw the members of a ruling clan living remote lives of immense luxury, assisted by a wealthy class that could afford the expense of a long and bookish education. There were no mechanisms for peaceful change of government, and so periodic rebellion was inevitable.

In the search for leaders, dissidents could easily be persuaded that things would not have gone wrong if only leadership had remained in the family of the Prophet. There were plenty of potential candidates. After the death of Ali's son Husayn, leadership had passed, some said to Husayn's descendants, known as sayyids, others said to Hasan's descendants, known as sharifs, and yet others said to Ali's son Muhammad Ibn al-Hanafiya (son not of Fatima but of 'the woman of the Bani Hanifa') – see Figure 4. There were even those who favoured the descendants of Ali's brother Jaafar or of the Prophet's uncle Abbas. A series of armed revolts took place in the second Islamic century, led by one or other of these claimants.

Unfortunately for the descendants of the Prophet through Fatima, it was the house of Abbas that launched the successful rebellion. The Abbasids were to prove far more oppressive than the Umayyads towards the Alids. In fact the Umayyads had on the whole behaved honourably. Even in the calamity of Karbala, after Husayn had been killed, the victorious commander spared the life of the Prophet's great-grandson Ali Zayn al-Abidin, the Shiite Fourth Imam, and sent him to the caliph Yazid, who had him escorted home to Medina to live in freedom.

Sixty years later it was a son of the same Ali Zayn al-Abidin, Zayd, the Fifth Imam of the Zaydi Shiites, who attempted to launch the next Alid revolt against the Umayyads in AH 122 (740). Like Husayn when he had met his death, he was about fifty, and had lived quietly in Medina as a respected religious authority. At last, unable to tolerate any longer the spectacle of unworthy caliphs, he came to Iraq to raise a rebellion, but he was caught and killed before he had even finished making contact with potential supporters. His young son Yahya was put to death three years later in eastern Iran, where he had taken refuge. The Abbasid revolutionaries cleverly secured Shiite support by adopting the slogan 'Vengeance for Zayd and Yahya!'.

There were two more Alid attempts at revolt after the Abbasids had come to power. Muhammad al-Nafs al-Zakiya ('the Pure Soul') and his brother Ibrahim, great-grandsons of Hasan, raised their standard in AH 144 (762) and were soon killed, as well as others in their family. Their cousin 'Husayn of Fakkh' was killed with many other Alids at Fakkh near Mecca during the Pilgrimage of AH 169 (786), in a mass martyrdom. This was the end of Hasanid hopes of the caliphate, but some of their descendants eventually established Sunni dynasties, including the Idrisids, the present-day Alawites in Morocco and the Sharifs of Mecca, who gave rise to the present Hashimite royal family of Jordan. Many other lines of descent from Hasan survive and most are Sunni.

After the death of Zayd, the Husaynid branch of the family lay low, pursuing a life of scholarship in Medina. Even this was not enough to protect them against Abbasid suspicions, and Musa al-Kazim, the seventh of the Twelve Imams, died in the prison of Harun al-Rashid in AH 188 (799). However, the family then experienced the most extraordinary change in its fortunes. Against all expectations, Harun's son, the revolutionary caliph al-Mamun, decided in AH 201 (817) to nominate Musa's son Ali al-Rida as his successor. The prospects of his actually succeeding seemed slender though, for Ali was already fifty – twenty years older than Mamun.

The joy of the Shiites was short-lived. Ali al-Rida died the following year at Meshhed in eastern Iran, allegedly poisoned by persons unknown. His tomb there was to become one of the greatest shrines of Shiite Islam, along with that of his sister Fatima at Qom. He left a partly African son aged eight, Muhammad al-Jawad, who died in his twenties, leaving a young son, Ali al-Hadi. Ali was arrested at the age of twenty on the orders of Caliph al-Mutawakkil and brought from Medina to the new Abbasid capital of Samarra. He lived the rest of his life a prisoner in the barracks, where his son Hasan al-Askari and his grandson Muhammad, known as 'al-Muntazar (the Expected One)' also spent their short lives. Muhammad, the last of the line, disappeared mysteriously aged about eighteen, in AH 264 (878). Other lines of descent from Husayn survived but had no pretensions to be Imams; most of them are Shiites.

The partisans of Ali al-Rida and his descendants developed the doctrine that there had been twelve rightful Imams, and that the twelfth, Muhammad al-Muntazar, lived on as the Hidden Imam and would come back at the end of history as the Mahdi (meaning 'the rightly guided one') to establish the rule of Allah. This is akin to the Christian doctrine of the Second Coming, and indeed the return of Jesus was envisaged in some Shiite scenarios. This school of thought – 'Twelver' Shiism – was fully worked out by two brothers Nawbakhti before the end of the third century of Islam.

In Twelver belief, religious authority after the death of the Prophet was vested entirely in the Imams by divine right. The claims made for them were far higher than those made for the caliphs, who ruled by consent of the community and had no religious law-giving authority. Once the Twelfth Imam had been hidden, legal decisions could be made on his behalf by an elaborator (Persian *mojtahed*), but these could never have the same authority. The main difference from the Sunni institution of the same name is that Twelver elaborators have continued to function down to the present day. In Iran they are usually called mullahs, from Arabic *mawla* (originally 'client' or 'slave', hence 'pupil' and eventually 'master'). There has been a slow inflation of titles down the ages, and the highest mullahs are today called ayatollahs (Arabic *ayat-Allah*, 'sign from Allah').

In theory, Twelver Law takes the Koran as the point of departure and supplements its rulings according to the decisions first of the Prophet and then of the Imams, instead of making Koran and Sunna two completed foundations. This meant accepting pre-Islamic custom only where it was expressly confirmed by these authorities, whereas Sunnis made use of customary rules wherever they were not explicitly abolished by the Koran or Sunna.

In practice, Twelver Islam differs remarkably little from Sunni Islam in spite of its different theory of authority. Each has its own version of the Sharia. The Shiites use their own law books and collections of Hadith, which differ mainly in the prominence of the Imams. Part of the reason for this similarity is that the two streams did not separate till very late. Jaafar al-Sadiq, the Sixth Imam, for example, who lived from about AH 80 (699) to 148 (765), is recognized as an authority by Sunnis. He studied with

Ata and Urwa, and he influenced Malik, Abu Hanifa and Wasil. His mother was a great-granddaughter of Abu Bakr, and he would not tolerate any criticism of the first two caliphs.

The Sunni and Twelver versions of the Sharia differ over certain questions of substance. The Twelver law of inheritance builds out from the Koranic rules and gives rights to certain female relations who in the Sunni systems are replaced by men related through the pre-Islamic patrilineal system. Women also benefit from formal requirements that make it more difficult for men to repudiate their wives. On the other hand, temporary marriage, which is accepted by some Twelver authorities, and which Sunnis denounce as illicit sex, seems unduly favourable to men. A feature that makes it difficult sometimes to be sure who is a Shiite is the acceptance of dissimulation to escape persecution; if in danger it is permissible to forswear one's beliefs.

Twelver Shiism is distinctive above all by its cult of martyrdom and its traditional mistrust of government. Its emotional tone has a melancholy that is absent from Sunni Islam. The killing of Husayn is commemorated each year, on the tenth of the first month by a day of universal mourning, marked by miracle plays, processions and mortification. The villains of the piece are the Umayyad caliph Yazid and his henchmen, and by implication all unjust rulers. Yet the solution offered was absolute submission to an alternative ruler – an unrealizable ideal starkly contrasting with the pragmatic Sunni accommodation.

Other Branches of Shia

Not all Shiites accepted all of the Twelve Imams. The followers of Zayd, son of Ali Zayn al-Abidin, remained faithful to his memory and revered him as the fifth and last Imam. A textbook of Islamic law is attributed to him and may be authentic, although much revised by later authors. He appears to have adopted positions close to those of the Mutazilites, holding notably that the Koran was created. The Zaydis eventually established states in northern Iran and more durably in Yemen, where Zaydism remains the dominant form of Islam. Their beliefs are closer than those of most Shiites to those of Sunni Islam.

A third main stream of Shiism took as Imam not Musa al-Kazim but his elder brother Ismail, who died before their father Ja'far, and whose son Muhammad al-Tamm disappeared mysteriously, much as the Twelfth Imam of the Twelvers was to do. There came to be many versions of Ismailism. Some held that Ismail was the Seventh Imam, in which case his son Muhammad was a prophet or higher than a prophet, others that he was the Sixth and Muhammad the Seventh, in which case Ali Ibn Abi Talib had been something higher than an Imam – even the incarnation of God, according to the Syrian Nusayris or Alawis (not to be confused with the Alawi sultans of Morocco, the Alawi Sayyids of Hadramawt, or the Alawi Sufis of Algeria). Some held that Muhammad al-Tamm was to return at the end of history as the Mahdi, others that his line had continued in secret and would emerge and found a dynasty in a later generation.

The many versions of Ismailism shared the characteristic Twelver features of belief in a hidden Imam and the right to dissimulation, but in addition they laid great stress on the transmission of esoteric knowledge to the elect few. There was an elaborate philosophy based on the number seven, with seven levels of existence, seven grades of religious authority, seven stages of initiation, and so on. The initiate obtained licence to break the strict letter of the law, like Ismail, whose drinking of wine was said by the Twelvers to have disqualified him from becoming the Seventh Imam. The effect of these doctrines is to make Ismailism the most different form of Islam, with some of its offshoots being scarcely Islamic.

What all forms of Shiism have in common is that they were initially a vehicle for protest against the established powers. They proved particularly popular from an early date with the Iranian and Iraqi descendants of the old Sasanian Empire, many of whom resented Arab domination. Other fertile grounds were Yemen and North Africa. The pattern of events, many times repeated, was that a Shiite missionary would establish himself in an area, secretly organizing support for armed rebellion, and eventually an attempt would be made either to obtain local autonomy or even to take over the central authority.

The most successful rebellions in classical times were those organized by Ismailis. In the last decades of the third Islamic century (around 900 CE), a sect called the Qarmatians (or Carmathians) after its leader, Hamdan Qarmat, founded a state centred on Bahrain and with outposts in Iraq and Syria. For the next two hundred years they terrorized their neighbours with raids and assassinations. They even carried off the sacred Black Stone from the Kaaba and kept it for twenty years. They appear to have rejected much of the fabric of Islam, though it is hard to be sure how much exaggeration there is in the accounts given by shocked orthodox Muslims. Their key beliefs – in the need for common ownership of property and in freedom for women – were close to those of Mazdak's followers, and this may have been a revival of Mazdakism in Islamic guise. It has been suggested that some of their ideas, coming into medieval Europe through Spain, contributed to the development of the movements that eventually gave rise to communism.

Even more consequential was the establishment of the Fatimid dynasty in Tunisia in AH 296 (909). Its leader, Ubayd-Allah, claimed to be descended from Imam Ismail and took the titles of Imam, Mahdi and Caliph. His successors conquered Egypt in AH 358 (969) and founded a new city, Cairo (*al-Qahira* – 'the Victorious') to be the seat of their caliphate. In it they built the Azhar Mosque and soon after installed there the world's first university, which was formally organized by AH 378 (988). The line of Fatimid caliphs continued till 567 (1172). Their influence reached into Syria, and on one occasion they entered Baghdad, but they did not produce any lasting conversion to Ismailism. Egypt in particular remained loyal to Sunni Islam in its Shafiite form.

Faith in Mahdist claims faded when the coming of a 'Mahdi' failed to bring the end of the world. In AH 400 (1009) the Fatimid caliph Hakim put in a bid to be the Renewer for the Fifth Century by renouncing the world and having the apparatus of luxury destroyed. Like Umar II and al-Mutawakkil, he instituted a brief period of persecution of Christians and Jews. Seven years later he declared himself divine, and five years after that he disappeared mysteriously. His worshippers became the Druzes. Meanwhile in Cairo the dynasty continued until there was a conflict for the succession between Nizar and Mustali. The Mustalids survive to this day in India. The followers of Nizar became the dreaded Assassins, who terrorized much of the Middle East between 483 (1090) and 670 (1292). They are said to have derived their name – *hasshashin*, 'smokers of hashish' – from their practice of drugging themselves before their killings. Their peaceful modern successors are the Khodjas or Mawlas, mostly concentrated in India and East Africa, whose head is the Agha Khan. From such episodes, Sunni folk culture has retained a fear of extremist Shiite movements.

For the first century of Fatimid power, it looked as though Shiism might take over the whole Islamic world. A dynasty of Persian Twelvers, the Buyids, controlled the Baghdad caliphate from 333 (945) to 447 (1055). That they did not trouble to abolish it shows how unimportant the institution had become. Part of the reason for the failure of Shiism to become the mainstream of Islam lies in the disagreement between the different factions, but a deeper reason may be that their strength lay in protest, and once they had constituted governments they became instead the targets of protest. The only lasting Shiite power has been in Iran, where the Safavids, claiming descent from Musa al-Kazim, the Seventh of the Twelver Imams, established a dynasty five hundred years ago. However, the peace of Shiite Iran has been shaken several times by religious protest against the government, most recently in 1979.

The Kharijites

It is a mistake to view any religion in terms of another, but there is a temptation to see the Shiites as the 'Protestants' of Islam, with Sunnis as equivalent to the Catholics or the Orthodox. There is an analogy in the way that Sunnism remained a 'broad church' while Shia divided into many sects. However, in an important respect the position is reversed, for Shiites look to living authorities with Pope-like prestige, while Sunnis look back to the authority of the founders, just as Protestants look back to the Bible and the definitions of faith by the early Church Fathers.

A closer analogy to the more extreme forms of Protestantism, is offered by the early Kharijites, with their rejection of any religious authority other than that of the virtuous Muslim, and with their emphasis on the Koran as the main source of Law. There were two tendencies among them from the beginning, and by AH 65 (685) they had divided into three main parties. The Azraqis (after their leader Ibn Azraq) held that all other Muslims were polytheists and targets for assassination. Successive governments fought them until they were eradicated. At the opposite extreme, the Ibadis (after their founder, Abd-Allah Ibn Ibad) considered other Muslims merely disbelievers on a par with Christians and Jews, and they lived in peace with them, even cooperating with the caliphs against the Azraqis. The third, Sufri, party stood between the two and were eventually absorbed by the Ibadis.

Ibadis could be called the Congregationalists of Islam. Their version is in practice not very different from Sunni Islam, but with its own version of the Sharia. Its chief authority, Jabir Ibn Zayd, was born in Oman about the year 18 (642) and moved to Basra, where he enjoyed a reputation second only to that of Hasan al Basri. He was a friend and follower of the Prophet's cousin Ibn Abbas, and he became an important authority for Sunnis. For a time he was valued by the Umayyads, but in his old age he was exiled back to Oman, which became one of the strongholds of Ibadism.

In general the Ibadi version of the Sharia is rather like that of the Malikis, an important difference being their rejection of the stoning of adulterers in favour of the Koranic punishment. With the Shiites they share acceptance of dissimulation. They lay particular emphasis on literacy, personal study of the Koran being so important for them that they teach all their children to read – girls as well as boys. However, this study is confined to the Koran and the Ibadi classics, and most secular books are proscribed as sources of error and sin. In doctrine they are close to the Mutazilites, believing notably that the Koran was created by Allah in the time of the Prophet.

The root of Ibadi differences from other Muslims is their concept of authority. They hold that the whole community should elect its Imam. In such elections family and tribe should count for nothing: the only qualification for a leader is to be morally the best Muslim; 'the noblest of you for Allah is the most pious of you.' (Koran 49:13). Such a person should be followed, even if he were 'an African slave with a head wrinkled like a raisin'. They very early ceased to believe in the need for a supreme leader for all Muslims; each community could have its own, and in times of persecution they could manage without any.

Ibadism remained centred on Basra for a couple of centuries, and it found favour with many of the learned in the heartland of Islam, but gradually its influence receded. It has had two enduring centres: in North Africa it was important in the early centuries as the focus for Berber resistance to Arab control, and it still predominates in a number of oases; in Oman it became the local orthodoxy, and it was carried from there to Zanzibar.

With their practice of universal literacy, their acceptance of rational philosophy and their advocacy of elected leadership, the Ibadis had a valuable contribution to make. With the shrinking of their numbers and their territory, their influence on mainstream Islam has been negligible, but their ideas remain an intellectual resource that could be tapped.

CHAPTER SEVENTEEN

THE SUFI DIMENSION

Early Sufis

The emphasis of the Sharia was on correct observance of outward forms, but many Muslims naturally wanted to go beyond this and to experience direct, inward knowledge of Allah. The distinction between *zahir* (outward, exoteric or literal) and *batin* (inward, esoteric or metaphorical) has always been important in Arab thought. The prevailing view has been that both aspects are necessary, since without outward form there is nothing to carry inner meaning, and without inward dedication the outer observance is a hollow shell. The Ismailis were peculiar in attaching such importance to inwardness that conformity with Islamic law became very lax. At the opposite extreme, some of the learned were so attached to outward observance that it alone seemed to matter. The school of Sharia founded by Daud Ibn Khalaf was actually called Zahiri, and Ibn Hanbal's school came close to it. The literalists condemned the idea that anyone could have privileged access to knowledge.

Those who most successfully cultivated inwardness, usually without abandoning outward observance, were the Sufis, as they came to be called. The Arabic word is thought to derive from *suf*, wool, and to refer to their adoption of a woollen habit like that of Christian monks. In English they are often referred to as 'mystics', but that is misleading, as the word has acquired overtones of mystification and introversion. There is a great difference between the Christian mystics, who have generally been isolated and other-worldly figures, and the Sufis, who have been organized into fraternities and orders, and who have often played an important role in public affairs.

It is difficult to give an account of Sufism that does not risk being misunderstood. It is not a set of beliefs or a movement but an experience – one that overturns common-sense ideas of the world and our place in it. Religious language is used in attempts to express it, but this will make no sense to anyone who supposes that the word 'Allah' has to mean a gigantic human-like person objectively existing outside the Universe, or that the word 'soul' must refer to a permanent 'thing' that each of us 'has'. The reader who is puzzled should try to remember experiences, probably in early childhood, in which he or she felt completely part of the world without a sharp boundary between world and self.

Like all Muslims, Sufis trace their beginnings back to the Prophet and the Koran. They point to his practice of solitary meditation in the hills of Mecca, his night vigils, his fasting and his simple way of life, and to his transcendent experience of being lifted up to Paradise. They take various passages in the Koran as expressing their experience of losing the self in an omnipresent Allah, for example:

> To Allah belong the East and the West, so wherever you turn, there is the face of Allah. Allah is indeed all-encompassing, all-knowing. (2:115).

> We indeed created humans, and We know what the self whispers in them, and We are closer to them than their jugular vein. (50:16).

> All on [Earth] perishes;
> But there endures the face of your Lord, glorious and honoured. (55:26-27; cf 28:88).

Sufis look constantly for the deeper meanings hidden beneath the literal surface sense of the Holy Book. Certain verses can be interpreted as containing a whole system of beliefs. For example, Sufis find inspiration and a mine of metaphor in the radiance of the Verse of Light (Koran 24:35):

> Allah is the Light of the heavens and the earth. The parable of this Light is as a niche in which is a lamp; the lamp is in a glass; the glass is as a brilliant star, lit from a blessed tree, an olive neither of the East nor of the West, whose oil seems to shine even

when fire has not touched it. Light on Light! Allah guides to the Light whoever Allah wills.

Later Sufis derive their authority from the Prophet through a chain of authorities. The first two links in virtually all the different chains were Ali and Hasan al-Basri. Any contact that Hasan ever had as an adult with Ali must have been very brief. He was born in Medina in about AH 21 (642), and so was only about fourteen when Ali left for his new capital in Kufa. Aged sixteen – three years before Ali's death – Hasan migrated to the other Iraqi garrison town of Basra, where he lived the rest of his life, dying in AH 110 (728) in his late eighties. He has already been mentioned for his scholarship and for his contribution to theological debates, but what gave him his authority was above all his intense religious feeling, which caused him to renounce the ordinary comforts of life for his devotions. At the heart of his spirituality was his practice of night vigils. His was not a joyful school, for he emphasized meditation on human sinfulness and the Day of Judgement. Indeed, these proto-Sufis were called 'the Weepers'.

There were early Sufis elsewhere, but it was again in Basra that the next important figure, Rabia al-Adawiya, appeared. She was born a Bedouin sometime near the end of the first century of Islam, was kidnapped as a young girl and sold into slavery. She eventually obtained her freedom and settled in Basra, where she lived, like al-Basri, into her late eighties, dying in AH 185 (801). She drew a large following with her teaching that Islam should centre on love for Allah, a love that should be without thought of reward or fear of punishment. One of the most famous remarks attributed to her was made when delayed on her way to Mecca: 'Oh Allah! My heart is heavy with sorrow. I am only a handful of dirt and your house is only a rock. You are my sole desire.'

The question of reward and punishment was central to the thinking of Abu Abd-Allah al-Muhasibi. He was outwardly a prosperous citizen of the newly established city of Baghdad, but inwardly he wrestled with the problem of how a pious and ascetic person can avoid pride and hypocrisy. His solution was to cultivate constant self-judgement (*muhasaba*), in which he transformed the notion of an objective Last Judgement at the end of time into the expression of an inner spiritual practice. In his later years he suffered the judgement of others, being condemned by the Mutazilites because he accepted that Allah had eternal Qualities, and by the Hanbalites because of his use of reason and his belief that the Koran was created. He died in obscurity in 243 (857), and only four people attended his funeral.

Sufism comes of age

It was in Egypt that the ideas of Sufism were first clearly stated, by a contemporary of al-Muhasibi, Dhu-'l-Nun al-Misri, a freed slave like Rabia, of Nubian origin. He was one of the greatest figures in the unfolding of Islam – a man who combined enormous learning, wisdom and piety. He was far ahead of his time in believing that the ancient Egyptians had possessed great knowledge, and he used to study the inscriptions on their monuments in the hope of deciphering their secrets. He was well versed in the sciences of his own age, and he practised medicine. He was also an eloquent speaker, and he composed hymns in which all creatures joined in the praise of Allah.

Dhu-'l-Nun introduced the distinction between outward knowledge, *ilm*, in which he included knowledge *about* religion, and inward knowledge, *marifa*, the direct experience of Allah within the self. The way to this knowledge was rapture (*wajd*), expressed in his saying that 'the person who knows Allah best is the one most lost in Allah'. However, the attempt to achieve this, using proven Sufi techniques, could be dangerous, and the way to it should be opened only to those who were already spiritually advanced. His caution was well founded, and eventually his literal-minded enemies succeeded in having him tried and imprisoned in Baghdad. However, he was released by order of the caliph, and returned to Egypt, where he died in AH 249 (859).

Other Sufis of this third Islamic century defined various spiritual states through which they passed. The ultimate states were perishing and enduring (from the verbs in Koran 55:26-27, quoted above). By this it was meant that the Sufi hopes eventually to lose the illusion of being a separate and autonomous self and to enjoy a timeless oneness with Allah. Many attempts were made to express this in words, for example by the Iranian, Abu Yazid al-Bistami, who died in AH 261 (875): 'I cast off Abu-Yazidness as a snake its skin. Then I looked and saw that lover, beloved and love are one, for in the world of union all can be one.'

In the lives and teachings of these early Sufis were present all the main techniques of Sufism. Their exercises involved the whole person. Alongside the bodily disciplines – night vigils, fasting, rhythmic movements, breathing control – there were two main spiritual exercises: meditation and recitation (*fikr* and *dhikr*). Meditation made use of the methods familiar from other cultures, fixing an object or idea, or seeking to empty the mind of thought. It has always tended to take second place to recitation, partly no doubt because Islam favours devotions that unite physical and mental acts.

In the earliest days, recitation was of whole passages from the Koran. With time the formulas were shortened, no doubt partly to free the mind from the distraction of reading or remembering, and later Sufi practice was to repeat over and over again one of a small number of phrases, such as '*la ilaha illa 'llah* (There is no god but Allah)'; '*al-hamdu li'llah* (Praise be to Allah)'; '*allahu akbar* (Allah is most great)'; '*astaghfiru-'llah* (I ask forgiveness of Allah)'; '*allahumma* (O Allah)'; or simply the name, Allah, pronounced as one long-drawn-out syllable, '*LLAAHH*, reminiscent of Hindu use of the sacred syllable, OM.

There were some Sufis who withdrew from normal living to spend their time in such practices, but the aim of most was to realize union with Allah constantly in everyday life, as the Prophet had done, being assisted and not hampered in practical action. They earned their living, married and raised children, travelled, studied and taught and involved themselves in public affairs just like anyone else, except that their inward experience gave a special quality to their lives.

Al-Hallaj

All the elements of later Sufism were present by the middle of the third century of Islam, but access to the teaching was still available only to a small elite with little influence on mainstream Islam. The first important attempt to bring Sufism to the general public was made by Husayn, known as 'al-Hallaj – the Carder'. He may at one point have carded wool (straightened the threads and brushed out the seeds and twigs), but he was later said to have been the 'carder of souls'. He was born in Iran in about AH 244 (858), of partly Arab descent. He studied with an Iranian Sufi master, Tustari, then moved to Basra, where he studied under Makki, and where he married the daughter of another Sufi. His final period of study was in Baghdad with Junayd, the leading Sufi of the age.

In his late thirties, al-Hallaj made the pilgrimage to Mecca and spent a year there, following a regime of arduous discipline. He then took up the life of an itinerant preacher for several years, culminating in a second pilgrimage to Mecca, on which many disciples followed him. After a spell with his family in Baghdad, he set off by sea on a new mission, in which he penetrated areas in India and Turkestan hitherto closed to Islam. Then came a third pilgrimage and another stay in Baghdad, after which this tireless man set off again. This time, however, he was arrested in Shush and brought back to the caliphal dungeons. After eleven years in prison, he was publicly gibbeted, beheaded and burnt in AH 309 (922).

The offence of al-Hallaj was to have taught openly an ecstatic vision in which the division between Creator and created seemed to be obliterated. His most famous declaration was 'I am the Truth', which the orthodox took to mean that he believed his human self to be Allah. There were even many fellow Sufis who disapproved on the grounds that he had offered to vulgar ears things that only the initiated could understand. The barbarity of his punishment resulted from the general political insecurity of the times, with the caliphate threatened by Qarmatians and Fatimids. The actual date of his arrest, just before the turn of the century, may have been dictated by the need to prevent him from being seen as the Renewer for AH 300.

Al-Hallaj had failed to turn Sufism into a popular movement, but in the long term his martyrdom was to add to the determination of Sufis. The immediate effect, however, was to shock them into operating very quietly. For the next two centuries they remained a spiritual elite, until they were brought into the mainstream of Islam by al-Ghazali. However, there was a price for their acceptance; they should adhere to orthodox theology and law. How far they did so will be discussed in the next chapter.

CHAPTER EIGHTEEN

A THOUSAND YEARS OF CONSTANCY

The End of Flux

By the year AH 300 (912-13), the Islam of the learned had taken the form it was to keep for a thousand years. Mainstream Islam had defined itself intellectually, though it still had not needed to name itself 'Sunni'. It had reconciled its internal differences, with its Seven Readings of the Koran, its Six Books of Hadith and its Four Schools of Sharia (though as yet there were still others). Learned versions of the other branches of Islam, too, were fully formed: Ibadism and Zaydi, Ismaili and Twelver Shiism. As yet ill-integrated with the rest, Sufism was a fully developed system of belief and practice. All that was left, in order to shape the Islamic world as we know it, was for the different branches to take up their present positions in relation to each other, and for Sufism to provide a bridge between learned and popular Islam.

Until the middle of the fifth century of Islam, it seemed uncertain whether Sunni Islam could survive as the mainstream. It was divided between two rival caliphates – that of the Abbasids being challenged by a revived Umayyad caliphate based in Spain. Both were threatened by the Fatimid caliphate, and Baghdad was still under attack from the Qarmatians, and its caliphs were controlled by the Iranian Buyids, who were Twelver Shiites. However, the structures of Sunni Islam were too solid for it to be seriously threatened by the divided Shiites. In political terms, the turning point was the final defeat of the Buyids by the Sunni Seljuq Turks in AH 447 (1055).

In intellectual terms the chief architect of the classical system was al-Ghazali, author of *The Confounding of the Philosophers*. After his years of lecturing in philosophy and theology at the Nizamia of Baghdad, a spiritual crisis rendered him unable to continue, and he abandoned his post after only four years. He made arrangements for his family, disposed of his wealth and became a wandering Sufi. After visits to Damascus and Jerusalem and a pilgrimage to Mecca, he settled back in his native Tus, where he founded a virtually monastic Sufi community. After ten years he was persuaded to return to teaching, at the Nizamiya College in Nishapur. The year was AH 499 (1106), and he was in effect putting in his claim to be seen as the Renewer for the next century. After a further five years teaching, he retired again to Tus, where he died shortly afterwards, in AH 505 (1111), aged only fifty-four.

The Spread of Popular Sufism

Al-Ghazali was an immensely learned man, and he wrote many books and pamphlets on a great variety of topics. However, his most important contribution was to reconcile Sufism with orthodox Islam, bringing to an end the period of marginalization that had begun with the imprisonment and execution of al-Hallaj. He also opened the way for the development of almost monastic communities, contrary to the tradition attributing to the Prophet the saying: 'Let there be no monasticism in Islam.' However, there was no move to introduce lifelong celibacy, which would have been contrary to the whole ethos of Islam. A negative feature of Ghazali's Sufism is that it was tending to become a male preserve, turning its back on the tradition of Rabia al-Adawiya and other great Sufi women.

The conflict between Sufism and orthodoxy was not completely ended by Ghazali, however. The most controversial figure was Muhyi-'l-Din Ibn al-Arabi, usually known simply as Ibn Arabi, who was born of pure Arab ancestry in AH 560 (1165) in Murcia, Spain. He spent the first half of his life in Spain and the Maghreb, studying with a number of spiritual masters. While still a beardless youth, he met the great Ibn Rushd (Averroes), who was so struck by the spiritual depth of the boy that he trembled and became speechless. At the age of thirty-five, Ibn Arabi had a vision instructing him to leave for the east. He spent a fruitful time in Mecca where he began his great compendium of Sufism, *Al Futuhat al-Makkiya*. He also shocked timid spirits by addressing a series of poems of spiritual love to the daughter of a respected sheikh. He eventually settled in Damascus, where he produced a copious succession of books. Despite the daring of his thought, he managed to avoid trouble with the authorities and lived into his seventies, dying in AH 638 (1240).

Ibn Arabi brought together the whole range of Sufi ideas in a philosophy of great depth, the foundation of which was the unity of all existence. He saw successive levels of phenomena descending from Absolute Being, which was beyond understanding. His opponents accused him of pantheism – of holding that every-thing is Allah – and to this day his works are banned in many countries. However, in religious observance he was strictly orthodox, and it was said of him that 'he followed the outward in religion and the inward in his speculative thought'. Sufis revere Ibn Arabi as 'the Greatest Master' and the Renewer for the Seventh Century.

From the time of al-Ghazali on, there was a rapid development of Sufi orders, each faithful to the teaching of its founder, whose authority derived from a chain reaching back through Ali to the Prophet. More than two hundred of these orders came into existence over the course of time, and several dozen of them are still active today. They spread to all parts of the Muslim world, providing large numbers of enthusiastic missionaries to revive and spread the religion. They transcended the divisions between the Sunni schools and between Sunni and Shiite. However, what they offered was diversity in unity, for several orders would usually be present in any one place, each with its own distinctive style and methods. Their chief limitation was that their membership was almost exclusively masculine.

The great achievement of the Sufi orders was to provide a framework within which the most spiritually gifted and intellectually informed could work humbly together with very ordinary people. Access to esoteric knowledge was not limited to a select few. All shared the hope of raising their consciousness, but the masters recognized that their followers existed at many different levels, and that for each there was an appropriate teaching. Many would stay all their lives at a level of literal understanding and child-like dependence, but their qualities and achievements were no less valued for this. There developed a rich literature of Sufi stories that could be enjoyed as entertaining folk tales, but which on reflection opened out deeper and deeper meanings.

The oldest Sufi order is that of the Qadiris, founded by the son of its first master, Abd-al-Qadir al-Jilani, a Hanbali scholar who was a younger contemporary of al-Ghazali. The best known to Westerners, though now shrunk to a mere remnant, is the order of the Mawlawis (or Mevlavis), the 'Dancing Dervishes', deriving from Mawlana (Our Master) Jalal-al-Din Rumi (AH 603-692; 1207-93), the greatest of the Iranian Sufis, author of a vast poem, the *Mathnawi* (Couplets) which is a compendium of Sufi wisdom. Their 'dance' is in fact a slow turning, accompanied by sacred music. The use of music is common to all the orders except the very orthodox Naqshbandis.

Many of the orders are linked through 'family trees'. The Shadhiliya, for example, founded by the disciples of Abu-'l-Hasan al-Shadhili, a Moroccan contemporary of Ibn Arabi, has given rise to numerous orders in North Africa. One of their offshoots, the Alawis, followers of a twentieth-century saint, Shaykh Ahmad al-Alawi of Mostaganem in Algeria, has attracted many Western Muslims through the biography of the shaykh by Martin Lings. The great Ibn Arabi himself founded no order, but many of the orders make use of his ideas, for example the Chishtis, whose faith in unity inspires them even to accept non-Muslim members, and whose philosophy makes them pacifists.

The orders mentioned above are primarily urban, which ensures that they are in keeping with the Islam of the learned. There were also orders, now virtually extinct, which were mostly rooted in the villages and which accepted all sorts of doctrines and practices derived from older religions. Perhaps the most famous of these was the Bektashi order, which flourished among the Janissaries (the European foot-soldiers) of the Ottoman Empire, and which mixed Shiite and Christian elements.

The spread of the rural Sufi orders, and even to some extent of the urban ones, was closely related to the development in many areas of the cult of saints, who were popularly believed to possess the power to communicate blessing, and even to intercede with Allah on behalf of ordinary people – a power granted by orthodox belief to the Prophet alone among human beings. Most of these saints were conveniently dead, so that all sorts of miracles could be attributed to them. The tombs or shrines of holy men or women became centres for pilgrimage and places of prayer. Many leading Sufis, sayyids and sharifs were transformed into saints after their death, and uneducated Muslims increasingly confused the categories of saint, Sufi master, and descendant of the Prophet. In remote districts there were even living saints – people who, without being learned in the Koran or Sunna, had sufficient reputation to wield authority over the local populace.

The Mature Landscape

Meanwhile, the various branches of Islam were consolidating themselves in their present geographical locations (Figure 5). The Seljuq Turks in the heartland of Islam and the Ghaznavid Turks in Afghanistan and India, followed later by the Ottoman Turks and the Moghuls, ensured that Sunni Islam in its Hanafi version prevailed over most of the eastern part of the Muslim world. The Ottomans also imposed Hanafi law on Egypt, but the people remained loyal to Shafii, whose rite spread down the Nile Valley and into East Africa, and also from the southern Arabian ports across the Indian Ocean to Indonesia and Malaysia. The Maliki school was carried from North Africa and Sudan into West Africa.

FIGURE FIVE

MAIN BRANCHES OF ISLAM

SUNNI
- ▨ Hanafi
- ▥ Hanbali
- ▨ Shafiʕ
- ▥ Maliki

SHIʕ
- ▦ Twelver
- ◦◦ Zaydi
- ●● Ismaʕli

KHARIJITE
- ✳ Ibaḍi

The fourth of the Sunni schools, that of Ibn Hanbal, might have become extinct without the influence of Ahmad Ibn Taymiya. He was born in Harran, now in Turkey, in AH 661 (1263), but he was educated in Damascus, a refugee from the Mongols. He lived simply, as a teacher, but obtained fame and a large following by his vast learning and his forceful presentation of ideas. He stood for a return to the pure Islam of the Koran and Sunna. Though he followed the Qadiri Sufi order, he denounced Ibn Arabi's brand of Sufism, the cult of saints, Shiism and lax morals. It is interesting to note, however, that this purest of Sunni Muslims had the first of many brushes with the authorities for protesting at the sentence passed on a Christian for allegedly insulting the Prophet. Like Ibn Hanbal, he suffered for his beliefs and was in and out of prison in Cairo and Damascus, finally dying a prisoner in Cairo in AH 729 (1328). In modern times, he has wrongly been held to have advocated generalized jihad.

The revival of Sunni Islam was matched by the dwindling of Shiism. The last Fatimid caliph was dethroned by Saladin (Salah-al-Din) in AH 567 (1171), and the power of the Assassins was broken a century later, leaving the Ismailis a scattered remnant. Twelver Shiites lived on in the Fertile Crescent and Iran, locally in the majority, but without political power. Their situation was changed only in Iran, with the advent of the Safavid Dynasty in AH 906 (1501), establishing there the one enduring Twelver regime. The only other Shiite state to last into modern times was the Zaydi Imamate of Yemen.

Ibadis fared even less well than Shiites. Their territory shrank down to the Mzab oases in Algeria, the Tunisian island of Djerba, the interior of Oman and the island of Zanzibar. They have been saved from extinction by their very great social solidarity, and by their cultivation of extreme thrift, honesty and devotion to work, which have made them indispensable to their neighbours as merchants and entrepreneurs.

The importance of the various schools, represented as a percentage of all Muslims, is at present approximately as follows:

Hanafi	47
Shafii	27
Maliki	17
Hanbali	1½
Sunni Total	**92½**
Twelver	5
Zaydi	1
Ismaili	<1
Shia Total	**<7**
Ibadi	<1

All these variants of Islam, except the Hanbalis and the Ibadis, tolerated rural Sufism and the cult of saints. The Islam of the learned and the Islam of the people coexisted more or less comfortably. The learned provided expert services as judges and lawyers, imams and preachers, copyists and teachers. The unlearned got on with their lives, made the economy work, paid their taxes and provided soldiers. As for governments and dynasties, they came and went, rose and fell, without having any great effect on religious life. The Abbasid caliphate was destroyed by the Mongols, was continued in shadow form by the Mamlukes of Egypt, and was taken over by the Ottoman Turks, but it had long since ceased to play any part in the life of Islam. It seemed that the religion had attained such stability and completeness that it could go on unchanged for ever. The only real innovation in this period was the annual celebration of the *mawlid*, the Prophet's birthday, on the 12th of First Rabi, first recorded in AH 604 (1207).

Islam was so stable that for several centuries it was difficult to find any generally acceptable candidates for the hundred-yearly role of Renewer. The nearest approach was perhaps Jalal-al-Din al-Suyuti, from Asyut in Upper Egypt, who died soon after the start of the tenth century of Islam, which began in CE 1495.

However, his achievement was chiefly to summarize the scholarship of the past in a series of massive compilations. He is remembered specially for having completed the 'Commentary of the two Jalals', started by Jalal-al-Din al-Mahalli, which remains the most widely used exegesis of the Koran in the Arab World. Like several of the Renewers, he was in trouble with the authorities, and he spent his last years under house arrest; however in his case it was not for anything heroic, but for having provoked a riot by trying to reduce the stipends of Sufis attached to a mosque.

The constancy of Islam did not mean that it was static – far from it! On most fronts there was steady expansion, mostly through a process of peaceful conversion. In India, under the Moghuls, Islam spread all over the continent from its early base in the Indus Valley, gaining many converts from Hinduism, particularly people from the lower castes, who found in the new religion the possibility of being treated as equals, at least by each other. Beyond India, Islam was carried by traders to Malaya and Indonesia, where it eventually gained the adherence of most of the population.

In Africa, Islam was hardly even an imported religion, despite the fact that the early migration of some of the Prophet's companions to Ethiopia had not established a community. From the beginning, many prominent Muslims had been at least partly of African ancestry, including Baraka Umm Ayman, the Prophet's nurse, and her son Usama, his 'adoptive grandson' through Zayd, Bilal the first muezzin, Ata the 'Father of Islamic Jurisprudence' and his son Wasil, the first Mutazilite, Dhu-'l-Nun the great Sufi master, and the last four of the Twelve Shiite Imams. From its bases in North Africa and on the east coast, Islam spread along the trade routes to become the dominant religion of powerful kingdoms in West and East Africa.

In these new territories in Asia and Africa, Islamic civilization absorbed elements of local culture to develop remarkable new forms. In such matters as women's dress and status, the freedom of the visual arts, and the place of music and dancing in popular culture, the outward appearance of society was often superficially very different. In many places, Sufi orders provided a vehicle for distinctive religious ideas and practices. However, the universality of the Five Pillars and of the study of the Koran and Hadith ensured the essential unity of the Muslim World.

Conflict with Europe

It was only on the European front that these successes were not matched. There, the greatest challenge to Islam was being prepared. At first, the Christian World was very similar to that of Islam – far more so than animist Africa, polytheist India or non-theistic China. Medieval Christians shared most of their essential concepts with the Muslims of the time: they thought in terms of a personalized God and Devil, literal revelation, immortal souls, saints and sinners, salvation and damnation, angels and demons, a physical Heaven and Hell, just war and death for apostates. In theory Christians were saved by faith in Jesus, but in practice their code of divinely sanctioned law was just as complex and central as the Islamic Sharia. In theory Muslims had no priesthood standing between the believer and Allah, but in practice the learned provided indispensable religious services. There was even a semblance of monasticism among the Sufis. The influence of Plato and Aristotle had been felt on both sides of the divide.

The most conspicuous difference was that there was a place for Christians in the Muslim scheme of things, but none for Muslims in the Christian view. In Muslim eyes, Christians and Jews were 'the People of Scripture', to be left free to practise their religion. In Christian eyes, Islam was the work of the Devil, and its Prophet was an imposter and charlatan, consigned by Dante, along with Ali, to the Eighth Circle of Hell. Fear, hatred and ignorance were built into the foundations of the European attitude. Magnified on to a vastly larger scale, this was the original tragedy of the encounter between the first Muslims and the Jews of Medina, the former expecting welcome, sympathy and friendship, the latter seeing themselves as threatened by an imposter.

The difference was particularly acute in marriage: Muslim men could marry Christian or Jewish women or take them as concubines, but Christian men could not marry Muslims or Jews. Christians, with their strict monogamy and impossible divorce, professed horror at Muslim polygamy, though they were probably often secretly fascinated and envious. Muslims, on the other hand, found Christian self-limitation merely perverse and rather comic. In reality the two sides were not so far apart; the Muslim ideal of love was the devotion of a man to one beloved woman, and the poetic forms that gave expression to this were brought from the courts of Muslim Spain by the troubadours and eagerly adopted by the rest of Europe.

The effect of these differences was to make Muslim-ruled countries very much more open and tolerant than those governed by Christians. Muslim Spain, in particular, lived a golden age with mutual stimulation and enrichment of its different religious communities. Muslim, Christian and Jewish thinkers debated on equal terms in a shared framework of ideas. Households of mixed religion were commonplace, and there was a wholesale mingling of European, Berber, Arab and African stock.

In philosophy, science and mathematics, the Muslim world started out with a marked advance on Western Europe, which had lost touch with the knowledge of the ancient Greeks. Christian scholars from Paris and Oxford came to the colleges and libraries of Toledo, Cordoba and Seville to study texts in Arabic and to translate them into Latin. Perhaps the only important disadvantage of the Muslims was the prohibition on drawing or painting living things, which was to limit their development of biology and anatomy.

There were intermittent wars between Muslims and Christians throughout this long period. Most traumatic was the series of crusades which brought repeated invasions of Palestine and the Levant between 1095 and 1291. The capture of Jerusalem in 1099 led to a general massacre of its inhabitants – Muslims, Oriental Christians and Jews – which left a terrible folk memory.

The Christian Kingdom of Jerusalem lasted until it was destroyed by Saladin in 1187. After a brief revival a couple of generations later, it was retaken along with the remaining Crusader outposts. The effect of this history was mainly psychological, and the seven-hundred-years reconquest of Spain was in the end more important, ending the last long-term cohabitation of the two religions in Europe.

The Turning of the Tables

The great turning point came in 1492 CE (897 AH), which saw the fall of Granada, the last Islamic state in Western Europe, and the expulsion of most Muslims and Jews from Spain. Later that same year, Columbus sailed the Atlantic and opened the way to the West European scramble for overseas empire, soon to be matched by Russian expansion eastwards. In the short term, this discovery took the pressure off the Muslims, for the Spaniards were diverted from pursuing their conquests into North Africa. Perhaps the place of Mexico and Peru in the history of human suffering would otherwise have been taken by a Hispanic Africa.

At first it seemed that the loss of Spain was compensated by Ottoman expansion into Eastern Europe, reaching the gates of Vienna in 936 (1529) and again in 1094 (1683). This in itself produced new misunderstandings, particularly because of differences between the Western and Islamic practice of slavery. West Europeans, who were to transport millions of Africans across the Atlantic to work till they dropped on colonial plantations, and who had enslaved so many East Europeans that the peoples there came to be called 'Slavs', were horrified when children from the Balkans were taken to serve Muslims until they earned their freedom. It was particularly degrading in the eyes of Europeans that female slaves in Muslim ownership could become concubines. Even now, long after the abolition of slavery on both sides, the memory rankles.

Muslims soon had to abandon the illusion that advance in the east of Europe would compensate for retreat in the west. The

Turks were slowly forced back in the Balkans, and Muslims also lost control of Moghul India to the British, of Central Asia to the Russians and of North Africa to the French.

Wahhabism

By the twelfth/eighteenth century, there was widespread consciousness of the relative weakness and immobility of the Muslim world, though few anticipated the scale of the disasters to come. The most interesting of the reformers of this period, and the one who left the most enduring legacy, was Muhammad Ibn Abd al-Wahhab, whose teaching was a bridge between medieval and modern. He was born in Nejd, Central Arabia, in 1114 (1702/3) and lived there all his life, apart from periods studying in Medina and in Basra. His father and grandfather were Hanbali judges, and he grew up in an atmosphere of piety and learning.

Although he is often portrayed as a latter-day Ibn Taymiya, Ibn Abd al-Wahhab was very much his own man, claiming the authority to interpret Islamic law, and he quoted Ibn Taymiya and Ibn Hanbal rather infrequently. Far from being a literalist, he tried to see texts in the context both of other texts and of their historical setting. He believed passionately in the need to renew Islam for his time, seeking the answers in the Koran and Hadith, and he called on others to do the same. He freely criticized contemporary jurists and local potentates, and was more than once expelled from a town.

The starting point of Ibn Abd al-Wahhab's doctrine was *tawhid*, the absolute Oneness of Allah, but he did not approach it from the Mutazilite point of view and was not concerned with questions such as the eternity of the Koran or the attributes of Allah. His focus was on misplaced reverence for human authorities and for objects such as tombs and shrines which symbolized such authority. He particularly criticized Shiites and Sufis for their veneration of past leaders. In symbolic actions of his own, he personally led the tearing down of the tomb of Zayd Ibn al-Khattab, brother of Caliph Umar, and the sawing down of a sacred tree.

Ibn Abd al-Wahhab was an immensely scholarly man and wrote copiously. In view of his subsequent reputation, his books on marriage and on jihad are of particular interest. As regards the position of women, he was concerned to restore the equality of rights in marriage, which he considered to have been abused by contemporary society. He regarded marriage as the only sexual relationship that safeguarded a woman's interests, and he condemned sex with concubines, denying the traditional interpretation of Koranic verses. He encouraged women to insist on marriage contracts specifying their requirements, for example that the husband should not take further wives. He refused the perfunctory divorce procedures that had become widespread, and he recalled the mechanism that existed for women to initiate divorce.

Ibn Abd al-Wahhab did not see jihad as a way to propagate Islam. On the contrary, that was to be accomplished by missionary work (*daawa*). He adopted the classic view that the function of jihad was defensive, and he recalled the limitations: that women, children and non-combatants must not be harmed. Jihad was a last resort, and the overriding concern was the protection of human, animal and plant life. Any jihad must be decided by the imam and devoid of any element of aggrandizement.

In 1156 (1744), he converted Muhammad Ibn Saud to his view of Islam, and the Saudi leader began the expansion of what was to become the First Saudi Kingdom. Ibn Abd al-Wahhab neither approved nor disapproved of these military activities, though he may have been uncomfortable with them. As imam to the Prince's amir, he did not declare them to be jihad. He saw his own role as guide on religious matters. When Muhammad was succeeded by his son Abd al-Aziz twenty years later, Ibn Abd al-Wahhab's discomfort with the partnership seems to have deepened, and he resigned his position as imam in 1186 (1773), after the conquest of Riyadh. However, the Kingdom continued to describe itself as Wahhabi, and after the death of Ibn Abd al-Wahhab in 1205 (1791) it went on to become internationally important with the sack of Kerbala in 1214 (1801), the occupation of Mecca and Medina two years later, and the destruction of shrines and tombs in all these places.

Ibn Abd al-Wahhab's life was spent deep in the Arabian desert. Meanwhile, in one of the high places of European civilization, events were stirring that were soon to shake the whole Islamic world. In 1213 (1798), Napoleon invaded Egypt. Though the occupation was short-lived, it was traumatic, for here suddenly were non-Muslim conquerors in what had been, ever since the Mongol sack of Baghdad, the greatest Arabic-speaking city, Cairo the Victorious.

CHAPTER NINETEEN

REFORM

Faced with the painful evidence of their weakness, Muslims awoke to the fact that they were in effect surrounded by a European world empire, and that their old adversary had acquired new sciences and new techniques that gave it great economic and military superiority. The first reaction was to try to obtain the enemy's arms. Muhammad Ali Pasha, ruler of Egypt after the retreat of the French, equipped his army with European weapons and founded schools and colleges to teach the new sciences and techniques. He reorganized Egyptian society along radically new lines, nationalizing the land, investing in industry, destroying the power of the Mamlukes and turning the religious authorities into state employees. He was rewarded with sufficient strength to seize Syria from the Ottoman Turks, spreading his reforms there.

The Egyptian revival soon faded, however. The European powers forced Muhammad Ali to withdraw from Syria after ten years, having their own designs there. After he became senile and was removed from office, his immediate successors abandoned many of his reforms, and his grandson, Ismail, was deposed under pressure from the French and British. Muslims began to wonder whether there was not something wrong with their conception or their practice of Islam to explain why the new sources of power seemed to be more accessible to Christian Europe than to themselves.

In the year of Muhammad Ali's death, 1849 (1265), was born the thinker who did most to re-examine Islam in a modern light, the Egyptian, Muhammad Abduh. He was a graduate of the Azhar University, but came under the influence of Jamal-al-Din al-Afghani, a shadowy, subversive figure, who in the course of his life was expelled from a succession of countries, including Egypt in 1879 (1296). Abduh was expelled in his turn after the British occupation in 1882 (1300), and for a few months he worked with Afghani in Paris, helping to produce a dissident periodical. This, incidentally, led some to regard him as the Renewer for the Fourteenth Century.

Abduh's interests, however, were very different from those of Afghani, who was essentially a secular pan-Islamicist. Abduh was concerned with the religious ideas underlying weakness in the secular domain. After further years in exile, he ended up advising collaboration with the British while Islam was being renewed. He was allowed back into Egypt in 1889 (1306), and had a distinguished career as a judge and finally as Mufti of Egypt, also giving lectures at the Azhar. His death aged only fifty-six in 1905 (1323) was a great loss to Islam.

The lasting expression of Abduh's thought is in his book, *The Epistle on Divine Unity*, and in his commentary on the Koran. His central message was that Islam is of all religions the most rational and the most compatible with science, and that Muslims must not be afraid to modernize their faith and to abandon antiquated beliefs and practices, which are not essential parts of the religion.

By using the expression 'Divine Unity' in the title of his book, Abduh was perhaps invoking the Mutazilites, for that was the term that they used to sum up their doctrine. However, it has always been one of the central concepts of Islam. He may be called a latter-day Mutazilite, for in the first edition of his *Epistle* he stated that the Koran is created and not eternal. He was obliged to remove this statement from later editions, but there seems no doubt that his view did not change. He also shared the Mutazilite view on such matters as free will and the role of reason in religion.

The Mutazilite tradition never completely died out, and many distinguished Muslims down the ages have shared their view on the createdness of the Koran, for example Bukhari and Muslim, the two great traditionists, Zamakhshari and Baydawi, the Koranic commentators (all of them Sunnis), not to mention the Zaydis (Shiites), the Ibadis, and many Sufis. The question is not trivial. The notion of the Koran as eternal is the central problem for anyone who seeks a rational Islam.

Abduh's commentary on the Koran was published in instalments in *Al-Manar* ('The Lighthouse'), a journal founded and edited by his friend and disciple Rashid Rida, 1865-1935 (1282-1354), who continued the commentary after Abduh's death. The emphasis throughout is on the rationality of the sacred text and its compatibility with modern ideas. An attempt is made consistently to find the deepest and most universal meaning behind the literal interpretation.

Abduh's great importance stems partly from the fact that his position in Cairo and at the Azhar enabled his influence to be very widely diffused. A parallel movement in India had in fact started earlier. Sayyid Ahmad Khan, 1817-1898 (1232-1316), found time in an active career as judge and educationist to write on the need for reform, and he too published parts of a modernist commentary on the Koran. Perhaps the most innovatory comments of all were those of Abul-Kalam Azad, 1888-1958 (1305-1378), Minister of Education in India after independence. These works were published in Urdu and did not reach so wide an audience as the Manar commentary.

There is no need here to examine the detail of who said what and when. The important thing is to understand the broad outlines of a set of ideas that were immensely important throughout the Muslim world in the twentieth century. At the base of the whole reformist structure was the assumption that Islam could learn from Western civilization – indeed, in the eyes of many, was part of it and should become again the leading part. The way forward was for Muslims to enter fully into the developments that had flowed from the scientific and industrial revolution. In religious terms, this meant applying modern concepts and techniques to Islam.

There is much to be said for the view that Islam is part of Western civilization. Christian Europe and the Muslim Near East and North Africa both developed partly on the territory of the Greco-Roman Empire, and they shared a heritage of Hebrew religion and Greek philosophy and science. There have been Christians in Muslim territory for fourteen centuries and Muslims in Europe for thirteen. For most of their history, the two religions had so much in common that an observer from a different civilization might have regarded them as two versions of the same. Nothing could be more natural than to suppose that they shared a common destiny.

Of the nineteenth-century Western ideas that Islamic reformists adopted, the most important was belief in progress. They saw all knowledge as developing over time, through observation, experiment and reason. There were certain eternal truths, and these had been communicated to humanity through the inspired medium of the prophets, but these truths came dressed in the forms appropriate to their time and place, and they needed to be reinterpreted for each new age and society.

Reinterpretation did not mean abandonment, on the contrary: the essential values of Islam would be not merely retained but rediscovered if they could be freed from the sediment of centuries of stagnation. The advancement of science, universal education, women's equality, investment in a modern economy and establishment of democratic government would give full expression to the Islamic virtues of humanity, tolerance and compassion. There were even those reformists who claimed to find specific references to such developments in the text of the Koran, but others saw them as the product of Allah-given reason.

In support of their views, reformists portrayed Muhammad as the supremely reasonable prophet. He did not overwhelm his followers' reason with miracles, but appealed to them on the basis of the practical organization of daily life. He did not overawe them by appearing remote and superhuman, but lived openly and humbly as a normal man. He explicitly addressed his message to all the known world, and he dealt equally with every believer, without regard for social status, nationality or race. In contrast with the complexity of Christian doctrine, Islam offered clarity and simplicity, resting on Five Pillars, of which one was the shortest possible creed.

Reformists stressed the lack of any contradiction between Islam and modern science. The Koran does, it is true, refer four times to creation 'in six days' but it compares a day of Allah in one place to a thousand years and in another to fifty thousand, so no arithmetic measure of time is to be understood. More generally the Koran represents creation as a continuous process and not a once-for-all act. There is nothing to prevent acceptance of the idea that natural selection is the divine principle for the evolution of species, that humans emerged from this process or that society evolves. Some Muslims point to 71:14, 'He has created you in stages' as implying such processes. In any case, the Holy Book of Islam is unequivocally about spiritual matters, and acceptance of it does not inhibit the use of experiment and reasoning to enquire into the working of the physical world.

If revelation and reason were separate and equal sources of knowledge, one consequence was the necessity to separate politics from religion, in the framework of a pluralist society. Muslims would, of course, have a religiously inspired view – not necessarily all of them the same view – on many political questions, but decisions should be left to a duly constituted secular government, and Muslims should organize themselves to exert influence through political parties in the same way as any other interested groups.

To the extent that the state was embodied in its laws, separation from religion implied the elaboration of a body of secular law to govern all the activities of modern society that fell outside the realm of the Sharia. There had always been such law, even under the Abbasids, but it had grown up on an ad hoc basis. What was needed was a comprehensive legal system deduced rationally from fundamental principles and integrated into a democratic political constitution.

As for the Sharia, the best features of the different schools should be combined to produce an optimal version of it, and the 'gate of elaboration' should be reopened to enable jurists to improve it still further. The fiercer punishments – death, flogging and amputation – should be interpreted away as contrary to the true intention of the Prophet. Polygamy should be either outlawed or made subject to such difficult conditions as to be virtually impossible. The administration of Sharia justice should be improved by bringing it into the ordinary courts or by adding to the Sharia courts a structure of appeal courts for which there is no classical precedent.

Flexibility with regard to the Sharia was justified by appeal to the Koran. It is part of the wisdom of the Holy Book that where a harsh punishment has been specified, it is usually followed by an escape clause, to the effect that if the offender repents, Allah will forgive (e.g. Koran 4:15-16; 5:34; 5:39; 24:5; 24:8-10). Similarly, polygamy can be outlawed on the grounds that the Koran (4:3) recommends monogamy to men who fear they will not deal justly with more than one wife, which in practice means everyone except the Prophet and a few saintly men.

Reformists gave priority to the Koran over the Sunna as a source of guidance. The techniques of scholarship which had shown the all-too-human process of the composition of the Bible could be applied with similar effect to Hadith and therefore to our knowledge of the Sunna. The Holy Koran on the other hand was proof against any such critique. Because it had all been revealed through a single person, it had few of the internal con-tradictions of the Bible, and these had long since been recognized and explained. There was no need to do detective work to discover the circumstances under which different passages had been revealed, since these had been painstakingly established by the early commentators. As for textual problems, there were none.

In their political thinking, reformists adopted the European ideal of the nation-state. This was partly a reflection of the fact that many of them came from Egypt, which is more easily conceived of as a nation than most parts of the Muslim world. There was nothing specifically Islamic about this idea, but it was a fact that

Muslims had been divided between several states since the end of the Umayyad caliphate. It therefore seemed realistic for each territory to seek its own salvation in its own way. In any case, it was much easier to solve the practical problems of organizing an economy, an education system and a modern network of communication and publication, if a government could work through a national language.

The emancipation of women played a central part in the reform programme, but there came to be an obsessive concern with one symbolic aspect – veiling. As the most visible sign of women's status, the veil had long been the focus of Western criticism, and this preoccupation was taken over by reformist Muslims. What no one seems to have seen however is that the imposition of unveiling is just as much an interference with women's autonomy as the imposition of veiling. Where the veil was prohibited, the consequence was that at first many women became embarrassed to go out, and those who did go out risked harassment by men who had not been psychologically prepared for such sudden change.

It would be wrong to speak of 'reformism' and to imply that reformists agreed on a common programme. Some were mainly concerned with religious renewal and others with the adoption of secular ideas. Among the latter some, especially earlier in the century, favoured liberal politics and economics, against a growing trend towards one-party government dedicated to Islamic socialism. There were deep differences over the extent to which the state should be neutral in respect of religion. However, whatever their divergences, all agreed on the need for change.

The culmination of the reformist programme was the transformation of Turkey into a secular nation-state with a Western-style constitution, a legal code based on Swiss law and the aspiration of being accepted fully as part of modern Europe. A symbolic move was the prohibition of veiling by women, and of the wearing by men of the fez (a brimless hat allowing the forehead to touch the ground in worship). Psychologically even more momentous was the abolition of the Ottoman caliphate in 1924 (1342). The shock waves rocked every country in the Muslim world, and strenuous efforts were made to create a new caliphate, but in the end everyone had to recognize that Islam could exist without this venerable institution, which had long since ceased to perform any real religious function.

CHAPTER TWENTY

THE TURNING TIDE

Middle Eastern Autonomy Lost

In the first half of the last century, reformist ideas of Islam seemed certain to carry all before them as they spread across the Islamic world. However, nothing fails like failure, and the twentieth century saw the scientific, technical, economic and military gulf between Western and Muslim-controlled societies grow wider and wider. The reformists began to be blamed.

The European empires, far from welcoming Muslim advancement, seemed intent on holding it back. Britain had already begun the process of setting up protectorates in the Persian Gulf, having begun to realize the potential oil wealth of the region. The unnecessary entry of the Ottomans into the World War in 1914 gave the British and French the chance to break up the state that was the direct successor of the original Islamic Umma. By the secret Sykes-Picot agreement of 1916, they arranged that France should have Syria, and Britain would take Iraq and Palestine. By the Balfour Declaration of 1917, secret from the Palestinians until 1920, the British agreed to develop a 'Jewish National Home' in Palestine.

Meanwhile, a different story was being told to the Hashemite Sharif Husayn of Mecca. If he would persuade the Arabs to revolt, the British would help them to achieve independence. Amazingly, he believed these promises – not that his compliance made much difference to the war, since he had little influence outside Mecca and Medina. The main consequence was the destruction of the Hijaz Railway, an engineering masterpiece opened in 1908, which linked Damascus and Medina. It was blown up in many places by Bedouin tribesmen aided by an English adventurer, T.E. Lawrence. The indirect result was that Mecca and Medina were left open to annexation by the Saudi Kingdom.

Britain and France were not permitted to take over the region as completely as they had planned. The League of Nations devised a system of mandates, under which 'Certain communities formerly belonging to the Turkish Empire have reached a stage of development where their existence as independent nations can be provisionally recognized subject to the rendering of administrative advice and assistance by a mandatory until such time as they are able to stand alone. The wishes of the inhabitants must be a principal consideration in the selection of the mandatory.' Their wishes were not consulted, but 'provisional independence' became a reality of sorts in 1932 for Iraq, in 1941 for Syria and Lebanon. The Wafdist Revolution in Egypt in 1919 reduced Britain's influence there too.

However, petroleum politics were weighing ever more heavily on the region. The huge reserves around the Gulf were rapidly yielding increasing profits for oil companies largely owned by Western shareholders. In 1918 Britain added Kuwait to its protectorates there, although Ottoman suzerainty had been recognized in 1913, so that it should have passed to Iraq as successor state. Most of the profits were invested in Europe and America, but a sufficient share was placed in the hands of the ruling families to maintain a grossly unequal social order. The most dramatic change was the enrichment of the Saudi Kingdom, enabling it to project its influence far beyond Arabia.

The Second World War brought the Anglo–Russian invasion of Iran and the imposition of a compliant new shah. The attempt of its post-war democratically elected government to nationalize the Anglo–Iranian Oil Company led Britain and America to organize a coup to oust Prime Minister Mossadegh in 1953. Three years later, in response to the nationalization of the Suez Canal, Britain and France colluded with Israel in a failed invasion of Egypt. This was for a period the last Western military adventure in the region, but the peoples of the Middle East had by then had time to conclude that Europeans and Americans were unwilling to treat them as equals.

Palestine

The event that did most to destroy good relations with the West was the establishment of Israel. It is doubtful whether anyone in Europe or America understood the central importance of Palestine for the whole Muslim world. It was not merely a matter of the Prophet's vision of his ascent from Jerusalem to the Seventh Heaven. Custodianship of the places associated with Abraham, Moses, Jesus and the other Biblical prophets was seen as confirmation that Islam was the final revelation, completing that given to the Jews and Christians. Possession of the land was taken as fulfilment of Allah's promise to Abraham and his descendants through Ishmael. Muslims prided themselves on the protection they had afforded to pilgrims of all religions to the holy sites.

Religious Jews had been content with this arrangement. Their presence in Palestine had persisted through the worst efforts of the Greeks and Romans and Crusaders, and they had no political ambitions. Zionist nationalism was invented in nineteenth-century Europe, where, as increasing numbers of Jews adopted secular ideas and practices, Christian anti-Jewish prejudice was increasingly supplemented or replaced by racism. This gave rise to Zionism, a secular movement that sought to transform Jews from a religion into a racially defined nation with its own territory. There was no reason in principle why this should be established in Palestine. At the end of his life, after he had understood that the Ottoman Sultan would never agree to a Zionist colony there, Theodore Herzl applied to the British government for land in East Africa. It was the British conquest of Palestine that unlocked the gate.

Lord Balfour, the Foreign Secretary who offered a 'national home' in Palestine to the Zionists, was a great cynic, who is said to have remarked 'Nothing matters very much, and few things matter at all.' Unfortunately for the Palestinians, one of these 'few things' was Zionism.

Balfour's letter included a commitment, never given effect, that 'nothing shall be done which may prejudice the civil and religious rights of existing non-Jewish communities in Palestine, or the rights and political status enjoyed by Jews in any other country.' Note that the indigenous people were defined by their quality of being 'non-Jewish', and there was no mention of their political rights. The hollowness of this assurance is revealed by a letter Balfour wrote to his successor as Foreign Secretary: '... in Palestine we do not propose to go through the form of consulting the wishes of the present inhabitants ... The four great powers are committed to Zionism; and Zionism, be it right or wrong, good or bad, is rooted in age-long tradition, in present needs, in future hopes, of far profounder import than the desires and prejudices of the 700,000 Arabs who now inhabit that ancient land.'

In fairness to the British, it has to be said that few of them foresaw the scale of the disaster that was to befall the Palestinians. The Zionists of 1917 seemed to be a small and eccentric group, which could be exploited for its diplomatic usefulness and financial clout. Through the 1920s there was only a trickle of Jewish immigrants to Palestine, and by the end of the decade they were outnumbered by emigrants. It was the arrival of Hitler in power that changed everything. Soon the flood of European settlers was provoking a powerful Arab reaction. Britain tried with its White Paper of 1939 to keep control of Jewish immigration, but the World War, the appalling treatment of Europe's Jews and the development of Zionist terrorism destroyed the British will to continue with the mandate.

Concerning the establishment of Israel, there should be a few plain facts that all can agree on, but after decades of hatred and propaganda even that may not be possible. For more than a thousand years, Palestine had been an Arabic-speaking and pre-dominantly Muslim country. Its Arabic-speaking Jewish minority had been protected by successive Muslim governments and had suffered persecution only under the Crusaders. The Zionists had no desire to assimilate to the indigenous Jewish community, seeing themselves as Europeans. Zionist terrorism was the chief factor leading the British to abandon their mandate, as detailed by Israeli historians such as Morris and Pappe. About three quarters of a million Palestinians lost their homes and most of their property in 1948, and Israel refused to allow them to return or to compensate them. Israel occupied areas that had not been allocated to them by the UN partition resolution, including much of Jerusalem, the whole of which had been designated to become an international city.

It is hard to deny that the UN vote for partition was contrary to the Organization's own principle of self-determination, in that Jews were the minority even in the areas allocated to a Jewish state. Even those who consider partition legitimate should agree that the last thing Jews needed after their disastrous history in Europe was new enemies, yet that is exactly what they got. If they had agreed to accept limitations on immigration and had been willing to become equal partners in a democratic and secular republic of Palestine, their conflict with the Arab world need never have happened. The trouble is that the only justification for a Jewish state is the doctrine that Jews, racially defined, will always and everywhere be in danger, so having enemies is part of the package. In mitigation, it must be pointed out that Jews in the 1940s were traumatized by the appalling events under Hitler and were psychologically in no condition to make rational decisions.

The success of the partition vote can be attributed partly to financial and political pressure on member states, but above all to what may be called Old Testament romanticism – the idea that the Zionists would fulfil God's promise to Abraham and Moses. This, and the fear of being branded anti-Jewish, attracted the support of many Christians. It also appeased religious Jews, many of whom mistrusted the secular nature of Zionism. Subsequent reluctance to criticize Israel owes much to the fear of being branded 'anti-Semitic', with powerful organizations such as the Anti-Defamation League, Bnai Brith and the American Israel Public Affairs Committee dedicated to stamp on any opposition.

Viewed from the Muslim point of view, Western mistreatment of Jews was an internal problem for the West, and there was absolutely no justification for seeking to solve it at the expense of Palestinians. Out of approximately 1.3 million Muslim and Christian Palestinians, more than half – over 726,000, according to UN figures – lost their homes and most of their property in 1948. By any standards, this was a catastrophe and demanded urgent remedy. Yet after seventy years, Israel has still not accepted any responsibility, claiming that the refugees left voluntarily, as if there were some principle of justice that allowed refugees to be deprived of their right to return home.

Not only did Western countries harden their hearts towards the Palestinians, they seemed ready to fall over backwards to placate Israel. They made no attempt to enforce UN General Assembly Resolution 194 of December 1948: 'refugees wishing to return to their homes and live at peace with their neighbours should be permitted to do so at the earliest practicable date.' After the war of 1967, they were similarly remiss over Security Council Resolution 242 of June 1967 calling for 'withdrawal of Israeli armed forces from territories occupied in the recent conflict' and subsequent resolutions requiring Israel to stop its illegal colonization of these territories. They even turned a blind eye to Israel's development of nuclear weapons (indeed France actively helped).

Since 1993, Palestinians have been fobbed off with the mirage of the 'Two-State-Solution', which is just a new name for the partition that failed so disastrously in 1948. It could conceivably have worked if Israel had not continued colonizing Palestinian territory, with American support, and if a compensation package had been offered to the refugees, on a vast scale commensurate with the value of their lost homes and their many decades of suffering. In practice, it has seemed that Israel is just playing for time, waiting for the death of the last who remember life before 1948 – a strange illusion for people who claim to be righting the wrongs of two thousand years ago! The only response the Israeli government seems to expect is total capitulation – Palestinian acceptance of all their losses in return for a small measure of autonomy without true sovereignty.

Protection of Israel affected Western policies throughout the Middle East. No Arabic-speaking country must be allowed to become strong enough to threaten the Jewish State. The compliance of the Egyptian and Jordanian governments has been bought at immense cost in terms of the good will of their populations. Lebanon has been devastated by repeated attempts to divide Christians and Muslims. Syria has been subject to endless diplomatic and economic pressure. As for Iraq, its virtual destruction undoubtedly owed as much to the threat it posed to Israel as to its attempt to keep control of its huge oil reserves. Relations with Iran too have been poisoned by the priority given to Israel's interests.

Meanwhile, elsewhere ...

Palestine was not the only country whose partition was decided in 1947. Britain, itself no secular state, had for half a century been practising religious politics in India, dividing the Indian National Congress by playing Muslims off against Hindus, putting them on separate electoral roles. During the Second World War, Nehru and the other Congress leaders had been in jail, while Jinnah, head of the Muslim League had been left free to organize his bid for a separate Islamic state. Britain granted his wish in August 1947, rushing through partition on the basis of a few weeks preparation. Objectively, partition greatly weakened the position of Islam in the Subcontinent. From being the largest Muslim community in the world, a third of the population of the Raj, they went to being divided into three, with those who remained in the Republic of India forming only 10% of the total.

Pakistan was an extraordinary construction, its two halves separated by a thousand miles of India, its peoples ranging from the ancient nation of Bengal to the tribesmen of the North-West Frontier, its early years burdened by the problem of integrating millions of refugees from the rest of India. Its birthright was the unsolved problem of Kashmir, and it was not long before it was torn apart by the secession of its eastern half. The only thing the peoples of Pakistan had in common was Islam, which inevitably became the defining feature of their state. Indian Muslims had been among the most open-minded and flexible in the world, after hundreds of years living in intimate proximity to Hindus, Sikhs, Jains, Parsees and Christians, but leadership passed to those who had the sharpest consciousness of their separateness, including many who had been schooled in the ultra-conservative Darul-Uloom Deoband. Pakistan, even more than Saudi Arabia, became the testing ground for attempts to create the Islamic state. It was even proposed that the language of Pakistan should be Arabic and its constitution the Koran.

Thanks to its proximity to the Soviet Union and China, Pakistan's largely military governments have always enjoyed the favour of the West. It became the launch pad for the drive to overthrow the Soviet-backed secular regime in Afghanistan. American and British money and arms poured in throughout the 1980s to help the Jihadists. This was the period when Bin Laden, reportedly a CIA agent, organized his 'Afghan Arabs', who were to become the nucleus of Al-Qaeda ('the Base'), founded in 1989.

At the same time, with almost schizophrenic inconsistency, America and Britain were helping the secular regime of Saddam Hussein in its war on the Islamic Republic of Iran, which had overthrown the all-too secular Shah. In fact, Iraq only fell out of favour when it tried to annexe Kuwait, after the American Ambassador, April Glaspie had reportedly told Saddam 'We have no opinion on your Arab-Arab conflicts. The Kuwait issue is not associated with America.' The American-led intervention of 1991 wisely stopped short of pushing on to Baghdad, but it was the beginning of twelve years of sanctions and bombardments, which, according to UNICEF, caused the death of half a million Iraqi children.

Unwilling to trust Muslim countries to choose their own governments, the West has over and over again relied on despotic rulers, providing them with the technology to help them maintain their grip on their populations, and becoming liable to be held responsible for their unpopular rule. The longer such local tyrants have stayed in power, the greater the danger that their overthrow will lead to chaos and to attacks on Western persons and property. There have been various occasions when the vicious circle could have been broken, for example after the Suez crisis or after the 1967 war, but each new crisis has led to a new strongman being backed to replace the old one.

The last thing that the West can be accused of during this whole period is clear-minded hostility to Islam or Muslims. There was even the intervention in Kosovo to prove the contrary. Indeed, clarity about anything was seriously lacking. However, America and Britain in particular showed a cynical indifference to the suffering aggravated by their policies throughout the region. The ultimate folly was the invasion of Iraq in 2003, undertaken on the basis of faulty intelligence, without plans for occupation and decided by leaders who were almost totally ignorant of the history of the country. The failure of their respective electorates to punish them in 2004 and 2005 added to the impression that Westerners generally do not care about Muslim misery, though it must be pointed out that the electoral system of both countries allows governments to be formed on the basis of a minority of the popular vote (a quarter of the electorate in the case of Blair's 'victory' in 2005).

CHAPTER TWENTY-ONE

REVIVALISM

Critiques of Reform

The events described in the last chapter have poisoned relations between the West and the whole Islamic world, but the failure of reformist governments to make people conspicuously happier cannot be blamed only on outside factors. It is not just in the Islamic world that many people are disillusioned with the secular state. Faith in human reason as a guide to conduct has been gravely weakened by the atrocities committed in supposedly advanced countries. Broken homes, delinquent children, violent crime, drug addiction, depression and suicide seem to be endemic in modern society. Even the economy, the golden idol of today's governments, seems to have worked to widen the gulf between the obscenely poor and the often undeservedly rich.

In any case, only a minority of reformists were conspicuously religious people concerned with preserving the values of Islam in lives of unselfish dedication to spiritual values. The majority seemed to be attracted merely by the outward manifestations of the Western way of life. For ordinary Muslims with a simple, literal faith, the abandonment of traditional beliefs and practices by their leaders was confusing and demoralizing.

The supposed cultural pluralism favoured by reformists is not in fact an equal competition between rival views. The vast economic power of America and Western Europe has flooded the world with manufacturers adapted to a way of life that gives priority to the satisfaction of material demands, and which fragments society into a multitude of separate specialist markets. The multi-national firms of the entertainment industry pour out films, videos, recordings, books and magazines that portray a world of glamorous youth, easy sex, gratuitous violence and luxurious living. It is no great comfort to Muslims to hear that many Westerners feel themselves to be exploited and misrepresented by such products.

Critics suggested that human reason cannot provide a foundation for morality, since a chain of reasoning must always have a starting point, which is subjectively chosen. Starting from the sovereignty of the individual, for example, reason arrives at liberalism. Starting from the priority of society, it constructs communism. Starting from the primacy of race, it invents nazism. Only revelation can provide a firm foundation beyond the reach of human subjectivity. The first duty of Muslims is to affirm the truth revealed in the Koran and Sunna.

If revelation takes priority over reason, then there can be no arguing away of the prescriptions of the Koran and Sunna in the name of 'progress'. The secular concept of progress constantly changes with the whims of fashion, and there is only one objective form of progress – towards the realization on earth of the revealed Will of Allah. Nor should Muslims stop at the Koran and Sunna; they should take inspiration from the whole of the Prophet's life. He spent his last eight years fighting against the enemies of Islam.

The idea of separating politics from religion has no place in Islam. Unlike Christianity, which was made the state religion by a secular emperor long after the death of Jesus, Islam was from the beginning concerned with the government of public as well as private life. The Prophet gave himself to the realization of the Will of Allah in the form of a state, the Umma, of which he was head and whose law was Sharia. His Companions understood after his death that they must maintain and expand the state that he had created. Differences of opinion soon appeared as to how this was to be achieved, but all Muslims agreed that proper government must be Islamic government. Followers of other religions have nothing to fear from this, since Islam was the first monotheistic religion to respect the rights of other faiths.

In any case, the end result of secular government is the decline of religion. If the state is agnostic it is in effect telling people that all beliefs are equally valid, and that it does not matter what you believe as long as you do not make yourself a nuisance to other people. In practice such governments are not really agnostic; they act according to a materialistic set of beliefs that see growth of economic consumption as the highest good. Christianity has declined steadily under such regimes, and it is the duty of Muslims to defend their religion against a similar fate.

The nation-state is a concept with no roots in Islam. Throughout their history Muslim states were multinational, until they were broken up by outside interference. Islam never discriminated between citizens on account of race or language, except that religious minorities were allowed, for their own comfort and security, to live in separate quarters. The attempt to divide the territories of defunct Islamic states along national lines has led many peoples, including non-Muslims, into terrible suffering, which shows no sign of ceasing.

The elements in the Sharia objected to by liberals are provided by revelation. Capital punishment was imposed by the Koran and Sunna in a few rare cases and is necessary if far more widespread killing is to be deterred. People are required to dress modestly to preserve everyone from the gratuitous arousal of feelings that would lead to either promiscuity or frustration, and if this is more restrictive for women than for men it is because men are more easily excited sexually. Polygamous marriages are an option for exceptional cases and circumstances, and are never imposed on anyone. The Prophet himself set an example of dealing justly with several wives. In all its provisions on sexual matters, Islam has regard for the difference between the natural behaviour of the male and that of the female, which is as important in human beings as in every other sexual species on earth.

Even the economy needs to be reorganized along Islamic lines. The division of the world into national economies, some grotesquely rich, others shamefully poor, has brought misery to the majority. Gross inequality is enhanced by a system based on the taking of interest and the treatment of paper tokens as if they were real assets. The application of Islamic principles would abolish the economic frontiers that preserve inequalities and would transfer resources from the rich to the poor, without taking away natural incentives to work hard to improve one's income.

Such ideas are by no means all home-grown. Some of them may have been borrowed from similar thinking in the West, where many Christians have sought to resist their declining influence on public life. More than a century after Abduh affirmed that Islam has no problem with the theory of evolution, it is galling to see Muslim groups producing glossy publications extolling American-style creationism.

Revivalist Movements

The sort of criticisms outlined above are broadly agreed to by many Muslims unhappy with the modern world. But there has been no general agreement on the response. Most Sunnis have adopted their traditional attitude that it is better to suffer bad governments than to let loose the evils of civil war. They have seen the answer as being religious – improving the Islamic quality of their personal lives and helping others to do the same. However, some believed in the necessity for political action to install an Islamic government. The first such Sunni movement was the Muslim Brotherhood, founded in Egypt in 1347 (1928) by a young schoolteacher, Hasan al-Banna. It grew rapidly through the 1930s and 40s, and became a major political force. The Brotherhood did not aim at violent revolution, but the activities of some members began to escape al-Banna's control, and in 1368 (1948) a group of them were implicated in the assassination of Prime Minister Nuqrashi. Al-Banna was himself assassinated two months later, probably with government connivance.

The intellectual pivot of the movement was a latecomer to it, Sayyid Qutb, born like al-Banna in 1324 (1906). He was a reformist until he went to the United States to study its education system; what he saw there drove him back to his Islamic roots. He returned to Egypt in 1950, joined the Brotherhood and was imprisoned with many others from 1954 to 1964. He was executed in 1966 for alleged involvement in a plot to kill Abdul-Nasser. In prison he wrote a widely admired commentary on the Koran, and a book, *Milestones*. The latter has been described as the charter for al-Qaeda, but it does not advocate generalized jihad nor attacks on civilians.

The Muslim Brotherhood has spread beyond Egypt and has been imitated by other Sunni movements. However, in Egypt it has been overtaken by the far more radical Islamic League (*al-jamaa 'l-islamiya*), held responsible for the assassination of President Sadat and for many other acts of violence. It became one of the main recruiters of Afghan Arabs in the 1980s and is implicated in the founding of al-Qaeda. All over the world, similar movements have come into being in bewildering variety, most of them secret societies. Almost every month some new group pops up to claim a bombing or a kidnapping. It is easy to have the impression that they have millions of followers, when in fact a few thousand suffice, rearranging themselves ceaselessly in new combinations under new names.

Some of these Sunni movements have succeeded in establishing Islamic governments. The oldest of course is Saudi Arabia, which defined itself as Islamic from the outset of the First Kingdom in 1744. It has never seen its mission as being the overthrow of other governments in Muslim-majority countries. General Zia's regime in Pakistan and the government of Sudan were established by military coup, not by popular revolution. The jihadist governments in Afghanistan are best seen as nationalist responses to foreign occupation, complicated by the involvement of outsiders.

It may seem surprising that the first modern movements of this kind came out of Sunni Islam, when their equivalents in earlier times (apart from the Azraqi Kharijites) were Shiite – the Alid revolts, the Carmathians, the Fatimids, the Assassins. A partial explanation may be that, once the divisions of the Muslim world had become fixed, Shiites were a minority in most areas. However, when it did come, the Shiites of Iran provided the first successful example of the revolutionary takeover of the state. Until the Anglo-American invasion of Iraq opened the door to Shiite militias there, it looked as though Iran would remain an isolated instance.

Sunni movements for a political Islam should be seen as a deviation from the tradition, which sees the need as being for spiritual renewal of individuals rather than imposition of an external conformity from above. In fact they are part of the worldwide politicization of public life. People expect governments to solve every kind of problem, from climate change to economic growth and from obesity to juvenile crime.

Even the Iranian Revolution owed much to Western models. The thinker who did most to prepare it was Ali Shariati 1352-97 (1933-77), a sociologist with a Paris doctorate, who developed a politicized concept of Islamic revolution. Many of the students who descended into the streets to bring down the Shah were the product of the strongly Westernized system of higher education that the government had introduced. The events of Teheran in 1979 were more like those of Paris in 1968 than like anything in previous Islamic history.

The Western Response

Ignorance of Islam has caused most Westerners to lump all these movements together under some general label such as 'fundamentalist', 'extremist', 'militant', 'Islamist', 'jihadist' or simply 'terrorist'. Any of them is liable to be branded a branch of al-Qaeda and seen as part of a worldwide conspiracy to 'destroy civilization'. This has been of immense help to those who really do want to shatter the current world order. The Western media have provided a free propaganda service to magnify their apparent importance and unity. In fact the only suitable term to cover all resistance to reform movements is something non-committal like 'revivalist'; but within this broad category, it is necessary to distinguish between Sunni and Shia forms and between spiritual and political tendencies. Jihadists stand out from the rest as being outside the mainstream of Islam. There is no precedent or authority for them in Sunni Islam nor in most Shiite history.

To make things worse, the same labels have been extended to national liberation movements such as those of Palestine, Chechnya or Kurdistan, which are Muslim in membership rather than ideology. Hamas, founded with Israeli encouragement as a foil to the Palestine Liberation Organization, is essentially another liberation movement and rose in popularity because of its effectiveness in organizing services for its people. It was ready to respect a ceasefire and enter into the democratic process, and has been recompensed with the assassination or imprisonment of many of its leaders by Israel. Even Hezbollah (Allah's Party) has no serious interests outside Lebanon.

Some Western governments have responded in ways that make things much worse, panicking their population with constant talk of terrorism, singling out Muslims repeatedly for special comment, making wide use of repressive legislation, condoning torture if not at home then at least abroad, adopting double standards in foreign policy. The effects have been particularly felt in Great Britain. At least a hundred thousand Muslims marched in London with more than a million others in the huge anti-war demonstration of 15th February 2003. They believed with the other marchers that Britain was a democracy and that their representatives in Parliament would pull the government back from the brink. Some of the young men who subsequently turned to violence were no doubt in that hopeful crowd.

The rhetoric of good versus evil, civilization versus barbarism, order versus chaos, is the same on both sides. George W. Bush's 'axis of evil' is the mirror image of Osama Bin Laden's Great Satan. Enemies are so demonized that it is not acceptable even to talk to them. Their motives are assumed as a matter of principle to be hostile. Those on one's own side who are suspected of sympathy with the enemy are not listened to. In Bush's America, knowledge of Arabic became a disqualification for service in intelligence or foreign affairs. In Britain, Middle East policy was run by the Prime Minister rather than the Foreign Office.

The proper response would be quiet and effective intelligence, careful distinction between different Muslim groups, discreet adjustment of foreign policy without appearance of giving in to violence, genuine pluralism with equal access for all religions to publicly funded media, abolition of public subsidies for segregated education, unwavering protection of civil liberties, active engagement with international institutions, effective measures to reduce the gross disparities of wealth and income between rich and poor countries and other forms of institutionalized injustice.

Instead, we were offered 'war on terrorism' – an utterly incoherent concept. Wars are fought by armies against whole states, in theory against opposing armies, but in practice very often doing immense harm to civilians. Terrorism is perpetrated by tiny, secret groups, attacking whatever targets they can with limited means and manpower, striking down civilians in order to spread panic, hoping to provoke governments into intensifying whatever policies make them appear hostile to the community out of which the terrorists have arisen. War is the supreme example of the response that terrorists desire. There are extremists on both sides who would welcome a world war between Muslims and the West.

In this light, a particularly alarming development is the involvement of troops from the North Atlantic Treaty Organization in Afghanistan. Early in 1995, Willy Claes, the organization's then Secretary General, told a security conference in Germany that Islamic fundamentalism was at least as great a threat to the West as communism had been. It seemed preposterous that anyone should compare the scattered little jihadist groups with the mighty, nuclear-armed Soviet Union and the vast armies of the Warsaw Pact; yet eight years later, European soldiers were out there fighting Afghans under a UN mandate in NATO's first ever mission outside the Euro-Atlantic area.

Meanwhile, the Israel-Palestine problem was left to fester, with bleatings about a 'two-state solution' that continuing colonization has rendered impossible. Israelis should be left alone to negotiate face to face with their neighbours the conditions for their continuing presence in the region. The Western powers should be prepared to underwrite the costs of settling a dispute that was created by them and to offer citizenship to any Israelis who are unwilling to live on equal terms with the rest of the population.

As for Muslims living in the West, all that the rest of us have a right to ask of them is to be good Muslims, to deepen their understanding of their religion and to use their special position to interpret one civilization to another.

CHAPTER TWENTY-TWO

THE NEW CENTURY

Remaking the Classic Synthesis

The Islamic reformist movements were born at a time when Western civilization seemed invincible. Abduh and his followers wanted to ensure that the Muslim world was part – indeed they hoped the leading part – of this new stage in human development. The revivalist movements matured a century later, at a time when disillusion with Western models was becoming widespread, not least in the West. Khomeini and other militants hoped to save Islam from what they saw as a worldwide spread of materialism and nihilism.

There is right on both sides. The reformists are right to see that religion must in future take account of the success of science and technology. Humanity cannot disacquire knowledge, nor disown the spirit of enquiry and the pursuit of rigorous intellectual honesty that have given rise to it. If people are not to live in a permanent state of doublethink, religion must be appropriate for a universe of more than a billion trillion stars swarming in a hundred billion galaxies – a universe at least fifteen billion years old and perhaps eternal – a universe in which complex life forms may evolve over and over and over again. Anyone who is ready to use such fruits of the application of science as computers, mobile phones and modern weapons, should also be ready to learn a scientific respect for evidence.

The revivalists are right to say that people cannot live by reason alone. Human beings have a powerful faculty for seeking pattern and meaning in everything, and are disturbed by the suggestion that life may be a succession of meaningless accidents. Our species is unique in being capable of suicide to escape a life without meaning, or martyrdom to ensure that a meaning lives. We can even deduce meaning from the fact that a government claims to be neutral between different beliefs, especially where its members transparently believe in enriching themselves and their friends as their highest aim. If religion is defined as the need to rise above the self and its material desires, then there is much evidence that the religious urge is universal, and this should be reflected in government.

However, the rise in popularity of revivalists at the expense of reformists cannot be explained only as part of a wider disillusion with agnostic government. Their success lies above all in the fact that they have managed to seem the more fervent Muslims, even where some measure of posing, sentimentality and hypocrisy may be involved. They are the ones who have been willing to risk imprisonment, torture and death rather than bow to oppressive governments. One should remember that there is a long history of the greatest Muslims suffering at the hands of unjust rulers, for example Malik, Abu Hanifa, Shafii, Ibn Hanbal, Dhu-'l-Nun, al-Hallaj and Ibn Taymiya, and of course the Shiite Imams.

Islam has been here before. The present conflict is remarkably like the one between the Mutazilites and the followers of Ibn Hanbal at the beginning of the third Islamic century. On one side are those who seek to benefit from applying a logic of European origin. On the other stand the defenders of strict loyalty to an unchanging view of the Koran and Sunna. There are of course important differences: the Muslim countries of today are weak and divided, unlike the mighty Abbasid state, and modern science and technology are far more powerful than Greek philosophy.

The most striking similarity between today's conflict and that of the third Islamic century is the absence of Sufism from the debate. It was absent then both because it was not yet a mass movement and because Mutazilites and Hanbalites were united in rejecting it. Both were essentially superficial systems of thought, subjecting everything to the flat measure either of pedestrian logic or of literal understanding. Both were threatened by the Sufis' reaching for a higher dimension. Sufism is absent now because of its collapse as a mass popular movement. This was brought about partly by the reformists who dominated intellectual life for generations, and whose Western philosophy had no place for the esoteric. The case of Abduh himself was typical, for he was an enthusiastic member of a Sufi order in his youth, but abandoned it later for a system based on reason. In Turkey, the government of Kemal Atatürk proceeded to the dissolution of the Sufi orders in 1925 (1343). The popular confusion between Sufism and the cult of saints led many of the revivalists to be as mistrustful as the reformists.

In the end, the uncompromising Mutazilites and Hanbalites of the third century were both marginalized, though there have been those who embraced their respective teachings down the ages. The future of mainstream Islam belonged to a threefold alliance of rational thought, of outward observance, and of Sufism, with its depth of feeling and understanding. Between them these three elements satisfied the full range of human faculties and provided the framework for a rich, tolerant and varied civilization.

If either the reformists or the revivalists were able to destroy their opponents, which seems unlikely, Islam would be diminished. To be fully itself, the religion needs to find a new balance between its three historic components: honesty towards the intellect, loyalty to the past and openness to the heights of spiritual experience. A revived Sufism, set free from the cult of saints, has an essential part to play in such a synthesis.

Into a New World

Meanwhile, developments in the wider world are creating the conditions for a new synthesis. In science, old-fashioned atomistic materialism has reached its limits. Physical scientists accept that common-sense categories like space and time, matter and energy, waves and particles do not properly describe our strange universe of interconnected disturbances in multidimensional fields. Human scientists are beginning to realize that their old mechanistic models do not account for the mystery of consciousness or human creativity. Some biologists are ready to abandon the dogma that the wonderful complexity of life is purely the product of blind accident in a random universe.

In politics, there is a loss of faith in institutions and mechanisms as a means to build a happier world. Democracy does not guarantee justice or humanity, being the expression of the values of the majority, whatever their moral condition and access to information. Nor do free elections guarantee democracy, often giving power to a minority, whether the party that wins by a first-past-the-post election or the one that holds the casting votes under proportional representation. With great disparity of wealth, the rich can buy undue influence. One-party government produces results that are usually no better, without even allowing the victims of injustice to complain. If a better world can be built, it will come not through the impossible attainment of an ideal political system but through the moral improvement of a large enough number of individuals.

In economics, there is widespread recognition that neither capitalism nor what is left of communism is going to narrow the monstrous gap between rich and poor, which is the greatest scandal of our world. Keynesianism has failed to end the cycle of inflation and depression, which spells periodic misery for many within each country. The world system of finance and commerce condemns the poorest in the poorer countries to permanent misery. Some economists now recognize that any economic system depends on the beliefs of the people who sustain it – beliefs about human needs, about the conditions for happiness and about the relation of the individual to society. Only if morality comes to control economic behaviour does there seem to be any hope of improvement.

In this new climate of ideas, it should be easier for reformists, revivalists and Sufis to reach an understanding. A reformist Islam no longer needs to see as progress the adoption of existing forms of science, politics and economics. A revivalist movement no longer needs to see all ideas coming out of the West as threatening. A renovated Sufism offers the way to combine depth of religious feeling with respect for science and a metaphorical understanding of the Koran and Sunna.

For such an understanding to be reached, it is necessary for each side to renounce violence against the other. Repression of revivalist movements is in any case counterproductive, making martyrs and giving the impression that government can impose itself only by force. Muslim leaders of all tendencies should remind their followers constantly that the Koran utterly condemns the killing of Muslims by Muslims, that jihad is a last resort, to be adopted only in self-defence, and that neither the Koran nor Sunna calls for people of other faiths to be attacked simply on account of their religion. Where war does break out, they should firmly recall the strict rules of engagement imposed on fighters in the time of the Prophet.

The outside world should not intervene in the internal conflicts of the Islamic world. Where the majority of the people clearly want to be ruled by a revivalist government, as happened, for example, in Algeria in 1992, they should be allowed to conduct the experiment, testing the theories against the difficult realities of running a country. As has happened in Iran, it would rapidly become clear that the forced unity of the revivalist movements in opposition hides a wide range of political ideas. Where there is conflict between a Muslim and a non-Muslim people, as in Israel and Palestine, former Yugoslavia, or Kashmir, the international community should apply the same principles of justice as should hold in any other conflict.

In a crowded world with modern weapons, the only tolerable relationship between cultures is peaceful coexistence. From an ecological standpoint, the survival and spread of any culture can be seen in terms of adaptation – of its fit with the reality of the surrounding world, including that of other cultures. Because some features of the world are constantly changing, in order to stay adapted a culture must itself change; but at the same time it must be able to keep those features that continue to have survival value. Too much flexibility, and a civilization will perish through loss of old adaptations; too much constancy, and it will die for want of new ones. The story of the unfolding of Islam shows how it has achieved its special balance of constancy and flexibility. The authority of the Koran and Sunna and the strength of the Muslim family give the religion an enduring central core. The absence of a priesthood, the tradition of tolerance and Sufi openness to new interpretations leave room for change.

Granted peace and its proper share of influence in the world, Islam should be able to regain its self-confidence and make its full contribution to solving the world's considerable problems. At present, growth of the global economy threatens to exhaust the planet's resources and destabilize its climates. 'Optimists' have forecast that the average income per head in a century's time will be six times what it is now. Assuming that population peaks at nine billion, that would require an increase of up to 730% in the supply of natural resources, which is probably impossible and certainly unsustainable.

The roots of this growth are discontent and inequality. The modern capitalist economy depends on continual growth, which requires people to be constantly discontented with what they have. The ever-increasing wealth of the rich both invites emulation by the relatively poor and leaves the vast needs of the destitute to be satisfied. Islam has an important contribution, with its concern for the weak and poor, and its distrust of material satisfaction: 'Know that the life of this world is only a game and a distraction and a trinket, out-boasting each other and competing to have much wealth and many children' (Koran 57:20). It warns explicitly against over-consumption: 'eat and drink, but not to excess; Allah does not love those who exceed' (Koran 7:31).

Even if consumption per head can be stabilized, there is also the question of the number of heads. With population growth rates well in excess of the world average, Muslims can make a disproportionate contribution to slowing the increase. Encouragement of family life is a strength, but strength will turn to weakness if population growth compromises education and exhausts resources. Most Muslim authorities accept contraception as a legitimate means of family planning. The persistence of high birth rates seems to result partly from a low level of women's education. There is nothing inherently Islamic in this; on the contrary, the civilization that centres on the Koran should inherently place the highest value on literacy, and indeed the Ibadis may have been the first people in the world to educate all their daughters. It is no doubt tempting to maintain high birth rates in order to increase the number of Muslims in the world, but the responsible way to achieve that will be to persuade more people to accept Islam.

Halting or slowly reversing the world's population growth will be only one aspect of solving the problems that our species poses for the planet. The long-term future of its resources of minerals, water, soil, plants and animals depends on wise stewardship. The message of Islam is clear, though it must be said that it has often not been heeded in the past. The Koran over and over again invites people to marvel at this miraculous world and to care for it gratefully. It calls the wonders of nature 'a vision and a reminder to every devoted servant' (50:8). It tells Muslims that 'all things that crawl on the earth or fly on their wings are communities like yours' (6:38). It warns them that 'corruption has appeared on land and sea by the action of human hands, to make them taste some of what they have done, that they may turn back.' (30:41)

All of this is of course secondary to the central message of Islam, which is the unity, majesty, goodness and mercy of Allah, whose grace is directly available to everyone at all times and in all places, without distinction of race, sex, age or social class, through simple acts of devotion. Even the most hardened atheist should be moved by the spectacle of a faith so humble and so egalitarian. The rest of the world should be ready to treat Muslims with affection and respect.

NOTE ON SOURCES

For the life of the Prophet and his Companions I have used primary sources, referenced in the text. By far the earliest of these is the Holy Koran, read in the light of the commentaries of al-Tabari and al-Baidawi. For the Sunna I have relied mainly on al-Bukhari and Malik. The *Sira* of Ibn Ishaq edited by Ibn Hisham has been invaluable, supplemented by citations from the *History* of al-Tabari. For further biographical information I have consulted the *Tabaqat* of Ibn Saad. Quotations from al-Bukhari are given by the numbers of book and chapter in the edition by Muhammad Muhsin Khan; those from the *Sira* are given by the page number in Guillaume's translation.

For the pre-Islamic period and the later history of Islam, I have relied on secondary sources, the more important of which I have included below under Further Reading. I have not quoted as fact anything that does not seem to be generally accepted, and where opinion differs, for example between Sunnis and Shiites, I have tried to present alternative views fairly. I hope I have made it clear where I am expressing my personal opinion.

For demographic data I used the statistics of the UN Population Bureau and also John R. Weeks, 'The Demography of Islamic Nations', *Population Bulletin*, Vol. 43, no. 4, 1988. Information on the heritability of religiosity comes from Niels G. Waller et al., 'Genetic and Environmental Influences, Attitudes and Values', *Psychological Science*, Vol. 1, no. 2, March 1990.

Among European books not included in Further Reading, either because they are not available in English or because they are too technical, I must mention specially Noeldeke's *Geschichte des Korans*, 2nd edition by Schwally et al. (Leipzig, 1909–1919), and John Burton's *The Collection of the Qur'an* (Cambridge University Press, 1977). For an up-to-date Muslim view I went to M. M. Azami, *The History of the Quranic Text* (UK Islamic Academy, 2003).

For information on Judaism I have used the *Encyclopaedia Judaica* (Jerusalem, 1972). I have tried to keep up with the kaleidoscopic shifts in New Testament scholarship, and I found a particularly helpful guide was Mark Alan Powell, *The Jesus Debates: Modern Historians Investigate the Life of Christ* (Lion, 1998).

FURTHER READING

Only books in English and accessible to the general reader are suggested in the following list.

1. General
The most useful general source is the *Encyclopaedia of Islam*, available in the larger public libraries. Words have to be looked for in a slightly non-standard transliteration, with K replacing the usual Q and DJ for the usual J.

A good outline history is that of Albert Hourani, *A History of the Arab Peoples* (Faber and Faber, 1991).

For the Crusades: *The Crusades Through Arab Eyes* by Amin Maalouf, Editor, J. Rothschild, Translator (Saqi Essentials, 2001).

A good general study of Western attitudes to Islam is given in *Muhammad in Europe* by Minou Reeves (Garnet, 2000).

2. The Holy Koran
The translation most widely used by English-speaking Muslims is that of Abdullah Yusuf Ali, which has copious notes (various editions). A more poetic version is that of A. J. Arberry (currently published by Oxford World's Classics). A new rendering by M. A. S. Abdel Haleem avoids the 'ye's and 'thee's of more conservative translations (also in the World's Classics).

For the traditional account of the writing down of the Koran, see *The History of the Qur'anic Text* by M. M. Al-Azami (UK Islamic Academy).

3. The Prophet

The oldest surviving biography of the Prophet, written about a century after his death by Ibn Ishaq, is the *Sirat Rasul Allah*, which exists only in the edition made by Ibn Hisham about another century later. It has been translated by A. Guillaume as *The Life of Muhammad* (Oxford).

Perhaps the best modern biography by a non-Muslim is *Mohammed* by Maxime Rodinson (Penguin). A recent Muslim account is *The Messenger* by Tariq Ramadan (Penguin).

Muhammad at Mecca and *Muhammad at Medina* by Montgomery Watt (currently in print in Pakistan) are not so much a biography of the Prophet as a series of studies of particular historical questions about his life.

4. Sunna, Sharia and Theology

The *Sahih* of Al-Bukhari – the most widely used collection of Hadith – is available in translation (Kitab Bhavan, New Delhi). Most accounts of Sharia available in English are very dry, very old or very unsympathetic or all three. The best is *A History of Islamic Law* by Noel J. Coulson (Edinburgh University Press, 1964), still in print. A readable account of Islamic thought is *Islamic Philosophy, Theology and Mysticism: A Short Introduction* by Majid Fakhri (Oneworld Publications).

5. Shia Islam

For the early history see *Origins and Early Development of Shi'a Islam* by S. H. M. Jafri. For a sympathetic account of Islam in modern Iran see *The Mantle of the Prophet* by Roy P. Mottahedeh.

6. Sufism

Sufism is best learnt about by personal communication. The best literary approach is through Sufi poetry; a recent collection in translation is *The Essential Rumi: Selected Poems* (Penguin

Classics). The humorous wisdom tales about Nasruddin exist in various collections, for example *Pleasantries of the Incredible Mulla Nasrudin*, translated by Idreis Shah.

7. Women in Islam
Fatima Mernissi produced a remarkable study of the place of women in the time of the Prophet: *Women and Islam: an Historical and Theological Enquiry* (Blackwell). She was continuing the tradition described by Mohammad Akram Nadwi in *al-Muhaddithat: the Women Scholars in Islam* (Interface Publications, 2007). The same theme of women in early Islam is treated in fictional form by Assia Djebar in *Far from Medina* (Quartet). The contribution of women to Sufism is described in *Sufi Women* by Javad Nurbakhsh (Khaniqahi–Nimatullahi Publications).

8. Islam in the Modern World
An enormous literature has been produced since the Iranian Revolution of 1979, still more since the Rushdie affair started in 1989, increasing to a torrent since the destruction of the World Trade Center in 2001. Much of this is not really about Islam but about whether or not there is a 'clash of civilizations' between Islam and the West, as described in a book of that title by Samuel P. Huntington.

Things are put in perspective by Albert Hourani, who shows how ready Muslims were to embrace the modern world, in *Arabic Thought in the Liberal Age 1798–1939* (Cambridge University Press). Perhaps the best study of the emergence of jihadists is *Unholy War: Terror in the Name of Islam* by John L. Esposito (Oxford University Press). The turning point in relations between Muslims and the British Empire is described in *The Last Mughal* by William Dalrymple. Robert Fisk gives a lively journalistic account of the history of Western intervention in the Middle East in *The Great War for Civilization: The Conquest of the Middle East* (Fourth Estate). The events that culminated in the creation of

Al-Qaeda are described in *The Siege of Mecca* by Yaroslav Trofimov. Thoughtful Muslims reflect on the future of their religion in *Voices of Islam* edited by John Bowker.

INDEX

Index

churches, 16
circumcision, female, 166
circumcision, male, 11, 12, 166
civil war, 154
Claes, Willy, 240
Columbus, Christopher, 210
commerce, 246
communism, 187, 234
Companions, 88, 132, 158, 163, 234, 251
concubines, 99, 100, 120
Confederation of Honour, 31, 127
Constantine I, 17
Constantinople, 17, 155
'Constitution of Medina', 72
Coptic Christians, 138
Cordoba, 209
creation, 219
creationism, 236
crime, 105, 160
criminal justice, 12
crusades, 209, 210, 225
Ctesiphon, 87
cult of saints, 203, 205, 206, 245
Cushitic language, 4
Cyrus the Great, 10, 18

D
Damascus, 144, 169, 170, 201, 223
'Dancing Dervishes', 202
Dar al-Harb, 167
Dar al-Islam, 167
Dar al-Sulh, 167
Darul-Uloom Deoband, 230
Daud Ibn Khalaf, 191
David, 9, 10, 14, 62
Day of Judgement, 13, 62, 176, 193
democracy, 246
demography, 251
Dhu-'l-Nun al-Misri, 194, 207, 244
diplomatic relations, 88
disciples, of Jesus, 14
divorce, 100, 101, 160, 165
Djerba, 205
dowries, 100, 101, 103, 104
dress, 102, 235
drinking, 94, 105

drunkenness, 160
Druzes, 188

E
East Africa, 166, 188, 203, 207
eating, *see* food
economics, 221, 246
economy, 106, 218, 233, 235, 236
  capitalist, 248
education, 218
Egypt, 87, 137, 138, 144, 147, 148, 166,
  194, 203, 206, 213, 215, 216, 220, 224,
  229, 236, 237
elections, 246
Elijah, 62
emirs, 153
Ethiopia, 149, 207
Ethiopic language, 4
Eurasia, 1, 3
Europe, 100, 208, 209, 210, 215, 217, 223,
  225
evolution, 236
Ezra, 8, 28

F
Fadak, 86, 130, 136
Fakkh, 182
family life, 98, 104
Al-Farabi, 179
Farewell Pilgrimage, 91, 124
farming, 4
fasting (as one of the Five Pillars), 47, 93,
  94, 97, 195
Fatima (Muhammad's daughter), 36, 122,
  128, 130, 148, 153, 199
Fatima (Muhammad's grandmother), 33
Fatimid dynasty, 187, 197, 199, 205, 237
fatwa, 171
fez, 221
finance, 246
First Convention of Aqaba, 65
First Saudi Kingdom, 212
First World War, 223
Five Pillars, 47, 53, 66, 74, 93, 97, 160, 164,
  181, 208, 219
Followers, 158